MESSAGE OF THE FATHERS OF THE CHURCH
General Editor: Thomas Halton

Volume 13

MESSAGE OF THE FATHERS OF THE CHURCH

WOMEN IN THE EARLY CHURCH

by

Elizabeth A. Clark

Michael Glazier, Inc.
Wilmington, Delaware

ABOUT THE AUTHOR

Elizabeth A. Clark is a graduate of Vassar College, and she received her doctorate in patristic studies from Columbia University. The recipient of many scholarship awards, she was founder of the Department of Religion at Mary Washington College. Internationally known as a patristic scholar, she is highly respected for her published works, among which is *Clement's Use of Aristotle: The Aristotelian Contribution to Clement of Alexandria's Refutation of Gnosticism.*

Second Printing, 1987

First published in 1983 by Michael Glazier, Inc.
1935 West Fourth Street, Wilmington, DE 19805

Library of Congress Catalog Card Number: 82-084410
International Standard Book Number:
  Message of the Fathers of the Church series:
    (0-89453-312-6, Paper; 0-89453-340-1, Cloth)
  WOMEN IN THE EARLY CHURCH:
    (0-89453-332-0, Paper)
    (0-89453-353-3, Cloth)

Cover design: Lillian Brulc
Typography by Richard Rein Smith
Printed in the United States of America

For
Audrey Clark Mayer
With thanks

CONTENTS

7

List of Abbreviations

CCL	*Corpus Christianorum, Series Latina*
CSEL	*Corpus Scriptorum Ecclesiasticorum Latinorum*
GC S	*Die griechischen christlichen Schriftsteller der ersten drei Jahrhunderte*
PG	*Patrologia Graeca*
PL	*Patrologia Latina*
SC	*Sources Chrétiennes*

EDITOR'S INTRODUCTION

The *Message of the Fathers of the Church* is a companion series to The *Old Testament Message* and The *New Testament Message*. It was conceived and planned in the belief that Scripture and Tradition worked hand in hand in the formation of the thought, life and worship of the primitive Church. Such a series, it was felt, would be a most effective way of opening up what has become virtually a closed book to present-day readers, and might serve to stimulate a revival in interest in Patristic studies in step with the recent, gratifying resurgence in Scriptural studies.

The term "Fathers" is usually reserved for Christian writers marked by orthodoxy of doctrine, holiness of life, ecclesiastical approval and antiquity. "Antiquity" is generally understood to include writers down to Gregory the Great (+604) or Isidore of Seville (+636) in the West, and John Damascene (+749) in the East. In the present series, however, greater elasticity has been encouraged, and quotations from writers not noted for orthodoxy will sometimes be included in order to illustrate the evolution of the Message on particular doctrinal matters. Likewise, writers later than the mid-eighth century will sometimes be used to illustrate the continuity of tradition on matters like sacramental theology or liturgical practice.

An earnest attempt was made to select collaborators on a broad inter-disciplinary and inter-confessional basis, the chief consideration being to match scholars who could handle the Fathers in their original languages with subjects in which they had already demonstrated a special interest and competence. About the only editorial directive given to the selected contributors was that the Fathers, for the most part, should be allowed to speak for themselves and that they should speak in readable, reliable modern English. Volumes on individual themes were considered more suitable than volumes devoted to individual Fathers, each theme, hopefully, contributing an important segment to the total mosaic of the Early Church, one, holy, catholic and apostolic. Each volume has an introductory essay outlining the historical and theological development of the theme, with the body of the work mainly occupied with liberal citations from the Fathers in modern English translation and a minimum of linking commentary. Short lists of Suggested Further Readings are included; but dense, scholarly footnotes were actively discouraged on the pragmatic grounds that such scholarly shorthand has other outlets and tends to lose all but the most relentlessly esoteric reader in a semipopular series.

At the outset of his *Against Heresies* Irenaeus of Lyons warns his readers "not to expect from me any display of rhetoric, which I have never learned, or any excellence of composition, which I have never practised, or any beauty or persuasiveness of style, to which I make no pretensions." Similarly, modest disclaimers can be found in many of the Greek and Latin Fathers and all too often, unfortunately, they have been taken at their word by an uninterested world. In fact, however, they were often highly educated products of the best rhetorical schools of their day in the Roman Empire, and what they have to say is often as much a lesson in literary and cultural, as well as in spiritual, edification.

St. Augustine, in *The City of God* (19.7), has interesting reflections on the need for a common language in an expanding world community; without a common language a man is more at home with his dog than with a foreigner as far as intercommunication goes, even in the Roman Empire, which imposes on the nations it conquers the yoke of both law and language with a resultant abundance of interpreters. It is hoped that in the present world of continuing language barriers the contributors to this series will prove opportune interpreters of the perennial Christian message.

ACKNOWLEDGMENTS

Thanks are due to several persons whose suggestions and criticisms were helpful in the preparation of this volume: Gregory Elftmann, Dennis Groh, Thomas Halton, Susan Hanna, Diane Hatch, Elizabeth Merrill and my father, Edmund Clark. Mary Ann Ellery provided special assistance with the Tertullian passages. These colleagues and friends are, of course, in no way responsible for any defects that remain in the translations. I also wish to thank the staff of the Dumbarton Oaks Library, especially Mrs. Irene Vaslef, for its assistance. Since the work for this volume was begun while I held a fellowship from the National Endowment for the Humanities, my thanks are again due to the Endowment for its generosity. In addition, I am grateful to Mary Washington College's Dean (Mary Ann T. Burns) and its Director of Graduate Studies (Donald E. Glover) for financing the secretarial services provided by Mrs. Una Crist, who typed the manuscript with her usual efficiency and cheerfulness.

One note seems in order regarding the contents of this volume: since the Virgin Mary is covered in another volume of this series, no special material pertaining to her is included in this book.

I thank The Edwin Mellen Press for permission to quote from my translations of the *Life of Olympias* and John Chrysostom's *On the Necessity of Guarding Virginity* that appeared in *Jerome, Chrysostom, and Friends: Essays and Translations* (New York, 1979), and Scholars Press for permission to quote from the translation of Faltonia Betitia Proba's *Cento* in *The Golden Bough, The Oaken Cross: The Virgilian Cento of Faltonia Betitia Proba* by Diane Hatch and myself (Chico, California, 1981).

August, 1982   Elizabeth A. Clark
                                          Duke University
                                          Durham, North Carolina

INTRODUCTION

The most fitting word with which to describe the Church Fathers' attitude toward women is ambivalence. Women were God's creation, his good gift to men—and the curse of the world. They were weak in both mind and character—and displayed dauntless courage, undertook prodigious feats of scholarship. Vain, deceitful, brimming with lust—they led men to Christ, fled sexual encounter, wavered not at the executioner's threats, adorned themselves with sackcloth and ashes. Leaving the examination of the Fathers' psyches to other specialists, this volume documents from an historical perspective the ways in which the Fathers praised and blamed, honored and disparaged the female sex.

One undoubted manifestation of this ambivalence lies in the Fathers' selective appeal to the Bible. Their interpretations of Genesis 1-3, for example, bespoke their views on women's subordination. Thus they consistently explicated the Genesis 2 account of woman's creation (in which Eve is created second, from Adam's rib) rather than Genesis 1, in which male and female are created at the same time, both "in the image and likeness" of God (Gen. 1:26). Similarly, when an opportunity arose to elucidate Eve's role as "helper" (Gen. 2:18), the Fathers failed to mention that the word *'ezer* is sometimes used in Scripture to designate God as the gracious helper of his Chosen People; given their weakness in Hebrew and their own inclinations, the Fathers concentrated on woman's "help" in childbearing, since they agreed that in other areas of human activity, her assistance was decidedly inferior to that of males.

Likewise for the New Testament: the Fathers usually focused on verses that provided a rationale for restricting, not for freeing, women. Thus the fact that in I Corinthians 11, Paul calls men "the image of God" but does not so designate women (to the neglect of Genesis 1:26) was taken by the Fathers to mean that women lacked some essential quality males shared with the Godhead. And since the Fathers believed that Paul had written such books as I Timothy, a view now rejected by most Biblical scholars, they accorded apostolic sanction to key verses reminding women to be silent and submissive to men (e.g., I Tim. 2:11). Thus the Fathers often quote the Bible in ways that serve to bolster and justify traditional attitudes toward women, attitudes derived from the Old Testament's adulation of the busy housewife and warnings against "loose women," pagan antiquity's ideal of the chaste and retiring matron, and the unfavorable representations of women in some classical literature, especially satire. One central purpose of this volume, then, is to highlight the Fathers' use of Scripture in their discussions of women. Readers can judge for themselves the extent to which exegesis sometimes played handmaiden to personal and cultural assumptions.

Although the Church Fathers did not quote such New Testament verses as Galatians 5:1, "For freedom Christ has set us free," in their commentaries on the female sex, Christian women of the patristic era who renounced traditional sexual and domestic roles did indeed find new worlds open to them, worlds of scholarship and contemplation, pilgrimage and charitable endeavor. Thinking of women such as these, the Fathers recalled verses about praiseworthy females in the New Testament: that women travelled with and helped support Jesus and the disciples, that women, not men, were last at Jesus' cross and first at his tomb, that Paul in various letters greeted women as his co-workers. Women who wholeheartedly dedicated their lives to such religious activities received extravagant accolades from the Fathers that provide a striking contrast to the denunciations many Fathers heaped on women in general.

The chief route to the acquisition of greater freedom for Christian women in the patristic era was asceticism. Most of the Fathers believed that women who renounced the sexual life were elevated above their natural abject condition to the degree that they almost constituted a "third sex," so much did they differ from females still in the thrall of Eve's birth pains and submission to husbands. Marriage by definition placed women in an inferior role; sexual functioning in itself made women subordinate. Thus it can be argued that one way in which the Fathers effectively encouraged greater freedom for women was in their championing of asceticism. If a girl could be convinced to espouse perpetual virginity, so much the better; if a woman was widowed, she could at least be encouraged not to return to the problems, indeed the vileness, of marriage.

Once again, the Fathers read the Scriptures selectively to find legitimation for their advocacy of asceticism. In the Old Testament, the fact that Adam and Eve were not depicted as actually engaging in sexual intercourse until after their expulsion from Eden (Gen. 4:1) was taken by some Fathers to mean that marriage and reproduction were lesser goods than celibacy, if they were goods at all. Likewise, Jesus' alleged words praising those who became "eunuchs for the sake of the Kingdom of Heaven" (Mt. 19:12), and his statement that "in the resurrection there will be no marrying nor giving in marriage" (Mk. 12:25 = Mt. 22:30 = Lk. 20:35) were taken as encouragements to the celibate life here and now. Indeed, the Fathers in their enthusiasm for virginity sometimes indulge in Scriptural interpretations that bear little or no relation to the historical meaning of the text. For example, Jerome's interpretation that the "onehundredfold harvest" in the parable of the sower (Mk. 4:1-9 = Mt. 13:1-9 = Lk. 8:4-8) indicates virginity, while the "sixtyfold" signifies widowhood, and the "thirtyfold" marriage, finds no basis in Jesus' message of the Kingdom's unexpected arrival and glorious abundance. In such ways were the Fathers' ascetic preferences bolstered by their appeal to certain texts, while other verses extolling marriage, sexual relations, and reproduction were either ignored or rejected as inappropriate to Christian ideals.

While such interpretations may more amuse than instruct modern readers, the point contained therein about women is important: if women were viewed almost solely in their sexual roles as allayers of male lust and as bearers of men's children, the essential point in raising women to personhood, to individuality, was through renunciation of their sexual function. Just as the Fathers' wariness about marriage stemmed first and foremost from their ambiguity about the goodness of the sexual act, so their ambiguous feelings about females revolved around woman as the symbol for sexuality, the lusts of the flesh, the downfall of rationality when confronted by desire. Although our contemporaries may reproach the Fathers for their denigration of married women and their excessive adulation of sexually continent ones, the fact seems clear that from an historical point of view, asceticism was an important factor in the improvement of some women's roles in the patristic era. Yet even for celibate women, the translation of that verbal elevation to elevation in the "real world" was only partial: the priesthood with its sacramental and public teaching offices was still closed to them.

So strong was the ascetic bias of early Christianity that it might well have become the norm for all Christians had not the Gnostic crisis intervened. Gnosticism was a movement that swept the Mediterranean world in the second and third centuries, promising to the "elect" salvation from the evils of this present life. Dozens of Gnostic sects flourished. Despite their bewildering variety, they shared a common loathing for the material world and the Creator who had made it. Over against this view, the mainstream orthodox Church appealed to the goodness of the created world and noted that God himself in Genesis 1 had pronounced the various aspects of creation "good." However wayward humans might be, our physical bodies were essentially part of that good creation. If the Creator gave humans sex organs and told the first couple to "reproduce and multiply" (Gen. 1:28), sexual intercourse and childbearing, when undertaken within the limits of the divinely ordained plan for human society and with the proper motivation, were not to be pronounced evil. Thus the Fathers' misgivings about sexual relations were guaranteed to run up against their theoretical claim that it was God who had given us bodies and an ordinance for reproduction: that claim was a deterrent to a wholesale advocacy of asceticism for all Christians.

The fourth Christian century, with its outburst of ascetic enthusiasm, brought new possibilities outside the domestic circle for women's lives. It is no accident, then, that the selections in this book are weighted toward the fourth and early fifth centuries: that is the period in which Christian women came into their own as models of the pious life and as mentors for others, setting examples of devout living that could be imitated by the next generations of females. The fact that many of the women praised by the Fathers came from the highest aristocracy and renounced wealth as well as social respectability in order to become Christian ascetics made their sacrifices all the more dramatic in the eyes of the men who wrote about them. That they also renounced natural family ties and sometimes deserted their children in order to pursue the ascetic life was seen by the Fathers as dramatic evidence of the force of will God gave even to females striving to follow their Lord.

Given the new avenues open to ascetic women, it is sobering to note that those avenues had definite roadblocks placed in them: women were not to be priests or public teachers. Although the Fathers indulge in much windy rhetoric about women's lack of intellect and scholarly ability as prime reasons for this exclusion, numerous testimonies reveal that some early Christian women outclassed men in their knowledge of Scripture, the Scriptural languages, and theology, as is revealed in Chapter Four below. The Fathers' rhetoric, in other words, is plainly contradicted by their own testimonies about the women's scholarly prowess.

Again leaving aside other possible motivations for the Fathers' exclusion of women from such offices, we can note an historical one: from the second century on, various sects on the fringes of mainstream Christianity, often proclaimed to be heretical or schismatic by the Church, allowed women high leadership positions, including sacramental ones. Various Gnostic sects probably let women baptize. Charismatic movements that appealed to the Holy Spirit's inspiration were also natural ones to allow women a larger role, for it could be argued that God did not discriminate sexually in distributing the *charismata,* the spiritual gifts. It is likely that the Catholic Church reacted to such sects, that were indeed a genuine danger to orthodox Christianity's survival and power, by drawing firm lines of differentiation between the types of church office permitted to women in the sects and the offices and roles permitted women in the Catholic Church. When the Fathers cite Biblical verses depicting Jesus' twelve male disciples as a justification for an all-male priesthood, we see that they are appealing to the norms of

Palestinian Judaism as a sanction for the practices of later Christian churches in the larger Graeco-Roman world. The historian might focus on the clash of Catholic Christianity with the heretical and schismatic movements as the immediate situation that led the Church Fathers to limit women's activities, and might understand their appeal to the customs of traditional Judaism and early Jewish Christianity as a legitimation for their practice.

The selections in this book are organized into five chapters. In Chapter One, the theoretical bases and Biblical justifications the Fathers gave for women's subordinate status are explored. Although the punishment placed on Eve for instigating the original sin is the chief reason given for women's subjection, many Fathers also believed that the Genesis 2 account of creation, in which the male was created first and the woman from him and for him, implied a God-given order of creation in which women were subjected to men right from the very beginning. With the Fall, that subjection was only increased. The Fathers were nonetheless eager to assert that the subjection was actually for the good of human society and resulted in a happy complementarity of male and female roles. Marriage, as the symbol of that female subjection, is appropriately considered in this chapter entitled "Paradise Lost."

Chapter Two investigates some phenomena pertaining to women in the second to early fourth centuries. This period saw the rise of a new class of Christian literature, the Apocryphal Acts, in which women were given the status of heroines. Interestingly enough, the type of Christianity represented in most of the Apocryphal Acts is already a highly ascetic one: apparently in the circles that produced the Apocryphal Acts, the coupling of ascetic motifs with larger roles for women had begun, a phenomenon manifested in the real, i.e., nonfictive, world chiefly during the fourth and fifth centuries of Christianity. In the Apocryphal Acts we find women frequently depicted as more devout than their male relations. They engage in functions traditionally thought of as reserved to males, such as teaching, and through them miraculous events occur, from the stilling of beasts in the arena to the raising of the dead. They are also often pictured as endangered: their decision for asceticism enrages husbands, fiancés, and family members who attempt to correct their behavior by drastic means, even by turning them over to the secular authorities for punishment. Chapter Two also investigates another class of "endangered women," those who gave themselves as martyrs. The Church Fathers agreed that in martyrdom, no difference of sex obtained. Women proved just as strong in faith and resistant to the threats of the Roman persecutors as men. Martyrdom not only provided an opportunity—if one may call it that—for the elevation of females; it also furnished heroic subject matter about women for writers of both prose and poetry, as Chapter Two explicates. The tales of valiant women who retained their dignity as well as their confessions of faith while tossed by wild beasts and stabbed by executioners supplied inspirational examples on which rhetorical talents might dwell.

Chapter Three presents material that suggests how asceticism, particularly from the fourth century on, provided avenues for female elevation. The theoretical justification for asceticism applied both to men and to women: the members of the Trinity, despite Fatherhood and Sonship, were "virginal"; Jesus was believed to have been born of a virgin and is depicted in the Gospels as devoid of sexual contact. If Christians aspired to regain their original created goodness, wished even to partake of divine qualities, virginity was the route to be chosen. Virginity was now seen as the equivalent of martyrdom, no longer an available means after the early fourth century of manifesting one's superior commitment to Christianity. In addition, asceticism had a special appeal to women: since subjection in marriage was the penalty for woman's role in the original sin, choosing celibacy meant that the bonds of that subjection were broken. The Fathers could, moreover, appeal to women on practical grounds: freedom from marriage meant freedom from the numerous duties and anxieties pertaining to husbands, children, in-laws, servants and household organization, all of which the Fathers thought cramped women's lives.

Practical issues about where and how women who wished to devote themselves to asceticism might live were pressing in a society that had no role for women other than that of wife and mother. The process by which Egyptian ascetic practices and lifestyles were transferred to western Europe, Palestine, and Byzantium are detailed in a variety of sources pertaining to female monasticism in Chapter Three. Part of the Church's advocacy of the ascetic life involved a strong criticism of second marriage, and selections relating to that theme are also here presented. Chapter Three thus explicates the Fathers' argument that women might win again through asceticism the status they had lost through the Fall and the institution of marriage: Paradise could be regained.

The fourth chapter documents both the restrictions and the opportunities facing women as they looked beyond the domestic scene to the larger world. The restrictions included female exclusion from the priesthood and from the teaching office, ostensibly because Eve once proved herself a bad teacher to Adam. Yet even here, private instruction was sanctioned and, in extraordinary cases, a woman was praised for her public instruction if that involved her successful refutation of heresy. Despite such restrictions, the women of the upper classes to whom our evidence pertains enjoyed classical literary educations, to which they added Scripture study, theological reading in both Greek and Latin, and even training in Hebrew.

Some clerical or semi-clerical roles were allowed women. From early times, the Church had an order of widows who performed various religious and charitable deeds. In the fourth century, there arose the order of deaconesses who aided the bishop with ritual and pedagogic functions pertaining to women. In eastern Christendom, if not in the west, deaconesses were ordained. Gradually, the various orders for women were subsumed in the office of nun. Material pertaining to these developments is included in Chapter Four. Lastly, the fourth century saw a rise of interest among Christians in pilgrimages to the Holy Places. Women as well as men were quick to travel the pilgrim routes to Palestine, Egypt, and other places, as is also described in Chapter Four.

The last chapter consists of individual portraits of the female friends, mothers, and sisters of various Church Fathers. The letters of Jerome, a late fourth-century Latin-writing Father, are especially rich in providing vignettes of distinguished Christian women in his circle of friends and acquaintances. The strong impact that mothers and sisters had on the religious development of their sons and brothers is revealed in selections by Augustine, John Chrysostom, and Gregory of Nyssa. Similarly striking is the way in which female ascetics came to serve as role models for younger generations of women. The praise heaped on the women whose stories are recounted in this chapter stands in stark contrast to the blame accorded Eve and her unworthy female descendants, as detailed especially in Chapters One and Three. We have thus come full circle in our exploration of the Church Fathers' ambivalence toward women. Women are extravagantly lauded and are inordinately denounced for the world's woes by one and the same author: rarely are they seen as persons with the same virtues and weaknesses as men. Time had to pass before male religious authorities could view women involved in the world of sexual functioning and reproduction as worthy of the same respect as women who chose the celibate course. Much also remained—and still remains—to open the avenues to women that the Church Fathers blocked, even as they hesitantly sanctioned new roles and opportunities for some members of the female sex.

Chapter One

PARADISE LOST: CREATION, FALL, AND MARRIAGE

Early Christianity accepted the Hebraic conviction that the world had been created by God and hence was essentially good, as Genesis 1 proclaimed. The first two chapters of Genesis, understood by the Church Fathers to be a connected unit written by one author, reported that woman as well as man was formed by God and hence shared in the goodness of the created order. How that goodness was manifested in the male-female relationship was a question demanding an answer, since the Fathers also firmly believed that Eve was responsible for sin's entrance to the world. How could she be called man's "helper" (Gen. 2:18) if she had led him to his doom? Yet most Fathers insisted that God had indeed intended there to be two sexes. The ambivalence of the patristic authors on these points is strikingly revealed in their discussions of creation.

Augustine (354-430 A.D.), bishop of Hippo Regius in North Africa, argued in his treatise *On the Good of Marriage,*[1] written in 401 A.D., that God created humans as social beings and that the first human "society" was that of man and woman.

[1] Text:CSEL 41.187.

1. Since every person is a part of the human race and human nature is something social and has in itself the power of friendship as a great good, God willed for this reason to create all humans from one person, so that they might be held fast in their society not only by likeness of descent, but also by the bond of relationship. Thus the first tie of natural human society is husband and wife. And yet God did not make each one separately and then join them as if they were strangers to each other. Rather, he created one from the other, yet he put a sign of their union's power in the side, from which the woman was drawn forth and formed (Gen. 2:21-22). For they were joined to each other from the sides, they who walk side by side, they who together look where it is they walk. The union of their society in children follows, which is the one decent result not of the marriage of man and woman, but of sexual intercourse. For there could have been between the sexes a kind of friendly, genuine relationship, one of them ruling and the other subject, even without such sexual intercourse.

> Despite this positive view of creation, the Biblical text forced Augustine to ponder Eve's role. In his *Literal Commentary On Genesis*,[2] composed in the early years of the fifth century, he reflected on the kind of "help" Eve was supposed to provide for Adam.

IX,5. If it were not the case that the woman was created to be man's helper specifically for the production of children, then why would she have been created as a "helper" (Gen. 2:18)? Was it so that she might work the land with him? No, because there did not yet exist any such labor for which he needed a helper, and even if such work had been required, a male would have made a better assistant. One can also posit that the reason for her creation as a helper had to do with the companionship she could provide for the man, if perhaps he

[2]Text: CSEL 28, 1, 273.

got bored with his solitude. Yet for company and conversation, how much more agreeable it is for two male friends to dwell together than for a man and a woman! If it is necessary for one of two people living together to rule and the other to obey so that an opposition of wills does not disturb their peaceful cohabitation, then nothing is missing from the order we see in Genesis directed to this restraint, for one person was created before, the other afterwards, and most significantly, the latter was created from the former, the woman from the man. And nobody wants to suggest, does he, that God, if he so willed, could only make a woman from a man's side, yet that he couldn't create a man as well? I cannot think of any reason for woman's being made as man's helper, if we dismiss the reason of procreation.

> The purpose of woman's creation, in view of her responsibility for the original sin, was also considered by Ambrose, bishop of Milan from 374-397 A.D. In his treatise *On Paradise*,[3] composed about 375 A.D., he paid close attention to the order of verses in Genesis 1 and 2, which he assumed to be a connected unit, as a way of arguing that Eve shared in the goodness of God's creation.

IV,24. "And God took the man he had created and placed him in Paradise to work it and keep it" (Gen. 2:15). Take note of who the man was who was "taken." He was, moreover, in the very land in which he was created. God by his power thus took the man and breathed into him in order to develop and increase the man's power. In short, God stationed him in Paradise so that you may know that he was "taken," breathed on by the divine power, so to speak. Note the point that man was made outside of Paradise and that woman was made inside Paradise. From this we are to gather that each person acquires grace not from his or her

[3]Text: CSEL 32, 1, 280.

geographical location, nor from the nobility of his or her family, but by virtue. In fact, even though man was created outside Paradise (i.e., in an inferior place), he is found to be superior, while woman, though created in a better place (i.e., inside Paradise) is found inferior. For the woman was the first to be deceived and she deceived the man. Whence the apostle Peter recounted that holy women were subject to the stronger vessel, obeying their husbands as lords (I Pet. 3:1-6). And Paul said, "Adam was not deceived, but the woman was deceived and was in sin" (I Tim. 2:14). Take note: from that time on, no one should have too easy a confidence in himself. For just look: she who was created to be a helper to man requires male protection! "The head of woman is man" (I Cor. 11:3). Although Adam believed that he would have his wife as a helper, he fell because of her. Therefore no one should lightly entrust himself to another person, unless he tests that person's virtue. Neither should he claim someone as his assistant whom he thinks of as a stranger. Rather, if he finds himself stronger, views himself as a protector, he can share his grace. Likewise the apostle Peter teaches that men should bestow honor on their wives when he says, "Husbands should in like manner live with their wives in understanding, bestowing honor on them as on weaker vessels, as on co-heirs of the grace of life, so that your prayers may not be impeded" (I Pet. 3:7).

X,46. Then here is another question, concerning which the Lord gave the saying, "It is not good for man to be alone" (Gen. 2:18). First of all, take note of what was said above, where God fashioned man from the mud of the earth (Gen. 2:7). At that point he did *not* add, "And God saw that it was good," the way he did with each of his other works.[4] For if God had here said that it was good for man to have been created, we would run into a contradiction when he later reports that "it is not good" (for man to be alone), since

---

[4]As in Genesis 1.

he would already have said in the previous passage that "it was good." Be aware of this at that place at which it says that God created Adam alone. When, moreover, he included the verses about man and woman being made together (Gen. 1:26), grant that not even then did he single them out for special treatment, for afterwards we have, "God saw all the things that he had made, and behold, they were very good" (Gen. 1:31). So it is clearly expressed: it is good that both man and woman were made.

X,47. From this question yet another comes to light. If Adam was created alone, why was it not said that Adam's creation was good?[5] Rather, it is only when woman was made from him that everything is then understood to be good. Granted that God had praised every created thing and had deemed the creation of the universe good: since man is included in God's commendation of nature in general, would it not have seemed superfluous to single out Adam's creation as something "good"? For this reason, at the time that Adam was created, by himself, God's praise of this particular good work would not have seemed to add in any way a further blessing. God even said that "it was *not* good for man to be alone." We know that Adam did not sin before the woman was created; indeed, after woman was made, she was the first to violate the divine command. She even dragged her husband along with her into sin and showed herself to be an incentive to him. If then, in truth, the woman is the author of sin, in what way does her addition seem to be for the good?

If you really think that the universe is in the care of God, you will infer that the Lord must have been more pleased about his being its cause than that the cause of sin, i.e., the woman, should have been condemned. So the Lord declared that it was "not good for man to be alone," because the

---

[5]Ambrose here reflects on the fact that God does not, in the Genesis 2 version of the creation story, pronounce a special blessing on Adam at his creation.

human race could not have been propagated from the man by himself. God preferred that there might be many people for whom he could work salvation and to whom he might forgive sin, than that there be only one person, Adam, even though he be sinless. In short, God is indeed the Author of both male and female, and he came into the world so that he might work the salvation of sinners.

Finally, God did not allow Cain, a man accused of fratricide (Gen. 4:8) to die before he begot children (Gen. 4:17). Thus for the sake of the succession of human reproduction, woman had to be added to the man. God's very words declare this when he says, "It is not good for man to be alone." For even if the woman was the first to sin, nevertheless, the fact that redemption was being prepared through her should not be excluded from the benefits of the divine action. Even though "Adam was not deceived, but the woman was deceived and was in sin, nonetheless," he says, "she shall be saved through the generation of children" (I Tim. 2:14-15), among whom she also brought forth Christ.

X,48. It is not beside the point to note that the woman was not made from the same earth from which Adam was formed, but from Adam's own rib. From this point we learn that the bodily nature of man and woman is one, one the source of the human race. Thus in the beginning man and woman were not created together as a couple, nor were two men nor two women created, but first a man and then a woman from him. Since God wished to constitute one human nature, he took away the possibility of multiple and diverse natures of this created being by beginning from one source. He said, "Let us make for him a helper like unto him" (Gen. 2:18). We take that to mean a helper for the purpose of generating human nature—and to do this is indeed to be a good helper! For if we take "helper" in the more favorable sense, the woman's work in the cause of procreation is found to be something very significant. It is like the earth's initial reception of the seed: it holds the seed and warms it, gradually making it grow and bringing it forth in the soil. This then is the way in which woman is a good helper, even though she may be called a helper of less importance. We also discover the same arrangement in human affairs, that powerful men in positions of authority generally enlist assistants of less importance.

XI,50. It is written, "And God sank Adam into a deep sleep and he slept" (Gen. 2:21). What does this "deep sleep" mean? Does it not mean that when we direct our minds for a while to the marital union, we seem to be turning expectant eyes to God's Kingdom? Do we not then seem to incline to a certain vision of that world and for a short time to sleep in God, even while we rest amid the worldly things of this present age? In short, after God "sank Adam into a deep sleep and he slept," then "the Lord God built the rib he took from Adam into a woman" (Gen. 2:21-22). "He built"[6] is well put in that verse where he was speaking of woman's creation, because the domestic edifice of man and woman seems to be rich in a certain kind of perfection. The man who is without a wife is accordingly considered to be without a home. Just as a man is thought to be more skillful at public duties, so a woman is thought more skillful in domestic services. Weigh the fact that God took a rib from Adam's body, not a piece from his soul: this is why woman is not called "soul of my soul" but "bone of my bones and flesh of my flesh" (Gen. 2:23).

John Chrysostom, bishop of Constantinople from 398-404 A.D., was of two minds about woman's status at the time of her creation. In some of his writings, such as in the following selection from his *Discourse 4 on Genesis*, he stressed that there had been an original "equality of honor" between Adam and Eve and took pains to argue

---

[6]*aedificavit.*

that Eve's role as "helper" was much superior to that of the animals whom God had also made to assist man.

1.[7] . . . Moreover, the first dominance and servitude was that in which men ruled over women. After the original sin, a need arose for this arrangement; before the sin, the woman was like the man. Indeed, when God molded the woman, he used the words in creating her that he had used when he fashioned man. Just as he said in the case of creating the male, "Let us make man after our image and likeness" (Gen. 1:26), rather than "Let there be man," so also in the case of woman, God did not say, "Let there be woman," but here he said in addition, "Let us make for him a helper" (Gen. 2:18). And he does not call her simply a "helper," but "a helper like him," once more showing the equality of honor.

Since God had introduced the animals as partners to help us with the many needs of our life and lest the woman also be considered in the ranks of these servants, note how clearly he makes the distinction between the animals and the woman. "He led the beasts to Adam and there was not found a helper resembling him, like unto him" (Gen. 2:19-20), he said. How can this be? Is not the horse a helper, who fights along with man in battle? Is not the ox a helper, who drags the plough and toils with us in the planting of the seed? The ass and the mule, are they not helpers, assisting in the transportation of our wares? To keep you from speaking this way, God makes a sharp distinction between the animals and the woman. He does not merely say, "There was found no helper for him" among the animals, but "There was found no helper like himself." Thus too in this passage he does not simply say, "Let us make a helper for him," but "Let us make a helper for him who resembles him."

But Chrysostom also believed that woman did not possess the "image of God" (Gen. 1:26) as man did, and

[7]Text: PG 54.594.

he linked her subordinate status to this deficiency; her status, in other words, was not simply a result of the Fall, but was an inferior one even at the moment of her creation. He argues his case in *Discourse 2 on Genesis*[8] against those who claim that both the man and the woman have the "image of God."

2. ...Certain others spring up to refute us, people who hold that we and God have the very same "image." Thus they misunderstand the meaning of Scripture. For the "image" is not meant in regard to essence, but in regard to authority, as we shall make clear by bringing forth arguments in an orderly manner. To grasp the point that the form of man is not that of God, listen to what Paul says: "For the man ought not to be veiled, for he is the image and glory of God. But woman is the glory of man. Therefore she ought to have a veil[9] on her head" (I Cor. 11:7-10). Indeed, if Paul here says this was the "image," making clear the unchangeableness of the form that is patterned on God,[10] then man is called the "image of God" because God has stamped him in this way.

Not so, according to our opponents, who argue that not only the man must have the "image," but the woman as well. Our answer is that the man and the woman do have one form, one distinctive character, one likeness. Then why is the man said to be in the "image of God" and the woman not? Because what Paul says about the "image" does not pertain to form. The "image" has rather to do with authority, and this only the man has; the woman has it no longer. For he is subjected to no one, while she is subjected to him; as God said, "Your inclination shall be for your husband and he shall rule over you" (Gen. 3:16). Therefore the man is

---

[8]Text: PG 54.589.

[9]The word for "veil" in Greek is also a word for "authority."

[10]Chrysostom here uses words sometimes employed by the Church Fathers to indicate that God is the "formal cause" of mankind.

in the "image of God" since he had no one above him, just as God has no superior but rules over everything. The woman, however, is "the glory of man," since she is subjected to him.

> In addition, Chrysostom thought that woman's inferior status made her more suited than man to assume the humbler responsibilities of life. Her sphere of activity was to be far more restricted than the man's. Chrysostom argues this point in a homily *The Kind of Women Who Ought To Be Taken As Wives.*[11]

4. Indeed, I have heard many people say, "So-and-so who used to be poor became very prosperous from his marriage. Since he married a rich woman, he's well off and now he fares sumptuously." What do you reply, O men? You neither feel shame nor do you blush, though you wish to make a profit from a wife? Why don't you prefer to sink into the ground, profiting in such a way? How can these be the words of a real man? A wife has just one purpose: to guard the possessions we have accumulated, to keep a close watch on the income, to take charge of the household. Indeed, this is why God gave her to you, that in these, plus all other matters, she might be a helper to you.

Our life is customarily organized into two spheres: public affairs and private matters, both of which were determined by God. To woman is assigned the presidency of the household; to man, all the business of state, the marketplace, the administration of justice, government, the military, and all other such enterprises. A woman is not able to hurl a spear or shoot an arrow, but she can grasp the distaff, weave at the loom; she correctly disposes of all such tasks that pertain to the household. She cannot express her opinion in a legislative assembly, but she can express it at home, and often she is more shrewd about household matters than her husband. She cannot handle state business well, but she can raise

11Text: PG 51.230.

children correctly, and children are our principal wealth. At a glance she can detect the bad behavior of the servants and can manage them carefully. She provides complete security for her husband and frees him from all such household concerns, concerns about money, woolworking, the preparation of food and decent clothing. She takes care of all other matters of this sort, that are neither fitting for her husband's concern nor would they be satisfactorily accomplished should he ever lay his hand to them—even if he struggled valiantly!

Indeed, this is a work of God's love and wisdom, that he who is skilled at the greater things is downright inept and useless in the performance of the less important ones, so that the woman's service is necessary. For if the man were adapted to undertake both sorts of activities, the female sex could easily be despised. Conversely, if the more important, most beneficial concerns were turned over to the woman, she would go quite mad. Therefore God did not apportion both duties to one sex, lest the other be displaced and be considered superfluous. Nor did God assign both to be equal in every way, lest from equality a kind of struggle and rivalry should again arise, for women in their contentiousness would deem themselves deserving of the front-row seats rather than the man! But taking precautions at one and the same time for peace and for decency, God maintained the order of each sex by dividing the business of human life into two parts and assigned the more necessary and beneficial aspects to the man and the less important, inferior matters to the woman. God's plan was extremely desirable for us, on the one hand because of our pressing needs and on the other, so that a woman would not rebel against her husband due to the inferiority of her service. Understanding all these things, let us thus strive for just one goal, virtue of soul and nobility of behavior, so that we may enjoy peace, live in concord, and maintain ourselves in love unto the end.

Whatever Eve's original role and purpose, the Church
Fathers agreed that she was responsible for the sin of
Genesis 3. One of the earliest expressions of this view in
patristic literature is found in the *Against Heresies,* a
polemical treatise against Gnostics composed by Irenaeus, bishop of Lyons, about 185 A.D. Although Irenaeus contrasts Eve's disobedience with the obedience of
Mary, he does not engage in vituperative declamations
against women on the basis of Eve's sin, as do some
Church Fathers.

III,22,4.[12] Moreover, it follows that Mary the Virgin is
found to be obedient. She says, "Behold your handmaid,
Lord; let it be done with me according to your word" (Lk.
1:38). Eve was disobedient, to be sure, since she did not obey
when she was still a virgin. Indeed, she had a husband,
Adam, but was still a virgin ("for they were both naked" in
Paradise "and were not ashamed" [Gen. 2:25], since they
had been created only a short time before and did not
understand about the production of children, for it was
proper for them first to reach maturity and thus henceforth
to multiply); Eve, having become disobedient, was made the
cause of death both for herself and for all the human race.
Thus also Mary had a husband selected for her and nonetheless was a virgin, yet by her obedience she was made the
cause of salvation both for herself and for all the human
race. For this reason the law calls a woman engaged to a
man his wife, while conceding that she is still a virgin. This
indicates a link that goes from Mary back to Eve.... Moreover, the knot of Eve's disobedience was loosened through
the obedience of Mary. For what the virgin Eve bound
through unbelief, this the Virgin Mary loosed through faith.

The view that blame for the first sin extended from Eve
to all other women soon became a commonplace in early

[12]Text: PG 7.958.

Christian literature. Tertullian, an important Christian writer from the North African city of Carthage, was particularly passionate in his denunciations, as is revealed in his treatise *On the Dress of Women* that dates from the opening years of the third century. Tertullian addresses a female audience.

I,1,1.[13] If such strong faith remained on earth, as strong as the reward of faith is expected in heaven, not one of you, dearest sisters, from the time she acknowledged the living God and learned about herself, that is, about the condition of women, would have desired a more charming dress, not to speak of a more exquisite one. She would rather go about in cheap clothes and strive for an appearance characterized by neglect. She would carry herself around like Eve, mourning and penitent, that she might more fully expiate by each garment of penitence that which she acquired from Eve—I mean the degradation of the first sin and the hatefulness of human perdition. "In pains and anxieties you bring forth children, woman, and your inclination is for your husband, and he rules over you" (Gen. 3:16)—and you know not that you also are an Eve?

I,1,2. God's judgment on this sex lives on in our age; the guilt necessarily lives on as well. *You* are the Devil's gateway; *you* are the unsealer of that tree; *you* are the first foresaker of the divine law; *you* are the one who persuaded him whom the Devil was not brave enough to approach; *you* so lightly crushed the image of God, the man Adam; because of *your* punishment, that is, death, even the Son of God had to die. And you think to adorn yourself beyond your "tunics of skins" (Gen. 3:21)?

Eve's particular responsibility for the first sin is also pressed home by Augustine in his *Literal Commentary*

[13]Text: CSEL 70.59.

on *Genesis*.[14] Augustine makes much of the biblical wording that Eve, not Adam, was the one who was led astray.

XI,42. . . . If Adam were already spiritual (in mind, at least, if not in body), how could he have believed what the serpent said? For the serpent said that God prohibited them from eating the fruit of that tree because he knew that if they did so, they would become as gods by their knowing good and evil (Gen. 3:5)—as if God begrudged his creatures so great a blessing! That a man endowed with a spiritual mind could have believed this is astonishing. And just because it is impossible to believe it, woman was given to man, woman who was of small intelligence and who perhaps still lives more in accordance with the promptings of the inferior flesh than by the superior reason. Is this why the apostle Paul does not attribute the image of God to her? For Paul speaks as follows: "The man ought not to cover his head, for he is the image and glory of God, but the woman is the glory of man" (I Cor. 11:7)—not in the sense that the woman's mind cannot receive the same "image," since he tells us that in a stage of grace there is "neither male nor female" (Gal. 3:28).

However, maybe the woman had not yet received this grace that comes with the knowledge of God, but would have acquired it only gradually, under the man's rule and management. The apostle Paul's words were not meaningless when he said, "For Adam was formed first, then Eve. And Adam was not led astray, but the woman was, and was made guilty of transgression" (I Tim. 2:13-14), i.e., that through her the man became guilty of transgression. For the apostle calls him a transgressor as well when he says, "In the likeness of the transgression of Adam, who is a figure of him who is to come"(Rom. 5:14), but he does *not* say that Adam was "led astray." For even when asked, Adam does not

[14]Text: CSEL 28, 1, 376.

reply, "The woman whom you gave me led me astray and I ate," but rather he says, "She gave me from the tree and I ate." She, to be sure, *did* speak the words, "The serpent led me astray" (Gen. 3:13).

Similar opinions about Eve's responsibility for the sin and the ensuing penalties God placed upon her, according to Genesis 3:16, were expressed by Ambrose in *On Paradise.*[15]

XII,56. ...We hold that it was Adam, not Eve, who received the command from God,[16] for the woman had not yet been created. Scripture does not transmit the specific words by which Adam told the woman the character and the sequence of the command. But we do understand that the sequence of the command was transmitted through the man to the woman. Although we should note what others have expressed on the matter, it seems to me nonetheless that the woman instigated the crime, originated the deceit. For even if there is some uncertainty about the two in this respect, nonetheless Scripture records which sex it was that first was liable to sin. Add that she is fettered by a previous condemnation when afterwards the earlier wrong is disclosed. The woman, therefore, is the originator of the man's wrongdoing, not the man of the woman's. Hence Paul also says, "Adam was not deceived, but the woman was deceived and committed sin" (I Tim. 2:14).

XIV,72. Because Eve herself confessed her fault, a milder and more advantageous sentence condemning her error followed, one that did not preclude forgiveness. Its intent was that she should devote herself to her husband, so as to serve him. There were two reasons for this: first, that she might not so easily delight in doing wrong, and second, that being placed under the stronger vessel, she might not expose her

15Text: CSEL 32, 1, 316;329.
16Not to eat of the tree of the knowledge of good and evil.

husband to ridicule, but might even more be ruled by his advice. Indeed, I clearly perceive in this the mystery of Christ and the Church. For the Church's future turning to Christ is indicated, and a pious servitude in subjection to the Word of God, far better than the freedom of this world. Hence it is written, "You shall honor the Lord your God and him alone shall you serve" (Deut. 6:13). This kind of servitude, then, is a gift of God. In fact, compliance with this servitude is counted among blessings. . . .

> Chrysostom made clear that whatever the inferior position of woman at creation, she was subjected to the man chiefly because of her role in the first sin. In *Homily 26 on I Corinthians*[17] he writes as follows:

2. . . . Among us the woman is fairly subjected to the man, for equality of honor produces strife. Not only for this reason is she subjected, but also because of the treachery that took place at the world's beginning. Therefore, I tell you, she was not subjected straightway upon her creation, nor yet when God led her to the man did she hear anything of this sort from him, nor did the man say anything like this to her, either. He rather said that she was "bone of his bones, flesh of his flesh" (Gen. 2:23), but rule or subjection he nowhere mentioned to her. When, however, she misused her power, and although created as a helper was found to be treacherous and to have ruined everything, then justly she hears the rest: "Your inclination shall be toward your husband" (Gen. 3:16).[18]

> Chrysostom, however, believed that woman's subjection was all for the good and was not burdensome to women who accepted it as God's will. Both the Old and the New Testaments agree on women's subordinate place

[17]Text: PG 61.215.
[18]"and he shall rule over you."

as a result of the sin, he argues in *Discourse 4 on Genesis*.[19]

1. ...After the sin came the words, "Your inclination shall be for your husband and he shall rule over you"(Gen. 3:16). God said in effect to Eve, "I made you equal in honor. You did not use your authority well, so consign yourself to a state of subordination. You have not borne your liberty, so accept servitude. Since you do not know how to rule—as you showed in your experiment with the business of life— henceforth be among the governed and acknowledge your husband as a lord." Note God's kindness here. For lest when she heard the words, "He shall rule over you," she might imagine them to mean a burdensome tyranny, God puts the words of caring first. He did this by saying, "Your inclination shall be for your husband," that is, "He is your refuge, your haven, and your security: he shall be these things to you. Amid all life's daily terrors, I give you the right to turn to him, to take refuge in him." This wasn't all. God also linked them together by their natural needs, linked them as if by an unbroken bond when he encircled them with the chain of desire. You see how sin introduced woman's subjection, but how God, so ingenious and wise, used the results of sin for our benefit.

Listen to how Paul speaks of this subjection, so that you may again be instructed on the agreement of the Old and the New Testaments. Paul says, "Let the woman learn in silence, in all subjection" (I Tim. 2:11). Do you see how he, too, submits the woman to the man? Hold on, and you will hear the reason. Why does Paul say, "in all subjection"? He asserts, "I do not permit a woman to teach a man" (I Tim. 2:12). Why not? Because she taught Adam once and for all, and taught him badly. "Nor should she have authority over the man" (I Tim. 2:12). What in the world is he getting at?

[19]Text: PG 54.594.

She exerted her authority once and exerted it badly. And she should be "in silence." Tell the reason for this as well. Paul says, "Adam was not deceived, but the woman was deceived and sinned" (I Tim. 2:14). Therefore let her descend from the professor's chair! Those who know not how to teach, let them learn, he says. If they don't want to learn but rather want to teach, they destroy both themselves and those who learn from them. This is the very thing that occurred through the woman's agency. So here it is evident that she is subjected to the man and that the subjection is because of sin. I want you to heed that verse, "Your inclination shall be for your husband and he shall rule over you."

2. I want to teach you how Paul speaks to this concern as well, how he mixes the authority with affection. How does he manage to do it? He says in the Epistle to the Corinthians,[20] "Men, love your wives" (Col. 3:19; Eph. 5:25). Behold, how like the Old Testament verse, "Your inclination shall be for your husband" (Gen. 3:16)! Paul then says, "Wives, respect your husbands" (Col. 3:18; Eph. 5:22). Behold, how like the Old Testament verse, "He shall rule over you" (Gen. 3:16)! You see how the tyranny is not burdensome when the master is the frenzied lover of the woman who serves, when fear is tempered with love? Thus the burdensome quality is removed from servitude.

> Augustine's views on the original sin were of prime importance for the development of western theology. He agreed with other Church Fathers that women's subjection was one result of that sin, but he analyzed in greater detail two other results of that sin, the entrance of death and of lust to the world. Augustine believed that lust, so irrational in its expression, would not have existed in Paradise had the sin not been committed, yet he affirmed that there would have been sexual intercourse and pro-

---

[20]Actually in Ephesians and Colossians.

creation even if the sin had not occurred. His phantasized description of the sexual relation between Adam and Eve had there been no sin is a fascinating piece of speculation. Despite Augustine's despair over the power of lust (his own early sexual experiences made him keenly aware of that about which he wrote), his hypothesis that sexual intercourse would have been part of God's world even if humans had remained sinless opened the way for a stronger appreciation of marriage than did the views of some other Church Fathers. Here are Augustine's musings on the subject from his lengthy theology of history, *The City of God:*

XIV,23.[21] . . . Therefore marriage, worthy of the bliss of Paradise had the sin not been committed, would have brought forth offspring to be loved without having had lust to shame us. But in what way this could have occurred, we cannot now demonstrate by example. Nonetheless, it ought not on this account to seem incredible that the will, which is now served by so many bodily members, could also have been served by this member, the sexual one, without that lust. For truly, we can move our hands and our feet when we want to; these bodily parts respond without any resistance. We see with what great ease they act, both in our own situation and in that of others. Most especially we note this among those who labor at some physical task, where by nimble diligence a somewhat weak and faltering nature accomplishes its task. Can we not also believe that those sexual organs, like our other bodily members, could have submissively served us through an inclination of the will in the task of producing children, if there had been no lust, the repayment for the sin of disobedience? . . .

XIV,26. Thus man was living in Paradise just as he wished, as long as he willed what God had commanded. He

21Text: CSEL 40, 2, 47.

lived in the enjoyment of God, from whose goodness he was good. He lived without lacking anything, and had it in his power always to live in the same way. He had food lest he hunger, drink lest he thirst, the tree of life lest he decay in old age. No vexations of any of his senses assailed him, vexations either arising from unsoundness in his body or arising from his body. No sickness from within nor wound from without caused him to fear. He was in the best of bodily health and in complete tranquillity of soul.

Just as in Paradise there was no summer or winter, even so within its inhabitant nothing came to pass from desire or from fear as a stumbling block to his good will. There was no sadness at all nor was there empty levity. True joy continued without interruption from God, for whom there glowed "love from a pure heart and a good conscience and a true faith" (I Tim. 1:5). And between the marriage partners there was a trusting community springing from chaste love; there was a peaceful alertness of mind and body, and an easy keeping of the command. Weariness was not vexing in leisure time, nor did sleep press upon them against their wills.

In such an easy situation, in such human happiness, we are far from suspecting that it was impossible for offspring to be begotten without the malady of lust. Rather, those bodily parts could have been moved by the same command of the will as the other members are. The husband, without the alluring sting of passion, with tranquil mind and no destruction of bodily wholeness, would have been poured out in the marital embrace. Even though we are not able to prove this through experience, it is not to be believed for this reason that when the wild fire of love did not drive those parts of the body, but that, as there was need, a voluntary power came to aid, the masculine seed then could not have been discharged into the wife's womb, preserving the wholeness of the female genitalia, just as now the flow of menstrual blood can be discharged from a virgin's uterus without injuring that same integrity. For the seed obviously could have been inserted through the same passage by which this other fluid can be ejected. Just as at childbirth the woman's womb would not have been dilated by a groan of pain, but by the impulse of fullness of term, so their sexual organs would have been joined for impregnation and conception not by lustful appetite, but by a natural exercise of the will.

Given the ambivalent opinions of the Church Fathers on sexual matters, it is obvious that marriage itself might need some defending. Especially in the second and third centuries, orthodox Christians struggled against various Gnostic groups which posited that the material world was evil. From this principle, the Gnostics derived either an ascetic sexual ethic that made no allowance for sexual functioning or a libertine morality that declared itself not beholden to the commandments of the evil God who made this pitiable world. Over against such Gnostic tenets, Clement of Alexandria, writing about 200 A.D., felt compelled to stress the relative goodness of marriage and procreation, despite his preference for celibacy. Clement's treatise on marriage, constituting Book 3 of his *Miscellanies*,[22] may sound like a lukewarm defense of its subject to the contemporary reader, yet it is in fact the strongest argument for the goodness of marriage to be found in the writings of the first three Christian centuries. Clement considers the various Gnostic positions on marriage and sets forth what he considers the orthodox Christian response.

III,1,1. Thus the Valentinians,[23] who believe that sexual union is patterned after the divine emanations on high, are

[22]Text: GCS 15.195.
[23]A Gnostic sect that flourished in the second century.

very pleased with marriage. In contrast, the followers of Basilides[24] say, "When the apostles inquired whether it would not be preferable not to marry, the Lord replied to them, 'Not all can accept this saying...for there are eunuchs who were so from birth, and others are eunuchs of necessity'" (Mt. 19:11-12). And their interpretation of the saying goes something like this: Some men from birth have a natural repulsion to women, and whatever men are so constituted with this sort of nature do well not to marry. Those, they say, are the "eunuchs from birth." The "eunuchs from necessity" are those theatrical ascetics who control themselves because of their counter-desire for fame. [And those castrated by chance have become "eunuchs by necessity."][25] These, then, who have become "eunuchs by necessity" have not done so by rational intent. But those who have made themselves "eunuchs for the sake of the eternal Kingdom" say they reached this conclusion, i.e., the decision for the ascetic life, because of the consequences of marriage: they fear the trouble involved in procuring the necessities marriage requires.

III,1,4. Continence, then, is a disdain for the body that agrees with our confession of God. For continence does not pertain just to sexual desire, but to everything that the soul wickedly desires when it rests discontent with the basic necessities. There is in addition a continence that pertains to the tongue, and ones concerning property, use, and desire. Continence not only teaches us chastity; indeed, it provides us with chastity, since it is a grace and power of God. Thus I must report something of our view on the proposed topic. We bless sexual abstinence in those to whom this condition has been given by God, but we also marvel at monogamy and the great majesty of a single marriage, for we think that

---

[24]A second-century Gnostic teacher.
[25]Possibly an interpolation in the Greek.

we should suffer with each other and "bear one another's burdens" (Gal. 6:2), lest anyone who believes he is standing firm all by himself should fall (I Cor. 10:12). It is of second marriage that the apostle Paul says, "If you burn, marry" (I Cor. 7:9).

III,2,5. But the disciples of Carpocrates and Epiphanes[26] think that wives should be held in common. Through them the greatest blasphemy has become current against the name of Christianity. This Epiphanes, whose writings I have in my possession, was a son of Carpocrates and his mother was Alexandria; his father's line was Alexandrian, and his mother's, Cephallenian. All together he lived only seventeen years and was honored as a god in Same in Cephallenia. ... His father taught him both his general education and Platonic thought, and he had expounded to him the knowledge of the Monad, from which stems the heresy of the Carpocratians.

> (Epiphanes in his book *Concerning Righteousness* wrote as follows, Clement reports:)

III,2,8. "God made everything for man to share in common; by bringing the female to the male in common and by joining all the animals in the same way, he proclaimed righteousness to consist of communality with equality. Yet those who have thus been born have denied the communality implied by their birth and say, 'Let him who took one woman have her, rather than all being able to share her, as the other animals do.'" These things I report in his own phrases. Next he goes on in the same way with his speech: "He created in males a vigorous and ardent desire in order to ensure the permanence of the race, a desire that neither law nor custom nor anything else can obliterate. For it is an ordinance of God."

---

[26]Leaders of libertine Gnostic groups.

How can this man still be estimated as one of us when by these sentiments he destroys both the Law and the Gospel? For the one says, "Do not commit adultery" (Ex. 20:14) and the other says, "Anyone who looks with desire has already committed adultery" (Mt. 5:28). The saying in the Law, "You shall not covet" (Ex. 20:17) shows that one God is proclaimed by the Law, the Prophets, and the Gospel, for it says, "You shall not covet your neighbor's wife...."

III,2,10. So these are the doctrines of the fine Carpocratians! It is reported that these people and some other zealots for the same sort of evil gather together for banquets (I for my part would not deem their assembly a Christian love-feast), men and women together. After they have gorged themselves on food ("upon being filled, then comes Cypris,"[27] as it says), by overturning the lamp and putting out the light, they think to hide the disgrace of this fornicating "righteousness": they have sexual intercourse in what manner they will and with what women they wish. Having rehearsed communality in this "love-feast," they now demand by day from whatever women they wish that they comply with the law of Carpocrates, although it cannot be called the ordinance of God. I think that such must be the ordinance that Carpocrates decreed for the lusts of dogs and pigs and goats! It appears to me that he wrongly interpreted Plato's words in the *Republic*, that the women of all are to be in common.[28] Rather, Plato meant that women before they marry are "in common" to those men who think of asking to marry them, just as the theatre is said to be "in common" for viewers, but when each man has fixed upon his own woman, then she is no longer available to be shared.

III,3,12. And if earlier, Plato himself and the Pythagoreans deemed birth as evil, as later on the Marcionites also

---

[27] Aphrodite, the love goddess: Euripides, *Frag. inc.* 895.
[28] *Republic* V, 457Dff.

did (although Marcion[29] did not go so far as to suggest that wives be in common), the Marcionites think nature is evil, that it was created out of evil matter and by a just agent. For the reason that they do not wish to fill up the world made by the Creator, they choose to refrain from marriage. They put themselves in opposition to their Maker and hasten to the God who is called good but not to the God of the other sort, as they phrase it. Since they desire to leave on earth nothing of their own after them, they remain chaste, not out of choice but from enmity to the Creator, not wanting to use the things created by him. But these people, in their impious warfare against God, have lost their natural reason, disdaining the patience and goodness of God. Even if they do not want to marry, they nonetheless use food that has been made and they breathe the Creator's air. These things are his works and they remain established in these things of his. . . .

III,4,25. Of the heretics, we mentioned Marcion of Pontus who deprecated using the things of the world because of opposition to the Creator. But the reason for his continence is thus the Creator himself, if indeed this can be labelled continence. This mighty man, who as God's foe sets himself in opposition to God, is continent against his will, ravaging the creation and the process of shaping life. . . .

III,5,40. . . . Let us bring forth all the heresies, dividing them into two classifications so we can respond to them. For either they teach that how we live is a matter of "indifference"[30] or they praise an extreme continence out of impiety and contentiousness. Let us first consider the former category. If it is possible to choose from all styles of life, it is clear that one may live in continence, and if any life is free from danger for the elect person, then it is also evident that a life with virtue and self-control is much more so. If the

[29]A second-century Christian often considered by the Church Fathers to be a Gnostic.
[30]A term from Stoic philosophy indicating a morally neutral category of actions.

"Lord of the Sabbath" (Mk. 2:28 = Mt. 12:8 = Lk. 6:5), Jesus, has been granted the right to be counted guiltless even if he lives dissolutely, how much more will the person who conducts himself in a decorous fashion not have to render an account? "All things are lawful, but not all things are expedient," says the apostle Paul (I Cor. 6:12; 10:23). But if "all things are lawful," clearly self-control is lawful as well.

III,5,43. It is not possible for those who are still swayed by their passions to have knowledge of God. Accordingly, neither can they obtain the hope, since they have not acquired any knowledge of God. And the person who fails to gain this end is rightly charged with ignorance. For it is altogether impossible both to be a wise person and not to feel ashamed at indulging the body....

III,6,49. There are people who openly say that marriage is fornication and decree that it was imparted by the Devil. These boasters say that they are imitating the Lord who neither married nor had any possessions in the world; they rather brag that they comprehend the Gospel better than other people. But Scripture says to them, "God resists the proud, but gives grace to the humble" (James 4:6; I Pet. 5:5). So, then, they do not know why the Lord did not marry. First of all, he had his own bride, the church (cf. Eph. 5:22-33), and second, he was not an ordinary man that he needed some helper after the flesh (Gen. 2:18). Nor was it necessary for him to beget offspring, since he remains eternally and was born the only Son of God....

(As part of his defense of marriage, Clement points out that notable Old and New Testament figures married:)

III,6,53. Indeed, Paul did not shrink from greeting his mate in a certain one of his letters (cf. Phil. 4:3).[31] He did not bring her around with him because it was advantageous for his ministry not to do so. Thus he says in one letter, "Do we

[31]Clement interprets the "yokefellow" Paul addresses to be his wife.

not have the authority to take along with us a wife that is a sister, as the rest of the apostles do?" (I Cor. 9:5). But these apostles, as was proper to their ministry, attended to preaching without distraction, took their wives with them not as marriage partners but as sisters, that they might be co-ministers to women at home. Through them the teaching of the Lord was introduced to the women's section of the household without incurring slander. For we know in addition the things pertaining to women deacons that the noble Paul drew up in one of his two letters to Timothy (I Tim. 3:11?). . . .

III,7,57. Thus the human notion of continence, I mean that held by the Greek philosophers, professes that we should fight desire and not assist its acts. Our notion, however, is that we should not even experience desire. It is not merely that someone should conquer desire, but that in some way he should be continent about desire itself. And there is no other way to receive this continence except by the grace of God. For this reason he said, "Ask and it shall be given to you" (Mt. 7:7 = Lk. 11:9). . . .

III,7,58. Our general line of reasoning about marriage and food and other things proposes that we should not act with desire as our motivation. We should rather will only those things that are necessary. For we are not children of desire, but of will (cf. John 1:13). And the man who desires to marry in order to beget children must discipline himself in continence, so that it is not desire he experiences for his wife, whom he ought to love, and so that he may beget children with a decorous and temperate will. For we have been taught not to "take thought for the flesh to satisfy its desires," and to "walk decently, as in the daylight," in Christ and in the enlightened training of the Lord, "not in revelling and drunkenness, not in chambering and wantonness, not in strife and envy" (Rom. 13:13-14).

III,12,79. . . . The proposed goal, both for the man who

adopts celibacy for himself and for the man who yokes himself in marriage for the sake of begetting children, should be to remain unyielding to lesser things. If he lives his life in devotion, he will obtain for himself great honor with God, as his continence is both pure and in accord with reason. But if he goes beyond the standard he chose to win greater glory, then he may lose hope. Thus celibacy and marriage each have their differing kinds of service and ministry to the Lord, I mean the taking care of children and a wife. It appears that for a man wishing a perfect marriage, the domestic relation allows him to take upon himself the care of everything in the household he and his wife share. To begin with, Paul says that bishops should be appointed who, by having practiced on their own households, can also govern the whole church (I Tim. 3:4-5). Therefore, let each person accomplish his ministry by the work in which he was called, in order that he may be free in Christ and receive the appropriate reward for his service.

(Clement argues against the Gnostics who say that Adam and Eve became like the beasts when they began to practice sexual intercourse. Clement retorts that the first couple performed the sex act "by nature." He continues:)

III,17,103. If, however, nature led them to the begetting of offspring, just as it does the irrational creatures, nonetheless they were impelled to do so more quickly than was fitting, for they were still young, having been led astray by deceit. God's condemnation of them was just, because they did not wait for his decision. But birth is holy. By it the world was established, as were the existences, natures, angels, powers, souls, commandments, the Law, the Gospel, and the knowledge of God.... How, apart from the body, could the plan for us in the Church reach its goal? Indeed, he himself who is the Head of the Church came in the flesh, lacking form, unsightly (Is. 53:2), in order to teach us to gaze upon the formless and incorporeal quality of the divine cause....

> Writers of the fourth and fifth centuries, such as John Chrysostom and Augustine, no longer needed to shape their treatises on marriage so directly in response to the Gnostic views. Yet by their time, the ascetic movement was in full flower and the life of asexual continence was being highly recommended to all Christians. How, in the light of the superior evaluation given to virginity, could a Christian theologian still explain marriage as God's good gift? Augustine's view of marriage, despite his condemnation of lust, is more positive than that of Chrysostom, who did not think God had intended humans to reproduce by sexual means and hence, with this claim, shut out a major argument on behalf of marriage. Augustine's views are here expressed in his treatise *On Marriage and Concupiscence,*[32] written around 420 A.D. Augustine's position on contraception and abortion as stated in this selection became determinative for much of later Catholic teaching.

I,4,5. The natural good of marriage is thus sexual intercourse between male and female for the sake of procreation. But a person uses this good of marriage badly if he uses it bestially, so that his purpose is in the pleasure of lust rather than in the desire for offspring. Nonetheless, in some of the irrational animals (for example, in most birds) there is preserved something that closely resembles a confederation of mates. The social skill involved in building a nest and also the birds' sharing the time for warming the eggs, and their taking turns in the work of feeding the young birds, makes them appear even more that in mating they put the task of procreation in the place of appeasement of their lust. Of

---

[32]Text: CSEL 42, 2, 215.

these two examples, one is the likeness of a human in a beast, the other is the likeness of a beast in a human.

What I said indeed pertained to the nature of marriage (that the male and female are joined in partnership for procreation and hence do not cheat each other, for by nature no association wants a deceptive partner), and does so to the extent that even unbelievers have this manifest good, yet since they use it without faith, they turn it to evil and sin. In the same way, then, the marriage of believers transforms that carnal lust by which the flesh lusts against the spirit (Gal. 5:17) to a righteous use. For believers have the intention of producing offspring to be regenerated, so that those who are born as children of the world may be born again as sons of God.

And for this reason, those who in begetting offspring do not have this intention, this will, this goal of transferring their children from being members of the first man into members of Christ, but pride themselves that they are unbelieving parents over unbelieving children, these people, however careful they may be in their matrimonial schedule to cohabitate only for the sake of producing children, do not in themselves truly have conjugal chastity. For since chastity is a virtue that has unchastity as its contrary vice, and since all the virtues, even those that act through the body, reside in the soul, how can the body be deemed chaste in any real sense when the soul itself fornicates against the true God? Such fornication that holy Psalmist condemns when he says, "Behold, for those that put themselves far from you shall perish; you have destroyed all who fornicate against you" (Ps. 73:27). Thus there cannot be said to be true chastity, whether in marriage, in widowhood, or in virginity, except that which is disposed to the true faith. For even though sound judgment prefers holy virginity to marriage, what Christian in sober mind would not prefer Catholic Christian women who had been married even more than once, not just to the Vestal Virgins, but even to the heretical virgins? So great is the power of faith, of which the Apostle says, "Everything that is not of faith is sin" (Rom. 14:23). The topic is also covered in the Epistle to the Hebrews: "Without faith it is impossible to please God" (Heb. 11:6).

I,10,11. What is commended to believers in marriage is certainly not so much fecundity, whose fruit is offspring, nor chastity, whose bond is fidelity, but also, in truth, a kind of sacramental tie, whence the Apostle says, "Husbands, love your wives, just as Christ also loved the Church" (Eph. 5:25). The essence of this marriage bond is doubtless that the man and woman joined in marriage should remain together as long as they live and that it is not lawful except for the sake of fornication for one spouse to be separated from the other (Mt. 5:32; 19:9). For this is maintained in the case of Christ and the Church, so as with two living entities, no divorce can ever separate them. And to such an extent is this bond kept in the City of our God, in his holy mountain (Ps. 48:1-2), i.e., in the Church of Christ, by all the believing married people, who doubtless are members of Christ, that although for the sake of bringing forth children women marry and men take wives, never is one permitted to abandon a sterile spouse in order to take another, fecund one. Anyone who does this is accused of adultery by the law of the Gospel, though not by the law of the world. According to secular law, when a divorce without charges takes place, the parties are permitted to enter into other marriages: the Lord even declares that the holy man Moses allowed such divorce to the Israelites because of their hardness of heart (Mt. 19:8, 9). The same judgment applies to the woman if she marries another man. And to such a degree do the laws of marriage remain for those who once for all entered upon them for as long as they should live, that they who have separated from each other are still looked on as spouses rather than the couple involved in the new partnership.

They would not, of course, be considered adulterers with these others if the former marriage did not remain permanent. Indeed, if the husband dies, i.e., the husband with whom a true marriage existed, then a true marriage can be made that earlier would have been adultery. Thus a certain conjugal relation remains while they are alive that cannot be destroyed either by separation or by coupling with another....

I,15,17. Nonetheless, it is one thing to have sexual intercourse only from the desire to bring forth children, which is not sinful; it is something else to long for the pleasure of carnal intercourse which entails venial sin, even when the act is done with no one but the spouse. In cases where the propagation of offspring is not the reason for sexual intercourse, even then there is, nonetheless, in this passion no prevention of the propagation of offspring, whether by evil desire or evil act. But those who take contraceptive measures, even if they are called spouses, are not; they retain nothing whatever of true marriage, but make the honored name a cover for shamefulness. They go so far as to expose their children born against their will, for they loathe to nourish or to keep those whom they were reluctant to bring forth. Thus when they rage against those whom in dark sinfulness they did not wish to beget, the sin is set forth in clear light and by the manifest cruelty is the hidden wickedness exposed. Furthermore sometimes this lustful cruelty or cruel lust even reaches the point that it arranges for sterility through drugs, and if nothing avails, tries to destroy and expel the fetus conceived within the womb in some way, wanting its offsping to die rather than live, or if the fetus were already living in the womb, to be killed before it was born. In short, if both partners are of this sort, they are not spouses, and if they were such from the beginning of the marriage, they have not united with each other by marriage but by defilement. However, if only one of the partners behaves this way, I dare to proclaim that either the woman is in a sense the husband's whore, or he is the wife's adulterer.

I,17,19. In marriage, however, let us esteem these nuptial

goods: offspring, fidelity, and the sacramental bond. Offspring, not so much that it simply be born, but born again, for it is born to punishment unless it is reborn to life. As for fidelity, I do not mean the sort that even unbelievers preserve with one another in their zeal for the flesh. For what man, however shameless, wants an adulterous wife? Or what woman, however shameless, wants an adulterous husband? Certainly there is in marriage a natural good, even though carnal. But a "member of Christ" (I Cor. 6:15) ought to fear adultery, because of the spouse, not because of himself, and to hope for a reward from Christ for the fidelity that he displays to his spouse. Assuredly since the sacramental bond is not lost either by separation or by adultery, the couple should keep it amicably and chastely. For it is the only good that even a sterile marriage retains by the law of piety, once the hope of fecundity is gone, the hope on account of which they became a couple. He who wishes to praise marriage, let him praise these nuptial goods of marriage. Lust of the flesh, however, should not be attributed to marriage, but is tolerated: it is not a good stemming from the nature of marriage, but an evil resulting from the ancient sin.

I,24,27. Therefore the devil holds infants guilty, infants born not from the good that pertains to marriage, but from the evil of lust. To be sure, marriage uses lust correctly, but nonetheless even marriage blushes with shame at it. In itself, marriage is honorable in all the goods that appropriately belong to it, but even when the partners have kept their bed pure (Heb. 13:4)—not only from fornication and adultery, which are damnable outrages, but also indeed from those excesses of the sexual relation that do not come about from a strong desire to have children, but rather from an overwhelming lust for pleasure, excesses that are venial sins in the married couple—nonetheless, when it comes to performing the act of generation, the very intercourse that is lawful and honorable cannot take place without the ardor of lust. As a result, the partners cannot carry out the act on the basis of reason, but rather proceed out of lust. Certainly this ardor, whether it follows or precedes the will, nonetheless somehow moves the members as if by its own power, members that cannot be moved by the will alone. The ardor thus shows that it is not the servant of a will that governs it, but the punishment of a disobedient will; it is not moved by free will but by some seductive stimulus and for this reason it is shameful. This lust of the flesh that is permitted in the regenerate and is no longer reckoned as sin nonetheless does not occur in nature apart from sin. I say that this fleshly lust is, so to speak, the daughter of sin, and when it consents to filthy acts, it is also the mother of many sins. Whatever offspring is born is liable to original sin unless it is reborn in him whom the Virgin conceived without this lust. On that account, when he deigned to be born in the flesh, he alone was born without sin.

II,20,35. ... However, what the apostle Paul says of the wanton, that "abandoning the natural use with women, they were aflame in their lust for one another, men doing disgraceful things with men" (Rom. 1:27), he does not speak of the marital act *per se* but of the "natural" sexual act, wishing us to understand that with the members created for this purpose, the two sexes can come together for procreation. From this it follows that when a man has intercourse with a prostitute using these members, the use is "natural," although it is not praiseworthy but blameworthy. But in truth, to use a part of the body that was not meant for procreation is against nature and disgraceful, even if a man is having sexual relations with his wife. For earlier, the same Apostle said of women, "For their women changed the natural use into that which was against nature" (Rom. 1:26); then about men he adds that they performed shameful acts with men, having left the natural use of women. Therefore that phrase "natural use" is not one meant to praise married sexual intercourse, but is intended to indicate (by contrast) those shameful deeds that are even more impure and defiled than those illicit ones that are performed with women but are nonetheless "natural."

Augustine's views on the relative goodness of marriage also emerge in his earlier treatise *On the Good of Marriage.*

9.[33] Certainly it is to be understood that God gives us some goods that are desirable for their own sake, such as wisdom, health, friendship, and others that are necessary for the sake of something else, such as learning, food, drink, sleep, marriage, sexual intercourse. For of these latter, some are necessary for the sake of wisdom, such as learning; some for the sake of health, such as food, drink, and sleep; some for the sake of friendship, such as marriage or sexual intercourse, for in them abides the propagation of the human race in which friendly association is a great good. Thus a person sins who uses these goods necessary for the sake of something else for a purpose other than that for which they were established; in some cases he sins venially, in others, mortally. To be sure, whoever uses them for the purpose for which they were given does well. Therefore, if the person to whom these things are not necessary abstains from using them, he does even better.

Thus when we need these goods, we can rightfully wish for them, but it is preferable that we do not so wish than that we do, for we ourselves are better people when we do not deem these goods to be necessary things. It is good to marry because it is good to bring forth children, to be the mother of a family (I Tim. 5:14; 2:15), but it is better not to marry, because it is better for human society itself not to need this activity.

For such is the human race at present that those others who cannot restrain themselves involve themselves in marriage; many as well now revel in illicit copulation, yet the good Creator brings good out of their evils. The result is that numerous offspring and an abundant succession do not cease to come forth, from which holy friendships are procured. From this is inferred that at the beginning of the human race, especially for the sake of propagating the

[33]Text: CSEL 41.199.

people of God through whom the Prince and Savior of all people should be both prophesied and born, holy people ought to have used marriage, not seeking it for its own sake, but as necessary for something else. But now, in fact, since everywhere in all nations spiritual relationship abundantly overflows, in order to devise a holy and pure society we should warn even those who wish to unite in marriage only for the sake of having children that they might rather use the larger good of continence.

10. But I know that some people mutter, asking, "What if all humans wished to abstain from sexual relationships entirely, how would the human race continue?" Would to heaven that everybody might wish this, at least if they did so "in love, from a pure heart, good conscience, and a genuine faith" (I Tim. 1:5)! The City of God would be more quickly filled and the end of the world hastened. For what else does it appear the apostle Paul was urging when he said in that passage, "I would that everyone were as I myself am" (I Cor. 7:7)? Or in that other passage where it says, "I tell you this, brethren, the time is short; it remains that those who have wives should be as if they had them not, and they who weep, as if not weeping, and they who rejoice, as if not rejoicing, and those who buy, as if not buying, and those who use the world, as if they used it not, for the form of this world is passing away. I want you to be without anxiety" (I Cor. 7:29-32). Next he adds: "He who is without a wife, thinks of the things that are of the Lord, how to please the Lord. But he who is joined in matrimony, thinks of the things of the world, how to please his wife. And an unmarried woman, a virgin, differs: she who is unmarried is concerned for the things of the Lord, that she may be holy both in body and spirit. But she that is married is concerned for the things of the world, how she may please her husband." (I Cor. 7:32-34). Whence it seems at this time that only those who do not have themselves under control should marry, according to the opinion of the same Apostle, "Therefore if they do not

restrain themselves, let them marry, for it is better to marry than to burn" (I Cor. 7:9).

Chrysostom's commendation of marriage in his *Homily on I Corinthians 7:2* ("But because of the temptation to immorality, each man should have his own wife and each woman her own husband") is more hesitant than Augustine's.

3.[34] . . . Here are the two reasons why marriage was established: so that there would be chastity, and so that we might become fathers. Of these, chastity is the reason that takes precedence. For once desire entered the scene, marriage also entered in order to curb over-indulgence and to persuade the man to have one woman. Marriage was not devised simply for the creation of children; it is rather the word of God that says "Increase and multiply and fill the earth" (Gen. 1:28). The proof of this is the number who married but yet did not become fathers. Therefore chastity is the preeminent reason for marriage, and is much more so at present, since our race has filled the whole world. At the beginning, to be sure, children were desired so that each person might leave behind a remembrance and a remnant of his own life. Since they had no hope of the resurrection (rather, death reigned), those people, destined to die, reckoned that all came to an end with the present life. God thus gave them the consolation of children so that when they departed, a living image of themselves remained and our race was preserved. For those about to die, as well as for their friends, their offspring were an immeasurable comfort. In order that we may thus learn that children were greatly desired, listen to how the wife of Job lamented bitterly after their many calamities: "The remembrance of you vanishes from the earth, that is, your sons and daugh-

[34]Text: PG 51.213.

ters" (Job 18:17).[35] And again, hear what Saul said to David: "Swear to me that you will not destroy my seed and my name after my time" (I Sam. 24:21).

Since the future resurrection is at the doors, the word of death is no more, and we will travel to another life that is much better than the present one, anxiety over these issues is superfluous. If you desire children, you can now acquire much better and much more serviceable ones. Spiritual birth pangs summon us, and worthier offspring, more useful to us in our old age. So there is one excuse for marriage, namely, avoiding fornication: this then was the medicine proffered.

> Despite Augustine's more positive evaluation of marriage, he makes clear in his commentary *On the Sermon on the Mount* that the asexual life is best. He here considers what Jesus meant when he said that we should "hate" our relatives (Lk. 14:26).

I,15,40.[36] ...Thus the Lord himself says, "For in the resurrection there will be no marrying nor giving in marriage, but they will be as the angels in Heaven" (Mk. 12:25 = Mt. 22:30 = Lk. 20:35). Therefore, whoever wishes to prepare himself here and now for that Kingdom must hate, not the humans themselves, but those temporal relationships by which this life of ours is supported, this life which is ephemeral, which is played out in being born and dying. For the person who does not hate them does not yet love that life where there will be no circumstance of being born and dying, that thing which joins people in earthly marriage.

I,15,41. Therefore, if I were to ask any good Christian man who has a wife, even one with whom he is still bringing forth children, whether he wants to have his wife in that Kingdom, especially remembering the promises of God and

[35]Actually said by one of Job's "comforters," Bildad the Shuhite.
[36]Text: CCL 35.44.

that life where "this corruptible shall put on incorruptibility and this mortal shall put on immortality" (I Cor. 15:53), although at the moment he may feel uncertain because of the greatness of his love (or at all events, a modicum of it), he will respond with a curse that he vehemently does *not* want it. If I were to ask him again, whether after the resurrection, when she had received that angelic transformation that is promised to the saints, he would want his wife to live with him there, he would respond that he wanted this as much as he did not want the other. Thus a good Christian is found to love in one woman the creature of God whom he desires to be molded again and renewed, but to hate in her the corruptible and mortal sexual connection, i.e., to love in her what is human, to hate in her what pertains to a wife. So, likewise, he loves his enemy, not insofar as he *is* an enemy, but insofar as he is a human, so that he wishes the same for him as he does for himself, namely, that he may arrive at the Kingdom of Heaven improved and renewed.

> Augustine firmly believed that God had willed women to be subject to their husbands in marriage. Even if they wished to live an ascetic life, one more in keeping with the monastic values of late ancient Christianity, they could not do so unless their husbands agreed. Augustine's *Letter 262*[37] to a Christian matron named Ecdicia reveals his insistence on wifely submission. Given Augustine's own bias toward the ascetic life, his sharp criticism of Ecdicia is particularly arresting.

1. I have read your Reverence's[38] letter and have inquired of the bearer concerning the matters that remained to be investigated, and I am extremely grieved that you decided to behave toward your husband in such a way that the edifice of continence, which had begun to be raised in him, should

---

[37]Text: CSEL 57.621.
[38]A term of polite respect.

have sunk into the wretched ruin of adultery by his slipping from perseverance. For if he had returned to carnal marital intercourse after taking a vow of continence to God, and upholding it in both act and character, it would have been lamentable, but how much more lamentable it is now that he is cast down into deeper ruin, committing adultery, breaking and dissolving the tie! In his anger at you, he was destructive to himself, as if by destroying himself he could vent his fury more sharply at you. This great evil occurred when you did not treat him with the moderation you ought, considering his state of mind, because even though by mutual consent you were not engaging in fleshly intercourse, nevertheless, you as the wife ought to have been subject to your husband in other things, accommodating yourself to the marriage bond, particularly since both of you are members of the body of Christ. And certainly if you, a believer, had had a husband who was not a believer, it would still have been proper for you to act in a submissive manner, so that you might win him for Christ, as the Apostle advises us (I Cor. 7:12-16).

2. I pass over the point that I know you undertook the continent state when he had not yet given his assent, and such an undertaking is not in accordance with sober teaching. For he ought not to have been cheated of the debt of your body before your wills were joined in that good that surpasses marital chastity. Except perhaps you had not read, or maybe had not paid attention, and thus did not hear, what the Apostle said:

> It is good for a man not to touch a woman, but because of fornication, let each man have his own wife and each woman her own husband. Let the husband pay the debt to his wife and in like manner the wife to her husband. The wife does not have power over her own body, but her husband does; likewise, the husband does not have power over his own body, but his wife does. Do not rob one

another except by consent, for a while, that you may have time for prayers, and again be together, lest Satan tempt you because of your incontinence (I Cor. 7:1-6).

According to these apostolic words, even if he had wanted to be continent and you had not, he would have been compelled to pay you the marital debt. God would have imputed continence to him if he, taking account of your weakness, not his own, did not deny you marital intercourse, lest you fall into the damnable sin of adultery. How much more suitable it would have been for you, to whom subjection is more proper, to comply with his wish in paying the debt in this way, lest he be dragged into adultery, since God would have admitted your desire to remain continent, the desire that you did not act upon, so that your husband would not perish?

4. But I am saddened that you observed another matter even less. You ought to have yielded to him in your domestic association with great humility and obedience, since he had so scrupulously conceded to you in an important matter, even imitating you. For just because you were together refraining from carnal intercourse, he did not cease to be your husband; quite the contrary, you remained in truth a married couple in a holier manner because you were amicably and agreeably preserving some holier goal. Therefore you ought not to have given away your clothes, or your gold or silver or any money, or any of your earthly belongings, without his decision, lest you set a stumbling block for a man who along with you vowed higher things to God and had chastely abstained from what he, by his legal power, could have required from your body....

9. Furthermore, you ought to have consulted with your husband, who was a believer, and who had undertaken with you the holy pact of continence, and not despised his wishes, concerning your plan for giving alms and devoting your possessions to the poor, a just and good deed about which

there are clear precepts from the Lord (cf., Mk. 10:21 = Mt. 19:21 = Lk. 18:22). And if you ought to have consulted him on this matter, how much more was it right for you not to change or assume anything pertaining to your costume and clothes contrary to his will, about which we read no divine commands? Indeed, it is written that women should wear dignified clothing, that wearing gold or curled hair and other such things that are customarily done for empty show, or to provide a seductive appearance, is worthy of reprimand (I Tim. 2:9). But there is a certain matronly attire geared to the person's station, distinct from widows' clothing and appropriate for married women who are believers, an attire that preserves religious respect. If your husband did not want you to discard this type of clothing, did not want you to display yourself as a widow while he was still living, I think he should not have been led to the point of a scandalous quarrel with you about this matter, with greater evil resulting from your disobedience than the good that might have come from any act of abstinence. For what is more ridiculous than for a woman to be filled with pride against her husband over the issue of a humble dress? Would it not have been more advantageous for you to comply with him in splendor of behavior than to fight against him in funeral garments? Even if it had been monastic garb that allured you, was it not possible for you to don it more graciously by respecting your husband and prevailing upon him, than you did in taking the matter for granted without consulting him and by disregarding him? And if he would absolutely not permit it, how would your resolution have been ruined? It is far from displeasing to God that while your husband is not yet dead, you are clothed, not like Anna, but like Susanna.[39]

11. Since you thought to consult me, I have written this to

---

[39]I.e., not like a widow, but like an attractive, pious matron: see Lk. 2:36-38 and the apocryphal book of Susanna, vs. 1-2.

you, not in order to break your upright intention by my discourse, but because I am saddened by your husband's behavior, behavior that came about by your unruly and reckless action. You ought to think earnestly about re- covering him, if in truth you want to belong to Christ. Therefore clothe youself with humility of mind so that God may keep you in perseverance; do not despise your husband in his failing. Pour forth pious and unceasing prayers for him, a sacrifice of tears like the blood of a wounded heart. Write to him, making amends, begging his forgiveness for the sin you committed against him by disposing of your possessions just as you thought fit, apart from his consent and wishes—not that you should repent for bestowing your property on the poor, but rather repent for not allowing him to share in and guide your good work. Promise that from now on, with the help of the Lord, if he will repent of his disgraceful activities and seek again the continence he forsook, you will be subject to him in everything, as is fitting. As the Apostle says, "Perchance God will give him penitence and he may recover from the snares of the Devil, by whom he is held captive according to his will" (II Tim. 2:25-26).

As for your son, since you bore him in lawful and honorable marriage, who does not know that he is more in his father's power than in yours? Therefore his father cannot be denied his rights once he learns where he is and makes a legal demand. And in accordance with your wish, he can be trained and taught the wisdom of God, but for this, your marital harmony is even more necessary for him.

It was not just marriage in general that early Christian writers criticized; special problems associated with marriage might arise for Christian women who lived in a world still dominated by pagan values and customs. When a women converted to Christianity but her husband did not, thorny difficulties could develop in their

relationship. Tertullian's *Exhortation to His Wife* presents some striking examples of the problems mixed
marriage, i.e., marriage between a Christian and a pagan,
might involve.

II,3.[40] . . . It is necessary for any Christian woman to
attend to God. How can she serve two masters (Mt. 6:24 =
Lk. 16:13), the Lord and her husband, and him a pagan in
addition? For in attending to a pagan she will carry out
pagan customs. She will be party to an artful appearance,
worldly elegances, shameful allurements, even the defiling
secrets of marriage themselves. This is not the situation
among the blessed, where the duties of sex are performed so
that honor is shown to their necessity; they are performed in
modesty and moderation, as if under the eyes of God.

II,4. But let us see how she weighs her duties to her
husband. Indeed, to the Lord she cannot give satisfaction as
far as habits go, for she has at her side a servant of the Devil,
the agent of *his* lord for impeding the activities and duties of
believers. Thus if a religious meeting is to be attended, at
dawn the husband makes an appointment for the baths. If
fasts are to be observed, that very day the husband organizes
a banquet. If there is to be a procession, never is family
business of more pressing concern. For what man allows his
wife, for the sake of visiting the brethren, to wander from
street to street, to strange places and even to the more
poverty-stricken huts? What man will voluntarily allow her
to be taken from his side for assemblies at night, if such were
necessary? What man, lastly, will serenely endure her
attendance at the all-night Easter solemnities? What man
will without suspicion send her out to that Lord's Supper
they try to bring into disrepute? What man will suffer her to
creep into prison to kiss the martyrs' chains? Indeed, to greet
any of the brethren with a kiss? To offer water for the saints'

[40]Text: CSEL 70.116.

feet? To wish to save something from her food, her cup, for them? To have them in her mind? If a brother from abroad arrives, what hospitality will there be for him in a strange home? If there is to be a distribution to the people, the storehouse, the cellars, are closed off.

> The wedding ceremony itself could endanger the moral purity of a Christian girl, argued John Chrysostom in *Homily 12 on I Corinthians*:

5.[41] . . . Marriage is deemed honorable by us as well as by those outside the church, and indeed it *is* honorable. But when wedding ceremonies are performed, ludicrous things occur about which you shall straightway hear. Most people, misled and held fast by custom, do not realize the peculiarity of these practices but need others to teach them. There is dancing, cymbals, flutes, shameless words and songs, drunkenness, carousing—and then all the enormous trash of the Devil is introduced.

I know that I seem ridiculous in attacking these practices and that I shall be convicted of great folly by the majority for disrupting the ancient laws. As I said earlier, the deception worked by custom is great. Nonetheless, I shall not cease making my point. For surely at least some people, if not everyone, will accept us and choose to be ridiculed along with us rather than have us join them in that laughter deserving of tears, harsh punishment, and retribution.

For how can it not be worthy of the strongest condemnation that a virgin who has lived entirely within the enclosure of her home and has been instructed in modesty from her early years, is forced all at once to cast off her modesty totally, and right from the start of marriage is taught shamelessness, is placed among licentious, crude, unchaste, and effeminate men? What sort of evil will not be implanted in

---

[41]Text: PG 61.103.

the bride from that day? Shamelessness, recklessness, inso-
lence, love of extravagant glory—for she will want all her
days to be like these! Hence women become extravagant
and lavish, hence result their myriad evils. . . .
    6. "What?" someone asks. "Are you criticizing marriage?
Speak up!" By no means—I am not *that* crazy! But I do
criticize the baggage wickedly dragged along in the wake of
marriage: the make-up, the eye-shadow, and all the other
superfluities of this sort. Indeed, from that day she will
receive many lovers, and these even before she receives her
bridegroom-to-be. . . .
    Then see what happens next. Not only during the day, but
also in the evening, drunken men, alternately stupefied and
inflamed by their carousing, are supplied to gape at the
beauty of the girl's face. And they show her off not just in the
house, but also strutting about in the marketplace. Late in
the evening they accompany her with torches, thus exhibit-
ing her to everyone. By these actions, they counsel nothing
other than that it henceforth behooves her to cast off all
modesty. And they don't call a halt even here, but they lead
her forth, uttering disgraceful words. This is a law with the
masses. Thousands of worthless runaway slaves and sorry
knaves henceforth fearlessly say whatever they wish, both to
her and to the man about to dwell with her. Nothing is
decent, everything is full of indecency. Will not the bride
have a lovely lesson in discretion, seeing and hearing such
things? A certain devilish rivalry prevails among the cham-
pions of these matters to surpass the others in uttering
reproaches and shameful words by which they dishonor the
group; those depart victors who hurl the most insults and
the greatest terms of disgrace. . . .
    "But this is the customary thing!" someone objects.
Indeed, for this very reason it deserves to be mourned,
because the Devil has enclosed the business in the guise of
custom. For since marriage is a decorous matter that mar-

shals our race and produces many benefits, that Evil One, being vexed and knowing that marriage was in effect a fortified outpost stationed against sexual immorality, here introduced anew in one way or another every kind of sexual immorality. In all events, many virgins have even been dishonored in such gatherings. And even if that is not always the case, for the time being it is enough for the Devil to have those evil words and songs, the exhibition of the bride, and the pompous escort of the groom through the marketplace. In addition, since these activities occur in the evening, many torches are brought in to prevent the unseemly events from remaining hidden, lest the darkness provide cover for these evils. For what do the great crowds portend? And what the drink? What the pipes? Is it not patently clear that these things take place so that those at home, sunk in deep sleep, cannot remain unaware of the events, but roused by the pipe, stooping to peer down over their balconies, become witnesses of the passing farce?

What can anyone say about the songs themselves, brimming with every sort of licentiousness, introducing disgusting amours and unlawful unions, the overthrow of households, myriad tragic episodes, frequently bandying about names like "my sweetie and boy-friend," "my darling and love"? And, what is yet sorrier, maidens who have taken off all their modesty as if their robes are present at these events. In honor of the bride, or more accurately as an insult to her, they even sacrifice their salvation, and in the midst of dissolute young men they behave disgracefully with their disorderly ditties, their shameful words, their satanic melody.

If you still are asking, *you* tell *me*: "Where do adulteries come from? Whence sexual immorality? Whence the ruining of marriages?"

The one way in which early Christian writers advanced the married woman's position was to press a single sexual standard, i.e., neither the man nor the woman was to engage in sexual relations outside of marriage. Men could not call themselves good Christians if they made use of the greater sexual freedom allowed them by Roman law and custom. Chrysostom expressed his views on the subject in *Homily 5 on I Thessalonians.*

2.[42] ... Therefore, I exhort you, let us keep ourselves from this sin. For just as we punish women when, although they are married to us, they give themselves to others, so too are we punished, if not by Roman laws, then by God. For this, too, is adultery. The sexual act is adulterous not only when the woman is bound to another man; it is also adultery for the man who is himself bound to a wife. Pay close attention to what I say. Even if my speech becomes tedious to many, it is still necessary for me to utter it to set you straight in the future. Not only is it adultery when we corrupt a woman yoked to a man; the deed is also adultery if married men corrupt a woman who is free and not constrained by any relationship with a man. "Why is this so, if the woman with whom we commit the act is not married?" someone may ask. But *you* are married. *You* have broken the law. *You* have injured your own flesh. Tell me, why do you punish your wife, if she has sexual relations with a man who is free, unmarried? Because it is adultery: even if the man who commits the act with her is unmarried, *she* is bound to a husband. But you also are bound to a wife, so, likewise, your deed is adultery. For it is said, "The man who divorces his wife, except for the cause of fornication, makes her an adultress. And the man who marries her when she is divorced commits adultery" (Mt. 5:32). If the man who marries a divorced woman commits adultery, what about the man who has his own wife yet corrupts himself with another woman: does he not even more do the same? That's

[42]Text: PG 62.425.

obvious to everyone. But to you men, what has been said on the matter suffices. Christ said about people who behave in this way, "Their worm will not die and their fire shall not be quenched" (Mk. 9:48).

> Chrysostom in fact believed that the single sexual standard was the one point at which Christian wives enjoyed equality with their husbands, as he asserts in *Homily 19 on I Corinthians.*

1.[43] . . ."Let the husband render to his wife the honor due her, and likewise the wife to her husband" (cf. I Cor. 7:3). And what is "the honor due her"? The wife does not exercise authority over her own body, but is both the servant and the wife of the husband. And if you as a woman refrain from the appropriate sexual service, you have offended God. If you wish to withhold yourself from the relationship, you may do so only if and when your husband sees fit, even if this is just for a brief period. This is why Paul calls the marital act a "debt," in order to show that no one is lord over himself or herself, but that couples are servants of each other. Therefore if you husbands ever spy a prostitute tempting you, say "My body is not mine, but my wife's." And the wife should likewise reply to those wishing to undermine her chastity, "My body is not mine, but my husband's." If neither husband nor wife has authority over his or her own body, how much more should this principle hold concerning possessions?

In other passages of Scripture, God gives to the husband great pre-eminence, both in the New and the Old Testaments, saying, "Your inclination shall be for your husband, and he shall rule over you" (Gen. 3:16). And Paul also differentiates in this way when he writes, "Husbands, love your wives, and let the wife stand in awe of her husband"

---

[43]Text: PG 61.152.

(Col. 3:18-19; Eph. 5: 24-25). But in the passage under consideration, it is not a question of greater or less: there is just one standard of authority. Why in the world is this? Because Paul's argument here pertained to chastity. "For in other things," he says, "let the man have the advantage, but when the argument is about chastity, this is no longer the case." The husband does not exert authority over his own body, nor does the wife over hers: great is the equality of honor, and no advantage for the man.

In such ways did the Church Fathers alternately praise the goodness of God's created order, condemn the woman responsible for the original sin, and consign her female descendants to a life of submission to men. According to them, marriage was a reminder to women of the Paradise they had lost.

Chapter Two

WOMEN ENDANGERED: THE APOCRYPHAL ACTS AND MARTYRDOM

In the late second and third centuries, a new type of Christian literature, the Apocryphal Acts, was created. Although the very titles of these apocryphal books suggest that they were modelled on the Biblical Acts of the Apostles and although their authors claim that their heroes *were* the Biblical apostles, now wandering as far afield as India, scholars think that there is in reality no direct line of development from the New Testament Acts to the apocryphal ones. Probably influenced by non-Christian literature, especially by the Hellenistic novels or romances, the books seem to have been composed both to provide entertainment and to inculcate certain Christian ideals, with an emphasis on asceticism and the miraculous.

Of particular interest is the central role occupied by women in the Apocryphal Acts. The women described in these books are from prominent families, married or engaged to powerful and wealthy men. They become spiritually enamored with one of the charismatic itinerant apostles and reject traditional social and domestic values for the sake of Christianity, understood as rigidly ascetic discipline. By no means are the women of the Apocryphal Acts the

docile housewives commended in I Timothy: these determined women are willing to risk social disapproval and life
itself to uphold their faith. It cannot be proved that these
popular tales found a major audience among women—the
leap from literature to "life" is always precarious—yet so
prominent are women in the Apocryphal Acts that a recent
monograph proposes that some of the Acts may have been
composed by females.[1]

One of the first such Acts is the *Acts of Paul and
Thecla,* a section of the longer *Acts of Paul.* Since Tertullian in a treatise dated about 200 A.D. refers to the work,[2]
scholars judge it to come from the late second century.
Thecla rapidly gained fame among Christians. Her name
became a virtual synonym for the heroic Christian
woman; Jerome and other writers urged their female
friends to imitate Thecla's ardent faith. A cult developed
around her and soon she was thought to have been an
historical person. By the time the pilgrim Egeria visited
Asia Minor in the late 300s, a shrine to Thecla existed in
Seleucia where Egeria was pleased to read the *Acts of
Thecla.*[3] In the fifth century, a *Life and Miracles of
Thecla* was composed that stressed the wondrous deeds
of its heroine.

Particularly interesting in the following selection are
the advocacy of asceticism; the unfavorable light in which
Paul is cast (e.g., far from helping Thecla when she is
sexually assaulted, he feigns ignorance of her); Thecla's
power over the animals, a trait characteristic of ascetic
heroes; and Thecla's self-baptism, a story that made difficulties for the Church later.[4]

---

[1]Stevan L. Davies, *The Revolt of the Widows: The Social World of the Apocryphal Acts* (Carbondale, Ill.: Southern Illinois University Press, 1980).
[2]See below, p. 173.
[3]See below, pp. 191-92.
[4]See below, p. 173.

(The apostle Paul goes to Iconium.)[5]

5. And when Paul entered the house of Onesiphorus, there was great joy, bowing, breaking of bread, and God's word pertaining to continence and the resurrection. Paul said,

> Blessed are the pure in heart, for they shall see God.
> Blessed are those who keep the flesh pure, for they shall become the temple of God.
> Blessed are those who remain continent, for to them shall God speak.
> Blessed are those who bid farewell to this world, for they shall be well-pleasing to God.
> Blessed are those who have wives as if they had them not, for they shall inherit God.
> Blessed are those that have fear of God, for they shall become angels of God.

6. Blessed are those who tremble at the oracles of God, for they shall be comforted.
> Blessed are those who receive the wisdom of Jesus Christ, for they shall be called sons of the Most High.
> Blessed are those who have preserved their baptism, for they shall find their rest with the Father and the Son.
> Blessed are those who have advanced to the sagacity of Jesus Christ, for they shall be in light.
> Blessed are those who for the love of God have left the way of the world, for they shall judge angels and shall be blessed at the right hand of the Father.
> Blessed are those who show mercy, for they shall be shown mercy and shall not see a cruel judgment.
> Blessed are the bodies of virgins, for they shall be well-pleasing to God and shall not lose the reward of their purity, for the Word of the Father shall be a work of

[5]Text: *Acta Apostolorum Apocrypha*, ed. R. Lipsius and M. Bonnet (Leipzig, 1891), I, 238.

salvation for them in the day of his Son, and they shall have rest for ever and ever.

7. And while Paul spoke these things in the midst of the assembly at Onesiphorus' house, a certain virgin named Thecla, whose mother was Theocleia, and who was wooed by a man named Thamyris, sat by a window of a nearby house and listened night and day to the message Paul spoke about chastity. And she did not turn away from the window, but led on by faith, she rejoiced greatly. Yet when she saw many women and virgins going to Paul, she also greatly desired that she be deemed worthy to stand before Paul, for she had not yet seen his physical appearance, but had only heard his voice.

8. Since she did not leave the window, her mother sent to Thamyris. He came rejoicing, as if he already were taking her to wife. Thamyris thus said to Theocleia, "Where is my Thecla?" and Theocleia said, "I have some news to tell you, Thamyris. For three days and three nights, Thecla has not risen from the window, neither to eat nor to drink, but she gazes as if she were seeing something delightful. She is thus devoted to the stranger who gives instruction in various and deceitful teachings, so that I am amazed at how such a modest virgin is so deeply upset."

9. "O Thamyris, this man is stirring up the city of the Iconians and your Thecla as well. For all the women and young men go in to him and are taught by him. He says you must fear the one and only God and live chastely. And my daughter, too, is like a spider at the window, bound by his words, and is seized by a new desire and an awesome passion. For she intently apprehends the things said by him and the virgin is conquered. But you go and speak to her for she is engaged to you."

10. And Thamyris went to her, both loving her and fearing her consternation, and said, "Thecla, my fiancée, why are you sitting like this? And what sort of passion has you so

stunned? Turn to me, your Thamyris, and be ashamed of yourself." And her mother also said the same thing, "My child, why are you sitting like this, eyes cast down, making no response, but behaving like a mad person?" And they wept powerfully, Thamyris missing his wife, Theocleia, her child, and the maid-servants, their mistress. Thus there was a great confusion of mourning in the house. And while these things went on, Thecla did not turn away, but paid rapt attention to Paul's message.

(Thamyris finds some enemies of Paul and with them conspires to have Paul brought before the governor. At the hearing, Paul speaks:)

17. And Paul lifted up his voice and said, "If today I am being investigated for what I teach, listen, O proconsul. The living God, the avenging God, the jealous God, the God who needs nothing, but desires the salvation of humans, has sent me so that I may tear them away from corruption and filthiness, and all pleasure and death, that they may sin no more. For this reason God sent his own Child, whom I preach and teach, that men may have hope in him, him who alone showed compassion for the world wandering in sin, in order that humans may no longer be under judgment but have faith and fear of God, knowledge of majesty and love of truth. Therefore if I teach the things revealed to me by God, how do I err, O proconsul?" And when the governor heard this, he commanded that Paul be bound and carried off to prison until he had the opportunity to hear him more attentively.

18. But at night Thecla removed her bracelets and gave them to the gatekeeper, and when the door was opened for her, she went into the prison. And giving the jailer a silver mirror, she went in to Paul. She sat by his feet and heard the great deeds of God. Paul did not fear at all, but lived freely in the perfect openness of God. And her faith was increased by kissing his bonds.

19. As Thecla was sought by her own people and by Thamyris, as she was searched for in the streets like a lost person, one of the fellow-servants of the gatekeeper revealed that she had gone out at night. And they inquired of the gatekeeper and he told them that she had gone to the stranger in prison. They went just as he told them and found her, bound to him in a manner of affection. And having departed from there, they drew together the crowd and showed it to the governor.

20. And he commanded Paul to be brought to the platform. Thecla, however, rolled around on the place where Paul had taught when he sat in prison. And the governor commanded that she also be brought to the platform. She went, exultant with joy. And the crowd, when Paul was brought in again, shouted inordinately, "He is a wizard, away with him!" But the governor gladly heard Paul on the subject of the holy deeds of Christ. And taking counsel, he called Thecla and said, "Why will you not marry Thamyris, according to the law of the Iconians?" But she just stood, gazing intently at Paul. When she did not reply, Theocleia, her mother, cried out, saying, "Burn the lawless woman, burn her who is not a bride in the middle of the theatre, so that all women who have been instructed by this man may be afraid!"

21. The governor was greatly affected and having scourged Paul, he sent him outside the city, but Thecla he sentenced to be burned. Immediately the governor arose and went to the theatre, and the entire mob went out for the distressing spectacle. But Thecla, like a lamb in the wilderness who looks about for the shepherd, sought Paul. And when she looked at the crowd, she saw the Lord sitting there, as if he were Paul, and she said, "As if I were not able to bear it, Paul came to watch me." And gazing at him, she kept intent on him. But he went away into the heavens.

22. And the boys and the virgins brought wood and hay in

order to burn Thecla. And as she was brought in naked, the governor wept and was astounded at the power in her. They spread the wood and the public executioners ordered her to climb on the pyre. She made the sign of the cross, went up on the wood, and they lighted it. A great flame blazed but the fire did not touch her. For God, showing compassion, produced a noise under the ground and a cloud threw a shadow from above, full of rain and hail, and the whole vessel was poured out so that many were endangered and died, and the fire being extinguished, Thecla was saved.

> (Thecla finds Paul after her miraculous rescue. She asks him to baptize her, but he tells her she must be patient. The story continues:)

26. And Paul sent away Onesiphorus with all his household to Iconium. Then he took Thecla and went into Antioch. And as they entered, a certain Syrian named Alexander saw Thecla, fell in love with her, and earnestly entreated Paul, bribing him with money and presents. But Paul said, "I do not know this woman of whom you speak, nor is she mine." But since the man was very powerful, he embraced her on the street. She, however, did not tolerate this, but sought Paul. And she cried out bitterly, saying, "Do not force a strange woman, do not force the servant of God. I am the first of the Iconians and because I did not want to be married to Thamyris, I am expelled from the city." And seizing Alexander, she ripped his mantle, removed the wreath from his head, and made him a scandal.

27. But he, loving her and ashamed of what had happened to him, brought her before the governor, and when she confessed that she had done these things, he sentenced her to the beasts. But the women were panic-stricken and shouted at the platform, "An evil judgment, an unholy judgment!" Thecla asked the governor that she might remain chaste until the time when she would fight the beasts. And a certain

wealthy queen named Tryphaena whose daughter had died took her into custody and had her as a solace. 28. And when the beasts were paraded forth, they bound Thecla to a fierce lioness and Queen Tryphaena followed close after her. But the lioness, when Thecla was seated on top of her, licked her feet all over, and the whole crowd was amazed. The charge that was written about her was "A committer of sacrilege." And the women with their children shouted from above, saying, "O God, an unholy judgment has taken place in this city!" And after the procession, Tryphaena received her once again. For her daughter Falconilla, who was dead, said to her in a dream, "Mother, you shall keep Thecla, the helpless stranger, in my place, so that she may pray for me and I may be transposed to the place of the righteous."

29. Thus when Tryphaena took her after the procession, she at once mourned because she was to fight the beasts on the next day and because she felt deep affection for her, as for her daughter Falconilla. And she said, "Thecla, my second child, come, pray for my child that she may live forever. For I saw this while sleeping." And without delaying, Thecla raised her voice and said, "O my God, the Son of the Most High, who is in heaven, give to her as she wills, so that her daughter Falconilla may live forever." And after Thecla said these things, Tryphaena wailed, seeing that such a beautiful woman was to be thrown to the beasts.

30. And when the dawn arrived, Alexander came to take her (for he was giving the wild-beast fights), saying, "The governor is seated and the crowd is raising a clamor at us. Give me the woman who is to fight the beasts that I may lead her away." But Tryphaena cried out so that he fled. She said, "In my house there has come about a second mourning for my Falconilla, and no one comes to give aid, neither child, for she is dead, nor relative, for I am a widow. O God of my child Thecla, come to Thecla's aid."

31. And the governor sent soldiers to bring Thecla. Tryphaena did not leave her, but she herself took her hand and led her up, saying, "I led away my daughter Falconilla to the tomb, but you, Thecla, I lead to fight the beasts." And Thecla wept bitterly and sighed unto the Lord, saying, "Lord, the God in whom I trust, with whom I have sought refuge, who rescued me from the fire, give a reward to Tryphaena who has had compassion on your servant, and because she has preserved me chaste."

32. Thus an uproar arose, and the noise of the beasts and a cry of the crowd, and of the women sitting together, some of whom said, "Bring in the woman who committed sacrilege!" while others said, "Away with the city for this lawless deed! Away with all of us, proconsul! A bitter sight, a wicked judgment!"

33. But Thecla, removed from the hand of Tryphaena, was stripped, and she wore a girdle, and was flung into the stadium. Lions and bears were put in against her. A fierce lioness ran up to her feet and lay down, and the crowd of women clamored greatly. A bear ran towards her, but the lioness ran to the bear, met him, and ripped him apart. And again, a lion trained to fight against humans, a lion that belonged to Alexander, ran to her. And the lioness joined him in a close fight in which both were killed. The women wept even more, since the lioness that had helped her was dead.

34. Then they threw in many beasts, while she stood and stretched out her hands and prayed. When she finished her prayer, she turned and saw a large pit filled with water and she said, "Now is the right time for me to baptize myself." And she threw herself in, saying, "In the name of Jesus Christ, I baptize myself on the last day." The women who saw it and all the crowd wept, saying, "Do not throw yourself into the water," so that even the governor shed tears that such beauty would be eaten by seals. Thus she cast

herself into the water in the name of Jesus Christ. But the seals, seeing the light of a flash of fire, floated dead. And around her there was a cloud of fire, so that neither did the animals touch her nor was she perceived as naked.

35. And the women, when other more dreadful beasts were cast in, cried loudly. Some flung petals, while others threw nard, others cassia and still others spice plants, so that there was a multitude of perfumes. All the animals were smitten so that they were held as if they were asleep and did not touch her. So Alexander said to the governor, "I have some extremely ferocious bulls; let us bind the woman condemned to fight the beasts to them." And the governor, although sullen, yielded and said, "Do what you will." And they tied her between the bulls' feet, put red hot irons on their genital organs, so that they might become even more agitated and kill her. Then they sprang forward, but the flame burning around her burned through the ropes, and she was as one not bound.

36. But Tryphaena, who was standing alongside the arena, fainted at the steps into the arena, so that her female servants said, "Queen Tryphaena is dead!" The governor stopped the procedures and the whole city was frightened. Alexander fell at the governor's feet and said, "Have mercy on me and the city, and release the woman condemned to fight the beasts, lest the city also be destroyed along with her. For if Caesar should hear about these things, he perhaps will destroy us and the city, for Queen Tryphaena, his relative, died at the steps into the arena."

37. And the governor called Thecla from the midst of the beasts and said to her, "Who are you? What is there about you that none of the beasts touched you?" And she replied, "I am a servant of the living God. And what there is about me, is that I have trusted in God's Son, in whom he is well-pleased. On account of him, not one of the beasts touched me. For he alone is the way of salvation and the

foundation of immortal life. He is a refuge for those who are distressed, a remission for the afflicted, a shelter for the despairing; in general, if anyone does not believe in him, he shall not live, but shall die forever."

38. And when the governor heard these things, he ordered clothes to be brought and said, "Put on the clothes." And she said, "The one who clothed me while I was naked among the beasts shall clothe me with salvation on the day of judgment." And taking the garments, she got dressed. Straightway the governor sent out an act proclaiming, "I release Thecla to you, the pious servant of God." And all the women cried out in a loud voice and as with one mouth, they gave praise to God, saying, "The God who saved Thecla is one," so that from their cry the whole city shook.

39. And when the good news was told to Tryphaena, she met Thecla with the crowd, embraced her, and said, "Now I believe that my child lives. Come inside, and I will sign over to you all my goods." Then Thecla went in with her and rested in her house for eight days, teaching her the word of God, so that the majority of the servants also believed, and there was great joy in the house.

40. But Thecla yearned for Paul and sought him, sending around everywhere. And it was reported to her that he was in Myra. Taking young men and maidens, she girded herself and sewed her mantle into a garment in the fashion of men. She departed for Myra, found Paul speaking the word of God, and went to him. He was amazed to see her and the crowd that was with her, wondering lest some other temptation had come to her. But she recognized it and said to him, "I have received baptism, Paul. For the One who worked together with you in the Gospel also worked with me for my being baptized."

41. And Paul took her by the hand, led her into the house of Hermias, and heard everything from her, so that he was much amazed and those who heard were confirmed and

prayed for Tryphaena. Thecla rose and said to Paul, "I go to Iconium." And Paul said, "Go and teach the word of God." Now the many garments and gold that Tryphaena had sent, Thecla left behind with Paul for the service of the poor. 42. She departed for Iconium. She entered the house of Onesiphorus and fell on the floor where Paul sat when he taught the oracles of God, and wept, saying, "O my God and God of this house where the light shone on me, Christ Jesus, the Son of God, my helper in prison, my helper before the governors, my helper in the fire, my helper amidst the beasts, you are God and to you be the glory for ever. Amen." 43. And she found Thamyris dead, but her mother alive. She summoned her mother and said to her, "Theocleia, my mother, can you believe that the Lord lives in the heavens? For if you desire money, the Lord will give it to you through me. Behold your child, I am here before you." And when she had witnessed to these things, she departed for Seleucia, and when she had enlightened many people with the word of God, she slept with a good sleep.

A second fascinating tale in the Apocryphal Acts is the Drusiana episode from the *Acts of John*. Scholars think that this book stemmed from Christian ascetic sects in Asia Minor. Although the earliest external evidence for the work dates to the fourth century, it may well have been composed earlier.

Drusiana is one of several heroines of the Apocryphal Acts whose husband or fiancé tried to prevent her from adopting the ascetic life. Other fragments of the Drusiana story than the one printed below reveal that Drusiana's husband shut her up in a sepulchre for fourteen days when she refused to accede to his sexual requests. Finally he was converted to an ascetic form of Christianity as well. Drusiana's next bad luck was to have a non-believer, Callimachus, fall in love with her. The story of his passion for her, her death, his attempted rape of her corpse, and the resurrections of all concerned makes for lively reading. Noteworthy is Drusiana's resurrecting of a dead man: nowhere in the New Testament itself is a woman the agent of such a miracle.

(John has come to Ephesus for a second visit and is staying at the house of Andronicus.[6])

63. And since there was much love and unsurpassing joy among the brethren, a certain man, a messenger of Satan, fell in love with Drusiana, although he saw and knew that she was Andronicus' wife. Many people said to him, "It is impossible for you to have this woman, since for a long time she has kept apart even from her husband because of her fear of God. Are you the only one who doesn't know that Andronicus, who formerly was not the God-fearing man he is now, shut her up in a tomb, saying, 'I must have you as a wife as I did before, or you shall die'? And she chose to die rather than to be involved in that filthiness. Thus if she would not agree to come together with her master and husband because of godliness, but even convinced him to consider the matter the same way she did, now will she consent to you who want to commit adultery with her? Abandon the madness that finds no rest in you; abandon the deed that you cannot carry through to a conclusion."

64. His close friends said these things to him, but they did not convince him. Indulging in shameless behavior, he sent messages to her. And when she learned of his dishonor and insults to her, she spent her time in listlessness. After two days, Drusiana became feverish and took to her bed from melancholy, saying, "Would that I had not returned to my homeland, for I have become a stumbling-block to a man uninitiated in godliness! For if he were a man who was filled with the Word, he would not have come to such a state of

[6]Text: *Acta Apostolorum Apocrypha*, ed. R. Lipsius and M. Bonnet (Leipzig, 1898), II, I, 181.

madness. But thus, Lord, since I have become in part the cause of a wound to an ignorant soul, deliver me from this bond and remove me to yourself speedily." And while John was there, who was completely ignorant of the matter, Drusiana departed from life, not at all happy, but indeed grieving because of the spiritual shattering of that man.

65. But Andronicus grieved with a hidden grief, mourned in his soul, and cried openly, so that John curbed him many times and said to him. "Drusiana has been removed to a better hope from this unrighteous life." Andronicus answered him, "I too am convinced of this, O John, and I feel no doubt at all about my trust in God. But above all I feel sure on this point, that she left this life in a state of purity."

66. And when she was buried, John took hold of Andronicus, and since he knew the cause, he grieved more than Andronicus. But he remained silent, having in full view the spiteful abuse of the Hostile One,[7] and he sat down for a little while. Since the brethren had gathered after to hear what words he would utter about the departed woman, he began to speak.

(John speaks on the need for perseverance in righteousness until the end.)

70. And as John was still talking at length to the brethren, saying that they should despise temporal things for the sake of these other ones, the man in love with Drusiana, inflamed with a horrible desire and by the power of the many-shaped Satan, bribed Andronicus' steward, an avaricious man, with a considerable amount of money. The steward opened Drusiana's tomb and would have permitted him to perform the forbidden act on the dead body. Not having succeeded while she was alive, he was persistent towards the body after her death, saying, "If while you were alive you would not agree to have intercourse with me, I will insult your corpse after your death." Thus considering the matter and having prepared himself for the indecent act through the agency of the

[7]Probably the Devil.

brutal steward, he burst into the tomb with him. And when they opened the door, they began to strip the shroud from the corpse, saying, "What did it profit you, miserable Drusiana? Could you not have done this while you were alive, for perhaps the deed would not have distressed you at all, had you done it willingly?"

71. And while these men were speaking these words and only the customary shift remained on her body, a strange sight was seen, such as those who do deeds of this sort deserve to experience. A snake appeared from somewhere and dealt the steward a single bite that killed him. But it did not strike that young man; rather, hissing dreadfully, it coiled itself around his feet and when he fell, it climbed up on him and sat on top of him.

72. Now on the next day, John, along with Andronicus and the brethren, came to the tomb at dawn, it being the third day after Drusiana's death, so that they might break bread there. And first, when they started out, the keys could not be found when a search was made for them. But John said to Andronicus, "It seems right that they should be lost, for Drusiana is not in the tomb. Let us go anyway, lest you be remiss, and the doors shall open by themselves, since the Lord has also provided many other things for us."

73. And when we came to the place, the doors opened at the command of our teacher, and by the grave of Drusiana we saw a certain handsome young man, smiling. When John saw him, he cried out and said, "And do you also arrive here first, before us, O beautiful one? And for what reason?" And he heard a voice saying to him, "For Drusiana's sake, whom you are about to raise up—for I found her nearly dishonored—and for the sake of the person lying nearby her grave." And when he had said these things to John, the beautiful man ascended into the heavens while all of us were watching. And John, turning to the other side of the tomb, saw a young man, a prominent Ephesian, Callimachus—for that was what he was called—and an immense snake lying asleep on him, and the steward of Andronicus, named Fortunatus, dead. And when he saw both of them, he stood

puzzled and said to the brothers, "What does such a sight mean? Or why did the Lord not show me what happened here, since he has never neglected me?"

74. And Andronicus, seeing those dead men, started up and went to Drusiana's tomb. When he saw her in only her shift, he said to John, "I know what has happened here, John, blessed servant of God. This Callimachus was in love with my sister,[8] and since he never succeeded with her, though he tried many times, he bribed this damnable steward of mine with a considerable sum of money, perhaps having in mind, as we now perceive, to fulfill his tragic scheme through him. Indeed, Callimachus admitted this to many people, saying, 'If while she lived she would not have sexual relations with me, she shall be violated when she is dead.' And perhaps, master, the beautiful one knew this and did not agree to having her remains be violated, and for this reason these men who dared to do this act are dead. And may it not be that the voice that said to you, 'Raise up Drusiana,' foretold this? For she departed this life in grief. But I am persuaded by the one who said that this man was among the men who had gone astray. Indeed, you have been commanded to raise him. For concerning the other man, I know that he is worthy of salvation. But in this I beg you: first raise Callimachus and he will confess to us what happened."

75. So John looked at the corpse and said to the poisonous reptile, "Get away from him who shall be a servant of Jesus Christ," and he stood and prayed thus: "O God, whose name deservedly is praised by us, O God who tames every noxious force, O God, whose will is carried out, who always hears us, now also let your gift be executed in this young man, and if there is some function to be brought about through him, let it be shown us when he is raised." And immediately the young man rose and was silent for a whole hour.

---

[8]Christian couples who practiced asceticism called each other "brother" and "sister."

76. But when he had come to his right mind, John asked him what his entry to the tomb meant. And learning from him what Andronicus had told him, that in truth he loved Drusiana, John asked him again if he had carried out his disgusting plan to violate a body so full of nobility. And he answered him, "How could I carry it out? This dreadful beast struck Fortunatus with a single blow before my eyes— and rightly, since he encouraged my mania after that untimely and horrible madness had already ceased. And it stopped me in a fright and made me such as I was, as you saw before I arose. And I will tell you something else, even more amazing, which undid me even more and was within a little of making me a corpse: when my soul was submitting to the plan and the unbridled sickness was greatly disturbing me, and when already I had stripped off the shroud in which she was clothed, and then came away from the grave and placed it as you see it, I returned again to my ill-omened work. And I saw a handsome young man covering her with his cloak. From his eyes, a shining light came to her eyes. And he also spoke to me and said, "Callimachus, die in order that you may live." Who he was I did not know, O servant of God. But by your appearing here, I perceive that he was an angel of God, I know that well. And I truly know this, that a true God is proclaimed by you; I am persuaded of this. But I exhort you lest you neglect to free me from such a hazardous state and fearful crime, and present me, a man deceived with a disgraceful and loathsome deceit, to your God. Thus I need your help; I grasp your feet. I wish to become a man among those who hope in Christ, so that also the voice may be true that said to me here, 'Die in order that you may live.' And the voice has also accomplished its work, for that faithless, undisciplined, and godless man is dead, and I have been raised by you, I who shall be faithful, God-fearing, knowing the truth, which I beg that you make known to me."

77. And John, seized with a great gladness and considering the whole spectacle of human salvation, said, "O, Lord Jesus Christ, I do not know what your power is; I am at a

loss about your great compassion and boundless patience. O, greatness came down into slavery! O, inexpressible freedom was brought into slavery by us! O, incomprehensible glory is ours! You have guarded the dead body from violation; you are the redeemer of the man who sprinkled himself with the blood of humans; you chastened him who would defile corruptible bodies. Father, you showed pity and compassion for a negligent man. We glorify, praise and honor you, we give thanks for your great goodness and patience, Holy Jesus, for you alone are God and no other, the power that is without plots, both now and for all eternity. Amen."

78. And when he had said this, John took Callimachus and kissed him, saying, "Glory be to our God, my child, who has pitied you and made me worthy to glorify his power, and also made you worthy in his way to abandon that madness and drunkenness of yours, and has called you to his own rest and reward of life."

79. But Andronicus, beholding the dead Callimachus raised up, begged John along with the brothers to raise Drusiana as well, saying, "O John, let Drusiana arise and prosper for a short while, as she was carried off in grief on account of Callimachus, imagining that she had been a stumbling block to him, and when the Lord wishes, he will take her to himself." Without hesitation, John went into her tomb, took her by the hand, and said, "I call upon you who are the only God, the exceedingly Great, the Inexpressible, the Incomprehensible, to whom every power of principalities is subjected, unto whom every authority bows, to whom every false pretension falls down and is silent, at whom the demons tremble, when they hear; all creation when it perceives him, keeps its bounds. Let your name be glorified by us, and raise Drusiana, that Callimachus may be further established in the One who furnishes to men what is very difficult and impossible, but to you alone is possible, salvation and resurrection, and that Drusiana may now come forth in peace, since the young man is converted, not bring-

ing with her the least impediment as she comes at the end to
you."

80. After he said these things, John said to Drusiana,
"Drusiana, arise." And she arose and left the tomb. When
she saw herself in only a shift, she was puzzled about the
matter. And when she learned everything accurately from
Andronicus, while John lay on his face and Callimachus
glorified God with voice and tears, she also rejoiced and
likewise glorified him.

(The decision is made to raise Fortunatus; the task is
assigned to Drusiana, who prays to God that Fortunatus
be raised.)

83. And taking the head of the dead man, she said, "Arise,
Fortunatus, in the name of our Lord Jesus Christ." And
Fortunatus arose, and when he saw John in the tomb, and
Andronicus, and Drusiana raised from the dead, and Callimachus a believer, and the rest of the brothers glorifying
God, he said, "O, how far have the powers of these dreadful
men advanced? I did not want to be raised but would rather
be dead, so that I might not see them." And having said
these things, he fled and left the sepulchre.

84. When John saw the unchanged soul of Fortunatus, he
said, "O, a nature not changed for the better! O fountain of
the soul that remains in filth! O essence of corruption, full of
darkness! O death, dancing in those who are yours! O
fruitless tree, full of fire! O wood full of coals for fruit! O
matter dwelling with the madness of matter and neighbor of
unbelief! You have proved who you are and you are convicted forever along with your children! And you are not
capable of knowing how to glorify what is better, for you do
not have the ability. So thus as your way is, so is your root
and nature. Be removed from the ones who hope in the
Lord, from their thoughts, from their minds, from their
souls, from their bodies, from their deeds, from their life,

from their conversation, from their occupations, from their pursuits, from their advice, from their resurrection to God, from their fragrance in which you would like to share, from their fasts, from their prayers, from their holy bath, from their Eucharist, from the nourishment of their flesh, from their drink, from their garments, from their love-feast, from their weariness, from their continence, from their righteousness, from all those things, you most unholy Satan and enemy of God, Jesus Christ, our God and the Judge of the ones like you who have your way of life, shall abolish you."

85. When he said these things, John prayed, and taking bread, he carried it into the tomb to break it, and said, "We glorify your name which converted us from error and merciless deceit. We glorify you who before our eyes has shown us what we have seen. We bear witness to your goodness that manifests itself in diverse ways. We praise your good name, Lord, who convicts those who stand convicted. We thank you, Lord Jesus Christ, that we are persuaded of your unchanging grace. We thank you for desiring our nature, by which our nature is saved. We thank you who has given us this immovable faith that you alone are God, both now and forever. As your servants, we thank you, we who are gathered and collected with a purpose, O Holy One."

86. Having thus prayed and glorified God, John went out of the tomb and shared the Eucharist of the Lord with all the brothers. And when he came to the house of Andronicus, he said to the brothers, "Brethren, some spirit in me has divined that Fortunatus is about to die, having turned black from the snake-bite. But let someone learn if this is then so by going quickly." And a certain one of the young men ran and found him henceforth dead and the blackness dispersing and reaching his heart; he came and announced to John that he had been dead for three hours. And John said, "Devil, you are receiving full payment in your child."

While the fictional women of the Apocryphal Acts were represented as endangered because of their conversions to Christian asceticism, real Christian women found that they, too, were endangered, in this case by the Roman persecutions. Major, empire-wide persecution did not begin until 250 A.D., but accounts exist from as early as 112 A.D. that indicate Christians were being persecuted simply because they bore the name of Christian. Although it is still subject to scholarly debate under what, if any, actual laws the persecutions up to 250 A.D. were carried out, we gather that Christians' refusal to offer sacrifices to the pagan gods and the pinch of incense to the emperor caused the Romans to suspect Christians of political disloyalty. In addition, their suspicion of Christian rituals such as the Lord's Supper and their annoyance at Christians' refusal to conform to the mores and pleasures of the age may also have contributed to their zeal as persecutors. And it was not only Christian men who became martyrs: women also felt called by their faith to risk death, not to deny their religion when put to the test. One of the most famous accounts of female martyrs is *The Martyrdom of Perpetua and Felicitas.* This martyrdom reports that Vibia Perpetua, its heroine, was from a prominent family in Thuburbo, North Africa. She, together with other Christians, including her slave Felicitas, was martyred probably in the year 203 A.D. The *Martyrdom* displays much enthusiasm for prophecy, revelations, and visions, typical emphases of the Montanist sect in the North African church during this era, a sect that emphasized the Holy Spirit's continued activity in its midst. In his introduction, the editor of the account indicates that these manifestations of the Spirit were in accordance with the Bible's predictions regarding ecstatic events that would occur before the coming of the Kingdom of God. If Perpetua herself wrote the first section of the *Martyrdom* that covers her early experiences and

visions, as the text claims, this account is one of the
earliest pieces of Christian literature written by a woman.
It perhaps suggests that women were allowed more freedom in the early Christian prophetic movements than
they later enjoyed.[9] In the third or fourth century, a
basilica dedicated to Perpetua's memory was constructed
in Carthage, and the Roman church incorporated the day
of her martyrdom into its calendar.[10]

2. Young catechumens were seized, Revocatus and his
fellow slave Felicitas, Saturninus, and Secundulus. And
among these was Vibia Perpetua, of distinguished birth,
with an upbringing befitting a free woman, recently married. She had a father, mother, and two brothers, one of
whom was likewise a catechumen, and an infant son at the
breast. Now she was about twenty-two years old. From here
on she recounts the whole series of events of the martyrdom;
it is just as she left it, written in her own hand, and it contains
her own thoughts.

3. When, she reported, we were still with the imperial
officials, my father wanted to break down my resolution by
his words and persisted in trying to fell me, out of his love
for me. "Father," I said, "Do you see this vase lying here, for
example, or this little pitcher, or whatever it is?" And he
said, "I see it." And I said to him, "Now can it be called by
any other name than what it is?" And he replied, "No." "Just
so, I cannot be said to be anything else than what I am, a
Christian." Then my father became so aroused by this name
that he started toward me as though he would tear out my
eyes; but having gotten irate to this degree, he left, conquered along with the diabolical arguments.

Then in a few days I thanked the Lord that I was free from
my father, and I was relieved by his absence. In this interval
of a few days I was baptized, and the Spirit suggested to me

[9]See below, p. 162, on the Montanists.
[10]Text: *The Acts of the Christian Martyrs*, ed. H. Musurillo (Oxford, 1972), 108.

not to seek anything else after the water except endurance of flesh. After a few days we were taken back to the prison, and I was terrified because I had never experienced such a dark place. O what a cruel time! Because of the mob, the heat was horrible; then there was also the soldiers' extortion. Last of all, I was tormented with anxiety there about my baby.

Then Tertius and Pomponius, blessed deacons who were serving us, offered a bribe so that for a few hours we were sent to a better place in the prison and could refresh ourselves. Then we went out from the prison and all of us were at our own leisure. I nursed my baby, already weak from lack of food. In my worry about him, I spoke to my mother and was comforting my brother, entrusting the child to them. Thus I was languishing because I saw them despondent because of me. Such were the anxieties I suffered for many days. And I got the opportunity for my baby to stay with me in prison. Immediately I became well and was freed from distress and anxiety over my baby; the prison suddenly had been made into a palace for me, so that I preferred to be there rather than somewhere else.

> (Perpetua next has a vision of her reception into heaven by a white-haired shepherd who gives her milk to drink: the practice of drinking milk after baptism was customary in North African churches in this period.)

5. After a few days a rumor went about that we would be given a hearing. Then my father also arrived from the city, eaten away with weariness. He came up to me to destroy my resolution, saying, "Have pity, daughter, on my gray hairs; pity your father, if I am worthy to be called your father, if by these hands I have raised you to your prime years, if I have preferred you to all your brothers: do not hand me over to the reproach of men. Consider your brothers, consider your mother and your aunt, think of your son who will not be able to live after you. Lay aside your purpose, lest you destroy all of us. For none of us will speak freely, should

something happen to you." My father was talking this way out of his affection; he was kissing my hands, throwing himself at my feet, and weeping; he was now calling me not "daughter" but "lady." And I was grieved for my father's sake, because alone of all my relatives, he would not be pleased at my suffering. And I was comforting him, saying, "What God wills will take place at that dock. For I know that we do not depend on our own power, but that we are in God's." And saddened, he departed from me.

6. One day as we were eating breakfast, we were suddenly whisked off for a hearing. And we came to the forum. At once a rumor went about the arena and a large number of people gathered. We climbed up the dock. The others confessed when they were questioned. Then it came my turn. My father appeared there with my son, and pulled me down the step, saying, "Perform the act of worship. Pity your baby." And the procurator Hilarianus, who then had received judicial power in place of the now dead proconsul Minucius Timinianus, said, "Spare your father's gray hairs; spare your infant boy. Offer the sacrifice for the emperors' well-being." And I responded, "I will not make it." Hilarianus asked, "Are you a Christian?" And I replied, "I am a Christian." And when my father continued his attempt to break my resolution, Hilarianus ordered him to be thrown down and beaten with a rod. And the misfortune of my father was painful to me, as if I myself had been beaten: thus I ached for his wretched old age. Then Hilarianus pronounced the verdict on all of us and condemned us to the beasts, and cheerfully we marched back down to the prison.

Now because my baby had gotten accustomed to nursing at the breast and to staying with me in prison, straightway I sent the deacon Pomponius to my father, asking for the baby, but my father would not give him up. And as God willed, the baby did not want my breasts anymore, nor did they suffer from inflammation, so I was neither tormented by anxiety over my baby nor by pain in my breasts.

(Perpetua has two visions of her brother Dinocrates who had died of cancer at age seven; in the second one, he had been healed and freed from his suffering. Perpetua's father also visited her again.)

10. The day before we were to fight the animals, I saw this in a vision: Pomponius the deacon came to the prison doors and was knocking on them vigorously. I went out to him and opened the door for him. He had on loose white clothing and complicated shoes. And he said to me, "Perpetua, we are awaiting you; come." He held my hand and we began to walk through harsh and winding territory. With difficulty we finally came to the amphitheatre, panting, and he led me to the center of the arena and said to me, "Fear not: I am with you and labor with you." And he departed. I looked about the vast, astounded crowd, and because I knew I had been condemned to the beasts, I was amazed that no beasts had been let loose against me. A certain Egyptian came out against me, loathsome in appearance, along with his assistants, to fight me. Comely young men came to me, to be my assistants and my promoters. And I was stripped and I was made a man. My assistants began to rub me down with oil, as is the custom in the contests. I saw the Egyptian across from me, rolling in the sand. And a certain man of amazing height came out. He was so tall that he topped the summit of the amphitheatre. He had on an unbelted purple tunic with two stripes spaced on the middle of his chest, and elaborate shoes made from silver and gold. He carried a stick like a gladiator-trainer, and a green branch on which there were golden apples. He asked for silence and said, "This Egyptian, should he conquer her, will kill her with a sword; if she defeats him, she will receive this branch." And he retired.

The Egyptian and I came close to each other and began to send blows. He wanted to seize my feet; I, however, was kicking him in the face with my shoes. Then I was raised into the air and began thus to strike him as if I were not standing

on the ground. When I saw there was a pause, I joined my
hands so that my fingers linked and I grabbed his head. And
he fell on his face and I stood on his head. The mob began to
shout, and my assistants, to sing Psalms. I approached the
gladiator-trainer and received the branch. He kissed me and
said to me, "Daughter, peace be with you." And I began to
go in triumph to the Porta Sanavivaria, the Gate of the
Living.[11] Then I woke up. I understood that I was to fight
not against the beasts but against the Devil, but I knew
myself to be the victor.

This is what I did up to the day before the public exhibition. However, for what happened at the contest itself, if
anyone so wishes, let him write about it.

15. About Felicitas, indeed the grace of the Lord was
furnished to her as well in this way. Since already the fetus
had come to the eighth month (for she was pregnant when
she was arrested), and as the day of the spectacle was at
hand, she was distressed lest her case be postponed because
of the fetus (for it is illegal for pregnant women to suffer the
death penalty), and lest she shed her holy and innocent
blood later on, amidst others who were just ordinary crimi-
nals. But her fellow martyrs were also deeply saddened lest
they leave behind so good a companion to follow alone on
the same path to hope. Thus they poured forth a prayer to
the Lord, united by a single groan, on the second day before
the spectacle. Straightway after the prayer, the labor pains
seized her. And when, because of the natural difficulty of an
eight-months' birth, she suffered in her labor, a certain one
of the jailers' helpers said to her, "If you suffer this much
now, what will you do when you are thrown about by the
beasts? Did you forget about them when you refused to

[11]One of the two major gates in an amphitheatre, through which the living
victors exited.

sacrifice?" And she answered, "What I suffer now, *I* am suffering; but yonder, another will be in me who will suffer for me, because I too will be suffering for him." Then she brought forth a girl, whom a certain sister raised as her own daughter.

18. The day of their triumph dawned, and they cheerfully came forth from the prison to the amphitheatre, as if to Heaven, with faces composed; if perchance they trembled, it was not from fear but from joy. Perpetua was following with a bright face and with calm gait, as the wife of Christ, as the woman pleasing to God, by the power of her gaze casting down everyone's stares. Also Felicitas came forth, rejoicing that she had safely borne her child, so that she could fight the beasts, going from blood to blood, from the midwife to the gladiator, about to wash after childbirth in a second baptism.

And when they were led to the gate, they were forced to put on garments: the men, those of the priests of Saturn, the woman, however, in those of the priestesses of Ceres. That noble woman fought this right up to the end. For she said, "It was for this reason that we arrived at this situation of our own accord, lest our freedom be smothered. We sacrificed our lives just so that we might not take part in such activities. We made an agreement about this!" Injustice recognized justice: the tribune yielded. They were to be brought in directly, just as they were. Perpetua began to sing a Psalm, already trampling on the head of the Egyptian. Revocatus, Saturninus, and Saturus were threatening the spectators. Next they fell under the gaze of Hilarianus, and began to indicate to him by gestures and nods: "You condemned us, but God will condemn you," they said. At this the crowd, provoked, demanded that they be attacked with scourges by a line of gladiators. They indeed rejoiced in the fact that they were to some extent imitators of the Lord's sufferings.

20. However, the Devil had prepared for the young

women a very savage heifer, on account of its sex contrary
to custom, just so their sex might rival that of the beast.
Thus stripped naked and tangled in nets, they were brought
forward. The mob was horrified, seeing that one was a
charming girl, the other a woman lately risen from childbirth, with dripping breasts. So they were called back and
clad in loose garments. First Perpetua was thrown and fell
on her back. And when she sat up, she pulled at her tunic,
torn down the side, in order to cover her thighs, having in
mind her modesty more than her pain. Next she asked for a
pin and clasped her straggling hair, for it was not proper for
a martyr to suffer with dishevelled hair, lest she appear to
lament while in her glory. Next she stood up, and when she
saw Felicitas dashed down, she went to her, gave her a hand,
and lifted her up. And both stood side by side. But since the
insensibility of the crowd was subdued, they were called
back to the Porta Sanavivaria, the Gate of Life. There
Perpetua was held up by a certain man by the name of
Rusticus, then a catechumen, who kept close to her. She
woke up as if from a sleep (so entirely had she been in the
Spirit and in ecstacy); she began to look around her and
said, to everybody's astonishment, "When are we being led
forth to that heifer or whatever it is?" And when she heard
that this had already happened, she at first did not believe it,
until she perceived some marks on her body and her garment. Next, having sent for her brother and that catechumen, she greeted them saying, "Stand firm in the faith
(I Cor. 16:13) and all love one another, and do not stumble
because of our sufferings."

21. In like manner, Saturus at another gate was exhorting
a soldier, Pudens, saying, "Down to the last detail, it is
exactly as I expected and predicted. Up to now, I haven't
experienced any beast at all. And now you may believe with
your whole heart: watch, I am going in there and I shall be
finished off in one bite of the leopard." And straightway, at

the end of the spectacle, a leopard was thrown in the way and in one bite Saturus was so bathed in blood that the crowd shouted as he turned around, as a testimony to his second baptism, "Well washed! Well washed!" Indeed he was entirely "well washed," he who had bathed in this way. Then he said to the soldier Pudens, "Farewell, remember the faith and me. These things should not upset you, but encourage you." And at once he asked him for a ring from his finger, and plunging it into his wound, he returned it to him as an inheritance, leaving him a pledge and a memorial of the bloodshed.

Now after that he was thrown to the ground, unconscious, and was with the others in the usual place to have his throat cut. And since the crowd demanded that they be put in the center so that their eyes might be added as attendants of murder to the sword that sunk in their flesh, they voluntarily got up and went over to where the crowd wished. Then finally they kissed each other so that they perfected their martyrdoms with the sacred kiss of peace. The others, indeed, received the sword without moving and in silence, especially Saturus, who climbed up first and was the first to give back his spirit. For he was also supporting Perpetua. She, however, was to taste some further pain. She howled as she was punctured between the bones and herself steered the erring hand of the novice gladiator to her own throat. Perhaps so great a woman, who was feared by the impure spirit, could not be killed in any other way than unless she herself wished it.

O, most brave and blessed martyrs! O, truly you are called in the glory of our Lord Jesus Christ! And whoever extols, honors, and adores his glory ought certainly also to read these examples for the edification of the church no less than the ones of older times, considering that these new virtues also will give witness to one and the same Holy Spirit who always is at work, right up to now, and to God the Father

Almighty and to his Son, Jesus Christ our Lord, to whom is splendor and boundless power for ages without end. Amen.

The last and most extensive of the persecutions began in 303 A.D. under the emperor Diocletian. Roman citizens were required to visit designated pagan temples in order to sacrifice to the gods and pay reverence to the emperor. Torture, imprisonment, forced labor in the mines, and other punishments of varying severity up to and including the death penalty were inflicted upon the non-compliant. The severity of Diocletian's persecution varied greatly from area to area, depending in part on the provincial or local officials' willingness to execute the imperial command. Although no accurate statistics exist for the number of Christians martyred during this last round of persecution, scholars have estimated that about three thousand Christians may have lost their lives. Yet even this "Great Persecution" did not last too long: in 305 A.D. Diocletian abdicated. Although persecution of Christians continued for several years more in the eastern portion of the empire, Christianity found itself in a favored position with Constantine's speedy rise to power. By the time Constantine called the Council of Nicaea in 325 A.D., he had already made numerous concessions to the Christians.

The cult of the martyrs was considerably strengthened by the events of Diocletian's persecution. Various cities and provinces revered their own martyrs, whose martyrdoms were commemorated as if they were "birthdays." In the city of Rome, a young woman named Agnes was counted among the notable local martyrs. Although historical evidence pertaining to Agnes' martyrdom is weak, tradition had it that she was martyred under Diocletian in about 304 A.D. Agnes fast became a popular saint in Rome and elsewhere. About 350 A.D., Constantine's daughter Constantina erected a church to her honor in

Rome. In the early fifth century, some highly unreliable *Acts* of her life were composed. Yet in the story of Agnes we see how the Christian imagination was fired, how the best literary talent of the times was expended on the glorification of a subject whose historicity scholars might doubt. The first selection is from Ambrose's treatise *On Virgins*. Ambrose wrote this work in 377 A.D. for his sister Marcellina who had taken a vow of virginity. In the work he takes the occasion to recount the tale of Agnes.

I,2,5.[12] It is fortunate that since today is the birthday of a virgin, it is about virgins I am to speak; the treatise has its introduction in such a commendation. It is the birthday of a virgin: let us imitate her integrity. It is the birthday of a martyr: let us sacrifice the victim. It is the birthday of Saint Agnes: let men marvel, let children not lose hope, let the married be astounded, let the unmarried seek to resemble her. What can we say worthy of her whose very name was not devoid of glowing praise? In piety, she excelled her years; in virtue, she was above nature. It seems to me that she bore not a human name but one that was a prophecy of her martyrdom by which she showed what she was to be.[13]

I,2,6. Nonetheless, I have at hand means for my assistance. The name of "virgin" is an appellation of modesty. I will entreat the martyr, I will herald the virgin. The eulogy is appropriate that is not sought after, but is held as a right. Thus let genius retire; let eloquence fall silent: one word is a commendation. Old men, youths, and boys sing this word. No one is more worthy of praise than he who can be praised by everybody. As many human beings as may exist, there are that many public criers who, when they speak, herald the martyr.

I,2,7. It is reported that she was martyred when she was

[12]Text: PL 16.189.
[13]Ambrose puns on her name: "agnus" means "lamb."

twelve years old. The more abominable the cruelty that did
not spare such meagre years, so much more the great power
of faith that even at her age found witness. Was there room
for a wound in that little body? Yet she, who had no room to
receive the sword, had that by which she conquered the
sword. Now girls of that age cannot even bear the stern
looks of their parents and are wont to weep at sharp pricks
of a needle, as if they were wounds. But this girl was
undaunted by the bloody hands of executioners; this girl
was unmoved by the heavy dragging of the creaking chains.
Now she offered her whole body to the raging soldier's
sword: she had been unaware of death until the present, but
she was ready for it. Or if she were carried off to the altars
unwillingly, she was still ready to stretch out her hands to
Christ in the midst of the fires and to make the sign of the
Lord, the Vanquisher, at the impious altars. Now she thrust
her neck and both her hands into the iron bands, but no
band could confine such slender limbs.

I,2,8. Is this a new type of martyrdom? Not yet of proper
age for punishment, she was already ripe for victory. Hard
to rival but easy to be crowned, she qualified for an instruc-
torship in courage while she yet bore the disadvantage of
youth. Thus she would not as a bride hasten to the nuptial
bed so that as a virgin with speedy step and joyful approach
she might march to the place of execution, her head not
adorned with curls but with Christ, redeemed not by orna-
ments but by deaths. All wept: she was without a tear. Most
marvelled that she was so promptly prodigal with her own
life, a life that she had not yet drunk in but now gave up as if
she had gone through it. All were astonished that already
there was a witness to God who until now could not herself
bear witness because of her youth. To sum up, she brought
it about that she should be believed concerning God, she
who as yet should not be believed concerning humans. What
is beyond nature is from the Father of nature.

I,2,9. What terror the executioner struck to make her afraid, what flatteries to persuade her! How many longed that she might come to them in marriage! But she replied, "It would be a wrong to my Spouse[14] to anticipate some man's pleasing me. The One who first chose me for himself shall receive me. For what, O murderer, do you delay? Let this body be destroyed, a body that can be loved by eyes of men I do not want." She stood, she prayed, she bent her neck. You could perceive the executioner tremble, as if he himself had been sentenced; the hand of the murderer shook, his face paled as he feared another's peril, when the girl did not fear her own. Thus you have in one victim a twofold martyrdom, of modesty and of piety: she both remained a virgin and acquired martyrdom.

> The second selection pertaining to Agnes illustrates how a prose legend could be turned into rhetorical poetry by the master hand of the early fifth-century Christian poet Prudentius. In the fourteenth chapter of his *Crowns of Maryrdom,*[15] a collection of poems he wrote about martyrs, he sings the praise of Agnes.

So brave a girl, a martyr famed
Was Agnes, who in Romulus'[16] home
Lies buried in a tomb. She sees
In death Rome's towering roofs
And so she keeps her people safe.
She also shields the pilgrims there
Who pray with pure and faithful hearts.
A double crown of martyrdom
Sets this noted girl apart:
Virginity free from any fault,
Then honor from a death she chose.

[14]Jesus as the heavenly bridegroom of virgins.
[15]Text:CSEL 61.427.
[16]The legendary founder of the city of Rome.

Hardly old enough to wed,   10
She was a little girl, they say,
By chance a child of tender years,
But aglow for Christ, with manly heart,
She defied the shameless laws.
For pagan idols she would not
Desert her holy, sacred faith.
First lured by many skillful tricks—   15
Now the lures of the fawning judge,
Now the raging butcher's threats—
She stood her ground tenaciously,
Of savage strength, she freely gave
Her body to the harsh abuse;
She did not flee impending death.   20
    Then the hardened tyrant said,
"If she bears the price with ease
And the pains that stem from it,
And if she scorns her life as cheap,
She cares about her precious vow,
The vow of chaste virginity.
I decree that she be sent
To a public brothel, unless she begs   25
Minerva's grace. Agnes must bow
To the altar of the virgin divine
Whom she, mortal virgin, continues to scorn.
Every youth will rush to seek
The new slave given for his sport!"   30
    "No," says Agnes, "By no means!
Christ does not forget his own
So that golden honor should be lost,
Nor does he now abandon us.
He guarantees to us, the chaste,
That he'll not let his gift be stained,
His gift of sacred purity.   35
You may stain your sword with blood,

As you will—but you will not
Stain my limbs with carnal lust."
   She spoke this way. He then decreed
Agnes be put in the public square.
The melancholy mob drew back,   40
With faces turned away, that no man's
Wanton leer should desecrate
The holy spot on which she stood.
As chance would have it, one man looked:
He boldly aimed his glance at her,
With rakish gaze and with no fear   45
He scrutinized her holy form.
Just look! A swift flame, like a flash
Of lightning, struck his eyes. Felled
And blinded by the branching light,
He quivered, trembling in the dusty square.
His comrades sobbed funereal laments
As weeping they raised up the half-dead man. 50
The virgin went triumphantly
To magnify in sacred song
God the Father and his Christ,
Since when unholy peril fell,
Virginity was Conqueress and
Found a brothel chaste and pure.   55
Some recall that on request
She poured forth earnest prayers to Christ
That the prostrate youth receive his sight:
The breath of life returned to him;
His sight was then restored unharmed.   60
   This was just the first of steps
That Agnes took toward Heaven's court:
A second ascent was granted soon.
For in the bloody foe, rage roused
A fury that brought forth his groan:
"I am outdone, go draw your sword,   65

O soldier there, and carry out
The highest prince's royal laws."
When Agnes saw the savage man
Standing with his sword unsheathed,
With greater joy she spoke these words:
"I revel more a wild man comes,
A cruel and violent man-at-arms,   70
Than if a softened youth came forth,
Faint and tender, bathed in scent,
To ruin me with chastity's death.
This is my lover, I confess,
A man who pleases me at last!
I shall rush to meet his steps   75
So I don't delay his hot desires.
I shall greet his blade's full length
Within my breast; and I shall draw
The force of sword to bosom's depth.
As bride of Christ,[17] I shall leap over
The gloom of sky, the aether's heights.   80
Eternal King, part Heaven's gates,
Barred before to earth-born folk,
And call, O Christ, a virgin soul,
A soul that aims to follow thee,
Now a sacrifice to Father God."
        Her fate thus sealed, she bent her head,   85
She worshiped Christ as suppliant,
That her sinking neck, more readily,
Might endure the threatened wound.
By the hand of the soldier she received
Fulfillment of her great desire,
For with one stroke he cleaved her head.
Swift death staved off a sense of pain.   90
        Then her spirit, bared, escapes,

[17]That virgins were brides of Christ was a common view in early Christianity.

And leaps in freedom to the air.
As the angels circle round,
She flies along the splendid path,
Admires the orb beneath her feet.
From on high she sees the dark below,   95
Smiles at the sun's disc wheeling on,
That moves and clasps the entire earth
On which we live in raging storm,
Whose vanities are snatched and seized
By the world's inconstancy:
Kings and despots, rule and rank,   100
Swollen, foolish pomp of honors,
The strength of silver, force of gold
That all folk seek with rabid greed,
Through impious deeds so manifold;
Dwellings built in sumptuous style;
The futility of wearing clothes   105
With lightly woven ornament;
Anger, fear, longings, harms,
Now long sadness, now short joy;
Gloomy envy's smoking brands
Darken human hope and worth;
And most base of all their ills,   110
The sordid clouds of pagan belief:
These Agnes treads and tramples down.
Standing, Agnes digs her heel
Into the head of the dragon fierce[18]
Who spreads his poison over all   115
The earthly things he sinks to Hell.
Now tamed by a virgin's foot alone,
The crests on his fiery head laid low,
Conquered, he dares not raise them up.
    Meanwhile, God with double crowns

[18]Cf. Gen. 3:15.

Wreathes the virgin martyr's brow: 120
One shows the sixtyfold reward
Sent forth from everlasting light,
The second shows fruit onehundredfold.[19]

   O happy virgin, glory new,
Famed dweller in the heavenly halls,   125
Turn your face with its twin crowns
Upon our vile impurities.
You only, Father of us all,
Can make the very brothel pure.
The brightness of your gracious face   130
Shall work atonement for my sins,
If you will satiate my heart.
All is pure that you may deign
To view with love, or condescend
To touch with your propitious foot.

Thus as martyrs and as ascetics, in real life and in literature, Christian women might see themselves both glorified and endangered.

---

[19]Martyrdom and virginity are the onehundredfold and sixtyfold harvests: an early Christian interpretation of the parable of the sower (Mk. 4:1-9 = Mt. 13:1-9 = Lk. 8:4-8).

Chapter Three

PARADISE REGAINED: ASCETICISM IN THEORY AND PRACTICE

Although celibacy and unpretentious living had been advocated by Christian writers from New Testament times on, the fourth century saw a flourishing of the ascetic movement. The demise of martyrdom as a way to manifest one's Christian commitment and the increased numbers of less-than-ardent Christians within the fourth-century Church are often given as reasons for the popularity of asceticism in this period. Indeed, the Church Fathers themselves saw the choice of a virginal life as a new kind of martyrdom and urged their followers to distinguish themselves from the rank and file of Christian believers by undertaking the "way of perfection."

Some authors also argued that the virginal life provided a means by which humans could recapture the purity of Paradise, a purity that Adam and Eve lost by their original sin and their subsequent involvement in marriage and reproduction. Especially was the ascetic opportunity lauded for women, who through it might cast off the subordination to a husband that was the married woman's lot. The Fathers argued that not only would ascetic women be freed from many domestic burdens, but also they would regain, at least in part, the bliss of Paradise.

> Given the enthusiasm for virginity among Christian writers, some explanation seemed called for why not just marriage, but even polygamy, was permitted in the Old Testament. One of the first attempts to resolve that problem was made by Methodius, a bishop who was martyred in 312 A.D. His most famous work, *The Banquet,* was modelled on Plato's *Symposium.* The crucial difference between the two works is that whereas Plato had his dinner guests discourse on the origin of love, Methodius imagines the ten female virgins at his "banquet" extolling the glories of Christian virginity. Marcella, one of the speakers, here explains the historical progress of the virginal ideal in human life.

I,2,16-18.[1] Truly it was by God's great extravagance that virginity's shoots were sent down from Heaven to human beings. For this reason, virginity was not revealed to the first generations. Since the human race was still very small in number, the multitude first needed to be increased and then perfected. That is why the ancients did not think it indecent to take their own sisters as wives, up till the time the Law came to define the situation and to prohibit the practice that at first had seemed right, plainly declaring it a sin and calling "accursed" the man who "uncovered the nakedness of his sister" (Lev. 18:9). God carefully brought help to our race at the right time and in a manner suited to the age, just as fathers help their sons. For fathers do not immediately, right from the start, set schoolmasters over their sons, but allow the children to frolic like little calves during their early years. When sons reach the age at which they stammer to each other, fathers send them to teachers and there they stay until the time they cast off the youthful down of their minds, much as they cast off their first whiskers. The fathers then send them on to the discipline of more advanced lessons, and from there, in turn, to those that are more difficult still.

We should reflect on the point that God, the Father of us all, also dealt with those who came before us in this way. For the world, when it was not yet fully peopled, was like an infant; it first needed to be filled with humans and attain its adulthood. However, when it came to be settled from one end to the other in later times, God no longer permitted humans to remain with these customs. He saw how they might advance closer to Heaven by passing from one point to another, until they arrived at the highest and most excellent lesson of virginity and were perfected. As a first step, they should refrain from marriage between brothers and sisters and should take wives from outside the family. After this, they should no longer indulge themselves by having many wives, the way animals do, as though impregnation was the purpose for which we were born. Next, they should not practice adultery. And from there they should pass on to continence and from continence to virginity, where, when they have studied how to despise the flesh, they may fearlessly drop anchor in the calm haven of incorruptibility.

I,5,25-26. What then did the Lord, who is the Truth and the Light (John 14:6; 8:12), undertake when he came to the world? He kept the flesh with which he adorned himself incorrupt and virginal. Thus we too, if we aim to be "in the likeness" of God (Gen. 1:26), should strive earnestly to honor Christ's virginity. For "likeness to God" is the flight from corruption. When the Word became incarnate, he was the chief of virgins, in the same way that he also was the chief shepherd and the chief prophet of the Church, as John, who was filled with Christ, also brings home in the book of Revelation (14:1-4)...in which he shows that the Lord leads the chorus of the virgins. . . .

But such an "historical" explanation was only one aspect of the Christian argument for virginity. Gregory of Nyssa,[2] a prominent fourth-century theologian whose writings reveal a subtle intellect, dwelt on the divine origins and analogues of virginity. His treatise *On Virginity*, dating from the 360's or early 370's A.D., argues that human virginity is modelled on the chaste relations of Father, Son, and Holy Spirit within the Godhead. Just as the Godhead is unchangeable, so does the adoption of virginity here on earth allow one to participate in the heavenly quality of "incorruptibility," i.e., the inability to change or decline. Moreover, Gregory pressed the notion that virginity was the original condition of the human race as an argument for its desirability in his own time. Whereas marriage involves humans in an ongoing succession of births and deaths, Gregory argues, virginity enables us to bypass that succession and associate ourselves with heavenly realities that do not perish.

2,1.[3] We need much astuteness to understand the superiority of this grace, the grace that is considered in association with the incorruptible Father. It is indeed a paradox to discover virginity in a Father who has a Son, who begot him apart from passion. Virginity is also perceived in the Only-Begotten God, i.e., the Son, the chorus-leader of incorruptibility, since it shone forth together with the purity and impassibility of his begetting. Here again the same paradox: through virginity, a Son is apprehended. In like manner, it is contemplated in the natural and incorruptible purity of the Holy Spirit. For you are only calling virginity by another name when you speak of the pure and the incorruptible. Virginity is a fellow-citizen of the entire celestial nature because its impassibility accompanies the superior powers and is inseparable from divine realities, in no way touching

[2]A Cappadocian see.
[3]Text: SC 119.262.

the opposites. For all things that by nature and choice incline to virtue beautify themselves totally in the purity of the incorruptible, and all the things that are rejected, cast into the opposite rank, are also called what they are by their falling short of purity. Then what power of words can suffice to equal such a grace? Or how can it not be feared that in a person's enthusiastic commendation of virginity, he not outrage the greatness of its honor, diminishing for his listeners the glory that they first associated with it?

2,3. The power of virginity, then, is such that it abides in the heavens with the Father of spirits; it is in the chorus of the celestial powers, it applies itself to human salvation, and by its power it leads God down to share in human life,[4] while it gives humans wings, so that in virginity we have a desire for heavenly things. It is as if virginity were a kind of bond in humans' relationship with God, and by its mediation leads into harmony things that by nature are separated from one another. What force of words, then, can we find that rises to match this wonder?...

4,7. ...How can a person enamoured of something in the present life possess the object of his longing to the end of his days? Of the things for which we are the most eager, which of them remain just as they now are? What is the bloom of youth? What is the happy possession of power or beauty? What is wealth? What glory? What power? Do not all such things flourish for a short time and then go, changing into their very opposites? Who has spent life entirely as a youth? For whom did power survive until the end? And what flower of beauty is there that nature has not made more ephemeral than the blossoms that appear in the spring? The things of the ongoing season shoot up, fade after a short time, again grow young, again fade, once more are decked out, then show again to a new year their present beauty. But the human flower, in contrast, once and for all shows itself in

---

[4]In the Incarnation of Jesus, his birth from a virgin.

the spring-time of youth; then nature extinguishes it and it fades into the winter of old age. Thus too with all other such things: for a time they deceive the flesh's sense, then pass on by, and are veiled in oblivion.

4,8. Since, then, such changes that occur in accordance with natural inevitability are totally distressing to the person who is passionately attached to them, there is one refuge from such evils: not to associate anything changeable with the soul. It is possible to remove yourself from any association with the life of passion, the carnal life, and even more, to be beyond sympathy with your own body, so as not to be subject to the life according to the flesh that accompanies a life in the flesh. But this involves living for the soul alone and imitating as far as possible the way of life of the incorporeal powers, with whom "there is neither marrying nor giving in marriage" (Mk. 12:25 = Mt. 22:30 = Lk. 20:35). Their work, exertion, and successful accomplishment is rather in the contemplation of the Father of incorruptibility and in establishing their own form through the imitation of the archetypal Beauty, as far as is possible.

4,9. As Scripture teaches, we say that virginity was given to humankind as a "helpmate" (cf. Gen 2:18), as an accomplice in thought and solemn desire. Just as in the other professions, certain skills are invented to execute each of the things zealously pursued, so it seems to me that the practice of virginity is a certain art, a power of the more divine kind of life, instructing those who live in the flesh to become like the incorporeal nature.

13,1. Therefore, if we are to "depart" from here and be "with Christ" (Phil. 1:23), it is proper to begin again at the last point from which the departure commenced, just as those who are far from their own people, when they start their return to the place whence they came, first leave behind the place that was the last one at which they happened to be as they departed. Since, then, marriage is the last point of separation from life in Paradise, the argument suggests to those "departing for Christ" that first they leave behind marriage as a kind of last station on the journey; next, to withdraw from the earthly misery in which humankind was placed after the sin; and after this, to strip off the coverings of the flesh, the "garments of skins" (Gen. 3:21), that is, they must strip off the "thought of the flesh" (Rom. 8:6)....

14,1. Such a virginal life should therefore be preferred, at least by rational people, since it is stronger than the power of death. For physical procreation—let no one be vexed at the argument—is more the occasion of death than of life for human beings. Corruption has its origin in generation; those who cease from procreation through virginity set a limit within themselves for death, preventing it from advancing further because of them. They set themselves as a boundary between life and death, so to speak; they hold death in check from further productivity. If death is then not able to outstrip virginity but ceases and is deposed, it is plainly demonstrated that virginity is stronger than death.

Also, it is appropriate to call a body "incorruptible" that has not rendered service in the life of corruptibility and has refused to become an instrument in the mortal succession. For in this way, the constant succession of corruption and death is broken, the succession that has been in effect from the first man through all intervening time down to the life of the One who lived as a virgin, i.e., Jesus. Indeed, it was never possible for death to be idle while human generation was active by means of marriage. Death found a limit to its activity in virginity, which it was at a loss to overcome, after having travelled the route with the preceding generations and having marched along with those forever entering life. Just as in the case of Mary, the Mother of God, "death had ruled from Adam" to her (Rom. 5:14), and when it also approached her, it was crushed by striking against the fruit of her virginity as against a rock, so in every soul, the power of death is somehow crushed and destroyed when the soul, through virginity, disregards life in the flesh, the power of death not having the means by which to vent its sting (I Cor. 15:55). Indeed, if wood, straw, hay, or some other combustible matter is not laid under a fire, the fire does not have it within its nature to continue on its own: so the power of death will not operate if marriage does not supply the underlying fuel and the people who must die, like those who have been condemned.

> John Chrysostom also wrote a treatise *On Virginity,* composed probably about twenty years after Gregory's. In addition to borrowing some of Gregory's theories, Chrysostom undertook to answer those partisans of marriage who argued that God had commanded us to "reproduce and multiply" (Gen. 1:28) and that without reproduction, the human race would die out. In responding to these objections, Chrysostom developed the unusual opinion, not held by other Church Fathers such as Augustine, that God could have multiplied the human race without sexual reproduction; besides, Chrysostom claims, it is always God's will, not human sexual activity, that creates new people. He also argues that virginity has practical advantages: the virgin escapes the anxieties and griefs that the married woman experiences over her family.

14,3.[5] For after this entire world had been completed and everything had been made ready for our refreshment and use, God formed man, for whom he also made the world. Man, when he had been fashioned, lived in Paradise; there was no reason for marriage. When he came to need a helper for himself (Gen. 2:18), one was supplied, but even then marriage did not seem to be necessary. It didn't make an appearance anywhere. Rather, Adam and Eve remained

[5]Text: SC 125.140.

apart from marriage, leading the sort of life in Paradise they would have led had they been in Heaven, luxuriating in their association with God. Desire for sexual relation, conception, labor pains, childbirth, and every form of corruptibility was removed from their souls. As a clear stream flows forth from a pure source, so in that place were they adorned with virginity.

14,5. At that time there were no cities, no professions, no houses. To be sure, we care about these things to an extraordinary degree, but then these things did not even exist. All the same, nothing caused Adam and Eve to retreat from or to drive back this blessed life, a life much better than the present one. When, however, they disregarded God and became earth and ashes (Gen. 3:19; 18:27), they also destroyed the beauty of virginity along with that blessed way of life, and along with God, virginity also abandoned them and withdrew.[6] So long as they were unconquered by the Devil and respected their Ruler, virginity also remained, adorning them more lavishly than diadems and golden garments adorn kings. But when they were taken prisoners, they were stripped of their royal raiment and laid aside their heavenly adornment. They received in exchange the corruptibility of death, the curse, suffering, and the life of toil (Gen. 3:16-19)—then, too, marriage, this mortal and servile garment,[7] entered along with these other things.

14,6. Paul says, "The married man is anxious for the things of the world" (I Cor. 7:33). Do you see where marriage had its origin, why it seemed necessary? Because of the disobedience, the curse, death. For where death is, there is marriage. If one of them does not step forward, the other does not exist. Virginity, in contrast is not followed by

---

[6]An echo of the classical theme of the departure of Reverence and Righteous Indignation at the close of the Golden Age; see, for example, Hesiod, *Works and Days*, ll. 197-200.

[7]Chrysostom interprets the "coats of skins" of Gen. 3:21 as meaning marriage.

death, but is always useful, always beautiful and blessed, before death and after death, before marriage and after marriage. For tell me, from what sort of marriage was Adam born? What sort of labor pains did he suffer in bringing forth Eve? You don't know what to say! Then why do you so heedlessly fear and tremble lest the cessation of marriage also entail the cessation of the human race? There are millions of angels who serve God, thousands upon thousands of archangels who stand beside him, and none of these was produced by generation, none from birth, labor pains, and conception! Is it not even more probable that God could make humans aside from marriage, just as he created the first people without marriage, those first people from whom all humans are derived?

15,1. Even now the force of marriage does not weld together our race. It is rather the word of the Lord pronounced at the beginning: "Reproduce and multiply and fill the earth" (Gen. 1:28). Tell me, did marriage profit Abraham so that he had children? Did he not exclaim after so many years of involvement in marriage, "Lord, what will you give me? Am I to depart without children?" (Gen. 15:2). Thus just as God at that time from the dead bodies of Abraham and Sarah gave the foundation and root of so many beings, so also at the beginning, if Adam and Eve had obeyed his commands and overcome the pleasure of the tree, he would not have been at a loss for a way to increase the human race. For marriage, without the will of God, cannot make many living beings; nor, had God wanted there to be many people, would virginity have caused the ruin of the population. But God wanted it this way, as Scripture says, because of us and our disobedience.

56,1. In virginity, it is difficult, indeed impossible, to encounter the woes of marriage, while in marriage it is difficult not to encounter them. If in apparently happy marriages so many disagreeable events and misfortunes occur, what can be said about those who agree about their distress? The woman has not just one death to fear, although she herself is going to die just once and for all; she has not just one soul to be anxious about, although she herself has only one. Rather, she trembles on behalf of her husband, she trembles on behalf of her children, she trembles for their families, the women and the children, and by as much as the root extends itself into many shoots, by that much are her anxieties more than sufficient for her. And in the case of each of these relatives, one of them will either sustain a loss, or a bodily illness, or some other undesirable accident; necessity makes us disconsolate and mournful no less than the victims themselves. If everyone dies before her, the sorrow is intolerable, but if those remain while others are carried away by untimely deaths, she does not in this way find a pure consolation.

56,2. For the ever-present fear on behalf of the living that shakes her soul is not less than the grief that occurs on behalf of the dead. If I must say something amazing, it is even harder to bear. For time softens the dispiritedness over the dead, but anxieties on behalf of the living always retain their force and come to an end only with death. And if our own sufferings are not enough, what sort of life do we live when we are compelled to grieve at the misfortunes of others? Many women are frequently born of illustrious parents, raised in great luxury, are given in marriage to some man who has great power; then suddenly, before the women could be deemed happy on account of these things, some danger arises, just like a tempest or a hurricane, and they too have sunk, they too partake in the horrors of shipwreck, and they who before marriage enjoyed thousands of good things, through marriage fall to ultimate misfortune. "But," an objector says, "these things are not likely to occur in all marriages, nor do they occur inevitably. And she's no different from anyone else!" Indeed, I will go over my point again:

it is all the same whether you are among the ones who come suddenly to the experience, or are among those who escape it, yet grieve about it through anticipation. Every virgin, in contrast, is set above both the experience itself and the anticipation of the experience.

> Given their enthusiasm for virginity, the Church Fathers could be criticized for disparaging marriage and for veering toward an heretical view of the inherent evil of the sexual relation. Although the Gnostic threat no longer dominated Christian consciousness, Christian writers had to defend their exhortations to virginity against accusations of heresy. Jerome, a late fourth-century Christian who lived in Rome and later in monastic retreat in Bethlehem, was one such author. An opponent named Jovinian had targeted Jerome's views as falling close to those of the heretics. Jovinian had written a popular book that defended marriage. In it he argued that virgins, widows, and married women were all equal once they passed through Christian baptism: superior merit was not to be accorded to celibacy. In 393 A.D., Jerome responded with his *Against Jovinian,* a work so sarcastic, so derogatory of marriage that his friends attempted to remove the book from circulation. Although Jerome strongly suspected that Jovinian simply wanted to disparage virginity by this enthusiastic exaltation of marriage, he nonetheless had to protect himself against the accusation of heresy, as the following selection makes clear.

I,3.[8] ... Indeed, we do not follow the teachings of Marcion and Mani; we do not disparage marriage, nor do we judge all sexual intercourse foul. We have not been deceived

[8]Text: PL 23.223.

by the error of Tatian, the head of the Encratites,[9] who condemns and rejects not only marriage, but food, which God created for our use. We know that in a great house there are vases not only of gold and silver, but also of wood and clay. And above the foundation of Christ that Paul the architect laid, some build with gold, silver, precious stones, while others, on the contrary, build with hay, wood, straw. We are not ignorant of: "Marriage is honorable and the bed undefiled" (Heb. 13:4). We read God's first judgment: "Increase and multiply and fill the earth" (Gen. 1:28), but just as we accept marriage, we prefer virginity, which is born of marriage. Now will silver not be silver, if gold is more precious than it? Or is it an insult to tree and corn, if we prefer the fruit to the root and leaves, and the ear to the stalk and the beard of the corn? As fruit is from the tree and grain from straw, so is virginity from marriage. Although the onehundredfold, sixtyfold and thirtyfold fruits are brought forth from one earth and from one sowing, nonetheless they differ much in number. The thirtyfold refers to marriage..., the sixtyfold to widows..., the onehundredfold...expresses the crown of virginity.[10]

(Jovinian argued his case in part on the basis of Biblical examples of people who married. Jerome thus responds:)

I,16. ...We also have to run through the same line of inquiry and show that chastity always was preferred to the business of marriage. Indeed, we must affirm about Adam and Eve that they were virgins in Paradise before the sin; however, after the sin, and outside of Paradise, immediately they were married.... Christ in the flesh is a virgin; in spirit, he was once-married. For he has one Church, about which

---

[9]An extremely ascetic sect of Christians that flourished in the late second century.

[10]An interpretation of the parable of the sower (Mk. 4:7-9 = Mt. 13:1-9 = Lk. 8:4-8); cf. p. 114.

the same apostle, Paul, says, "Husbands, love your wives, just as also Christ loved the Church" (Col. 3:19; Eph. 5:25)....The "image" of the Creator is not found in the bond of marriage. When difference of sex is taken away and we put off the "old man" and put on the "new" (Col. 3:9-10), then we shall be reborn in Christ, a virgin, he who is both born from a virgin and is reborn through a virgin[11].... Marriage fills the earth, virginity fills Paradise....

I,33. "Let it be granted," Jovinian says, "that the situations of marriage and virginity are different. What can you reply to this point: if a virgin and a widow were baptized and remained such, what would be the difference between them?" What we have said above about Peter and John, Anna and Mary, may be useful in this present discussion. For if there is no distinction between a baptized virgin and a baptized widow (since baptism makes a "new man"), on the same principle harlots and prostitutes, if they were baptized, would be equal to virgins. For if an earlier marriage does no harm to a widow if she is baptized, so should it be in the case of harlots. Despite their earlier pleasures and the exposing of their bodies to vulgar licentiousness, if they received baptism, it would follow (by Jovinian's argument) that they would have the rewards of virginity. To unite with God with the purest mind and with no defiling recollection is one thing; it is quite another to do so remembering the repulsive and unavoidable embraces of a man and to replay in memory what you are no longer doing in the body....I do not deny that widows are blessed who remain in the state of widowhood after their baptisms; nor do I detract from the honor of those women who remain with their husbands in sexual abstinence. Yet just as these women have a higher reward with God than married women who comply with the marriage duty, so also let them with impartial mind allow virginity to be preferred to their own situations. For if they

[11]Probably a reference to John the Baptist's baptism of Jesus.

rise up against married women after a belated chastity skims off bodily pleasures, why do they not recognize themselves to be below the rank of perpetual virginity?

I,36. But you will say, "If all people were virgins, how would the human race continue?" I shall submit for consideration like for like. If all were widows or remained abstinent in marriage, how would human progeny be propagated? On this line of reasoning, there will be nothing at all, lest something might cease to be. For example, if all were philosophers, there would be no farmers. Why do I speak of farmers? There would be no orators, no lawyers, no teachers of the other professions. If all were officers, who would be the soldiers? If all were the head, whose head would they be called when the other members were lacking? Are you afraid that if many had an inclination for virginity, prostitutes would cease, adulterous women would cease, that there would be no squalling infants in cities and towns? Daily the blood of adulterers is poured forth and adulteries are condemned, yet blazing lust rules amidst the very laws, authorities, and judgment seats. Do not fear that all will become virgins: virginity is a difficult business and is rare just because it is hard. "Many are called but few are chosen" (Mt. 22:14). To undertake virginity is for the many, to stick with it is for the few—whence also the reward for those who have persevered is great. If all were able to be virgins, the Lord never would have said, "He who can receive this, let him receive it" (Mt. 19:12), and the Apostle would not have wavered in his recommendation, "About virgins, however, I have no commandment from the Lord" (I Cor. 7:25).

"And why," you will ask, "were the genital organs created, and why were we thus made by a most wise Creator so that we experience a burning for each other and feel joy in natural intercourse?" We risk our modesty in responding; as if we were between two rocks, the Symplegades[12] of neces-

---

[12]Two rocks that crashed together at the entrance to the Black Sea, through which the Argonauts had to pass.

sity and of modesty, one on each side, and we suffer shipwreck either of our modesty or of our cause. If we reply to the
point, we blush with shame. But if modesty succeeds in
silencing us, we seem as if we were conceding our position
and give opportunity to the attacking adversary. Nevertheless, it is better, as they say, to close our eyes and fight in the
fashion of the Andabatae[13] than not to repel aimed arrows
with the shield of truth.

Indeed, I could say, the hind part of the body and the
passage through which the belly's excrement is discharged
are hidden from the eyes, are placed at our backs, and thus
also that which is under the belly, parts that are for separat-
ing the fluids and liquid that water the body's inner vessels:
they are made by God. But seeing that the very construction
of these organs and genitals, that which differentiates us
from women, and the receptacle of the womb that is fashioned for receiving and coalescing the fetus, proclaims the
difference of sex, I will respond to the point briefly.

Let us never cease from lust, lest we bear members of this
sort in vain! For why should a husband refrain from sexual
relations with his wife, why should a widow keep chaste, if
we are born especially for this, that we may live in the
fashion of the beasts? Or how does it hurt me, if another
man sleeps with my wife? For even as the function of the
teeth is to chew and to pass along that which has been
chewed to the stomach, and it is no crime for a man to give
my wife food, thus if it is the function of the genitals that
their nature should always be used and when I am weary, let
another man take over, and if I may put it thus, let my wife
slake her burning lustful appetite as chance would have it!
However, what does the Apostle intend, that he urges us to
continence, if continence is against nature? What does the
Lord himself intend, who teaches about the varieties of
eunuchs? (Mt. 19:12). Certainly the Apostle, who challenges

[13]Gladiators who fought blindfolded.

us to his own chastity (I Cor. 7:7), ought to be resolutely obeyed. Why do you have genitals, O Paul? Why are you distinguished from the female sex by your beard, your hair, and your other bodily properties? Why do your breasts not swell; why do you not broaden at the hips, narrow at the chest? Your voice is lower, your speech more fierce, your eyebrows hairier. It is in vain that you have all these masculine properties if you do not make use of women's embraces!

I am compelled to speak out and become foolish, but you have driven me so I dare to do so: Our Lord and Savior, who though he was "in the form of God, deigned to assume the form of a servant, becoming obedient to the Father, even unto death, death on a cross" (Phil. 2:6-8)—what necessity was there that he be born with those members that he would not use? Furthermore, he was in fact circumcised to show his sex (Lk. 2:21). . . .

"In the resurrection of the dead, they shall neither marry nor give in marriage, but they shall be like the angels"(Mt. 22:30). Virgins begin to be on earth what others will be afterwards in Heaven. If it is promised us that we shall be as the angels (however, among angels there is no difference of sex), either we shall be without sex, as the angels are, or assuredly, as is plainly attested, we may be resurrected in our own sex but shall not perform the sexual function.

> In his celebrated *Letter 22* to Eustochium, daughter of his aristocratic Roman friend Paula, Jerome further reveals his preference for virginity over marriage. Eustochium in early adolescence had opted for a life of perpetual virginity. Jerome, in his letter of congratulation to her, dated 384 A.D., makes the following points, among others:

20.[14] I praise weddings, I praise marriage—but because they produce virgins for me. I gather roses from the thorns,

[14]Text: CSEL 54.170.

gold from the earth, a pearl from the shell. "Does he who plows, plow all day?" (Is. 28:24). Shall he not also enjoy the fruit of his labor? Marriages are more honored when what is born from them is loved the more. Why, mother, do you begrudge your daughter? She was nursed with your milk, brought forth from your womb, grew up in your lap. You have kept her safe by your careful devotion. Are you offended that she does not want to be the wife of a soldier but of a King? She has shown you a great honor: you have begun to be the mother-in-law of God. . . .

(Jerome explains the different ideas of blessedness found in the Old and the New Testaments):

21. In the law of the Old Testament, there was another happiness: "Blessed is he who has seed in Zion and a family in Jerusalem" (Is. 31:9 LXX), and cursed is the barren, who does not give birth; "Your children are as an olive shoot around your table" (Ps. 128:3). A promise of riches was also given: "There will not be a weak one among your tribes" (Ps. 104:37 Vg.). But now it is said, "Do not suppose that you are dry wood; instead of sons and daughters you have an ever-lasting place in heaven" (cf. Is. 56:3-5). Now the poor are blessed and Lazarus is preferred to the rich man in purple (cf. Lk. 16:19-31). The world was empty, and, not to indulge in symbolic interpretation, the only blessing was that of children. . . . Therefore, as we have said, this so great good of continence was found only among men, and Eve went on bringing forth continually in pains. However, after a virgin conceived in her womb and bore a son for us, of whom it is said, "the government shall be upon his shoulders" (Is. 9:6), mighty God, Father of ages to come, the curse was dissolved. Death came through Eve, life through Mary. And for that reason, too, the gift of virginity pours forth more richly upon women, because it began with a woman. Straightway when the Son of God made his entrance to

earth, he established for himself a new family, so that he who was adored by angels in Heaven might also have angels on earth. . . .

Living arrangements for women who undertook the life of Christian asceticism posed a problem for the Church. By the early fourth century, communities of female ascetics had grown up in Egypt modelled on the monasteries for men founded by Pachomius, who began the trend away from the solitary asceticism of the desert hermits toward the practice of communal monasticism. The Coptic *Life of Pachomius* reveals that its hero built the first such monastery for women for his sister Mary a short distance from the men's monastery he had founded. At first, we gather, the Rules used in the men's monastery were also used by the women ascetics. These desert ascetics of the early fourth century were a powerful influence on the development of the ascetic ideal in both Latin and Greek Christianity. Jerome's eulogy of his friend Marcella, for example, relates that her primary impulse to the ascetic life came from hearing tales of the desert monks.[15] Palladius, a fifth century writer who described the lives of notable Christian ascetics in his *Lausiac History*, here provides a glimpse of life in the women's community founded by Pachomius at Tabennisi.

33.[16] With these men there was also a monastery of about four hundred women, who had the same arrangement and the same way of life, excepting the cloak. The women were across the river, with the men on the opposite side. Whenever a virgin died, the virgins prepared her for burial; they carried her body and placed it on the riverbank. The brothers crossed over on a ferry and with palms and olive

[15]See pp. 206-207 below.
[16]Text: *The Lausiac History of Palladius*, ed. C. Butler (Cambridge, 1898; rp. Hildesheim, 1967), 96.

branches, and singing Psalms, they would bring her to the opposite side, burying the body in the common cemetery. No one, however, except for the priest and the deacon, crosses over to the women's monastery, and this happens only on Sundays.

The following thing happened to the women in this monastery. A tailor from the outside world who was looking for work crossed over, out of ignorance. One of the younger sisters came out (for the place was a desert), listened to what had befallen him, and gave him the retort, "We have our own tailors." Another woman saw this occurrence; after some time had passed, a fight occurred, and she, out of diabolical intent, from great evil and seething with anger, falsely accused this woman to the sisterhood. A few of the others concurred with her in the evil. The accused woman was thus distressed at enduring this sort of slander (for she had no intention of doing a deed of the type of which she was accused). Since she was not able to bear it, she secretly threw herself into the river and died. Likewise, the woman who had slandered her, knowing that she had falsely accused her out of evil and was responsible for this guilt, was not able to endure the event either, and strangled herself. The other sisters therefore reported the matter to the priest when he came. And he commanded that the Offering not be made for either of them. He separated out those sisters who would not live peaceably, those who, even when they became aware that the charge was slander believed the tales, and excommunicated them for seven years.

In the later fourth century, when the ascetic spirit had pervaded Rome, several Roman aristocratic women renounced their worldly lives and possessions, and journeyed to the Holy Land where they founded monasteries for both men and women near the sites sacred to Christians. Melania the Elder, whose life is recounted in Chapter Five, started a monastery for women at Jerusalem in the last quarter of the fourth century. Another female monastic founder was Jerome's friend Paula, who established a monastery for women at Bethlehem in the closing years of the fourth century. Jerome's *Epistle 108* constitutes a memorial to Paula. In it Jerome describes the organization and routine of Paula's monastery.

20.[17] I shall also speak about the order of her monastery, how she turned the continence of the holy to her own advantage. She sowed carnal things that she might reap spiritual ones (cf. I Cor. 9:11); she gave earthly things that she might assume heavenly ones; she renounced short-lived things that she might exchange them for things eternal. After she established a monastery for men, whose governance she handed over to them, she divided the many virgins whom she had assembled from diverse provinces (as many from the nobility as from the middle and lower classes) into three bands and monasteries. As far as work and meals were concerned, they were separate, but they joined together for Psalm-singing and for prayers. After the singing of the Allelulia, by which sign they were called to the assembly, no one was allowed to retreat, but Paula, first or among the first, used to wait for the others who were coming to the assembly, rousing them to their work not by fear but by her modesty and her example. In the early morning, at the third, the sixth, the ninth hours, in the evening, and at midnight, they chanted the Psalter in order. None of the sisters was allowed to be ignorant of the Psalms and daily they were to learn something from the Holy Scriptures. Only on the Lord's Day did they go out to the church, which was next to where they were living, each troop following its own mother superior; from there in like manner they returned and pursued their set tasks, and made clothes either for themselves or for others.

[17]Text: CSEL 55.334.

If a sister were high-born, she was not permitted to have a maid from her home, lest by frequent conversation the recollection of former deeds and the jollity of childhood might re-excite and renew old errors. All dressed the same; they used linen only for drying their hands. To such an extent were they kept apart from men that Paula separated them even from eunuchs, lest she give any occasion to abusive tongues, so apt to censure holy people as a solace for their own failings. If a sister were too slow in congregating for the Psalms or sluggish about her work, Paula approached her in various ways: if the sister were hot-tempered, with enticements; if she were unyielding, with reproaches. Thus she imitated that apostolic saying, "What do you want? Shall I come to you with a rod or in a spirit of gentleness and mildness? (I Cor 4:21).

Aside from food and clothing, she permitted no one to have anything—as Paul said, "Having food and clothing, we are content with them" (I Tim. 6:8)—lest the habit of having more should furnish an occasion for avarice, which is not filled by any amount of riches: the more it has, the more it wants, and neither prosperity nor poverty lessens it. When the sisters quarreled among themselves, she united them with the softest speech. Often when the younger sisters had fleshly lusts, she crushed them with doubled fasts, preferring that they suffer in the stomach than in the mind. If Paula saw some sister overly adorned, with a frown and a sad face she used to censure her error, saying, "A clean body and a clean dress imply an unclean soul. A shameful or lewd word should never be brought forth from a virgin's mouth; by those signs a wanton mind is shown, and by the outer person the faults of the inner person are manifested."

When Paula noticed a sister who was talkative, garrulous, bold, and delighting in disputes, after she had often impressed the point upon her without her making any change, she put her among those ranked lowest, outside the assembly of sisters, making her pray at the doors of the dining hall and take her food separately, so that shame might correct her since she had not reformed by remonstrance. She hated stealing as if it were sacrilege. She said that what among worldly people is thought of either lightly or as nothing, in the monastery was a very serious offense. How should I recall her kindness and care for the sick, with what marvellous indulgences and services she pampered them? When others were ailing, she supplied them abundantly with everything and even furnished meat for them to eat, but when she herself got sick, she did not indulge herself and seemed quite different in this situation: she replaced what was kindness to others with harshness toward herself.

> Jerome does not tell us about any specific Rule that was in effect at Paula's monastery, although surely some disciplinary regulations must have been laid down. Our first written account of such Rules for female monastics comes from Augustine. He had established a monastery for women after his return from Italy to North Africa and had given the directorship of it into the hands of his sister. Her successor as Superior apparently encountered some disciplinary problems that occasioned Augustine's *Epistle 211* in the year 423 A.D. Among the regulations he sets forth for the nuns in the monastery are the following:

5.[18] These are the rules that we lay down for observance in the monastery. First, because you are in one community, you should have concord within the house and "be with one heart and one soul" in God (Acts 4:32). You should not call anything your own but should have everything in common. You should let your Superior distribute food and covering to each of you, not the same to everyone, because you are not all of equal vigor, but to each as she has need. For thus

[18]Text: CSEL 57.359.

you read in the Acts of the Apostles that there were "all things in common to them and distribution was made to each in proportion to his need" (Acts 4:32, 35). Those who had something in the world, when they enter the monastery, let them freely will it to be in common. However, those who did not have such things, let them not seek in the monastery for what they could not have outside. Nonetheless, if they are among the sick, let what is needed be allowed, even if, when they were in the outside world, their poverty could not have acquired these things they need, but they should not now think themselves fortunate for this reason, because they have gotten food and clothing of the sort they could not have had outside.

6. Let them not raise their necks in pride because they are associating with women whom they would not have dared to approach outside the monastery, but let them lift up their heart and not seek worldly goods, lest monasteries begin to be advantageous for the rich but not for the poor, if in them the rich are humiliated but the poor are puffed up. On the other hand, let those who seem to be something in the world not express distaste for their sisters who came to that holy fellowship out of poverty; moreover, they should take pains to pride themselves on the company of the poor sisters rather than on the eminence of their rich parents. Let them not grow proud if they have contributed to the communal life something of their own riches, lest they plume themselves more on their riches because they share them with the monastery than if they were enjoying them in the world. For in fact, every other sort of wickedness makes use of evil deeds to accomplish its ends; pride, in truth, rather creeps into good deeds, so that they are done in vain. What is the use of dispersing one's goods by giving to the poor and of becoming poor oneself, if the wretched soul is made prouder by its light esteem for wealth than it would have been by its possession? Thus all should live in concord and harmony,

honoring God in each other, for you were made as his temples (I Cor. 3:16; II Cor 6:16).

8. Master your flesh by fasting and abstinence from food and drink to the extent that your health permits. However, when some sister is not able to fast, she should not for all that consume any nourishment outside the meal hours, except when she is sick. From the time you approach the table until your rising from it, listen to what is read to you, as is the custom, without disorder or contention, so that not only do your throats consume food, but also your ears take in the word of God.

10. You should not let your clothing be conspicuous, nor should you strive to please by your clothes but by your behavior. Do not have such delicate headcoverings that your hairnets show underneath. Do not let any part of your hair remain uncovered nor should you be outside with hair either carelessly strewn or painstakingly arranged. When you go out, walk together; when you reach the place you are going, stop together. In your gait, in your stance, in your clothing, in all your motions, let there be nothing that could entice anyone's lust, but rather let there be what is fitting for your purity. . . .

12. Have your clothing under the care of one or two women, or however many as may be needed for shaking them so that moths do not damage them. Just as you are fed from one storeroom, so you should be clothed from one closet. And if it is possible, do not be concerned what clothing appropriate to the season is supplied you, whether each individual received the garment that she had turned in or another garment that someone else had worn, as long as each woman still is not denied what she needs. . . . Thus it also follows that what any man or woman gives to those living in the monastery, whether they are daughters or are linked to them by some other relationship, and whether they give clothes or any other thing deemed necessary, let the gift

not be secretly received, but let it be taken under the Superior's authority so that when it is brought into the common supply, she may offer it to a woman who needs it. If any woman hides what has been brought to her, let her be condemned with a sentence of theft.

13. According to the decision of the Superior, let your clothing be washed either by you or by a cloth worker, lest an excessive desire for clean clothing produces inner uncleanness for your soul. Even the washing of the body and the use of baths should not be habitual, but allowed at the customary interval of time, that is, once a month. However, in the case of sickness, when necessity compels the washing of the body, let it not be delayed by very much; let it be done according to medical advice, without grumbling. Thus even if a sister does not want such a bath, let her do what should be done for the sake of her health, at the command of the Superior. If, however, she wants it and perhaps it is not beneficial, let there be no bending to her desire, because sometimes we believe that what delights us is profitable, although it actually causes harm. . . . Moreover, those who are keepers of the storeroom, or of the clothes, or of the books, should serve their sisters without grumbling. Let books be requested at a set hour every day; those who request them outside that time may not receive them. However, as pertains to clothing and shoes, when they are essential for someone in need, let those who have these things in their care not delay to give what is requested.

15. Let the Superior be obeyed as a mother, held in honor, lest God be offended in her, and much more should you so honor the priest, who shoulders the care of all of you. Thus all these rules are to be kept by her, and if something is not observed, she is not to disregard it negligently, but let her take care to amend and correct it. It concerns the Superior chiefly, that what exceeds the limits of her authority or power, she thus report to the priest who directs you. . . .

Augustine's various Rules were used by later Christians to develop new monastic Rules for both men and women. In the first decades of the sixth century, bishop Caesarius of Arles laid down this Rule for nuns in a monastery he had founded and dedicated to John the Baptist. Following a now familiar pattern, the leadership of the new monastery was turned over to his sister, Caesaria. Caesarius' *Rule for the Holy Virgins* is heavily dependent on Augustine's and shows that the women were becoming more "enclosed" in their monasteries. The ideal he sets forth is one of contemplation, not of active service. By the time Caesarius died in about 542 A.D., the convent had more than two hundred women in it. Some of his rules for the women's monastery are as follows:

2.[19] And because there are many things in women's monasteries that seem to be unlike the arrangements for monks, we have selected a few points from the many, by which the older members may live with the younger ones under a Rule and so that they may aim to fulfill spiritually what they see as especially suited for their sex.

These things first are suited to your holy souls: if a girl, having left her parents, should wish to renounce the world and enter the holy sheepfold, in order that by God's assistance she may escape from the jaws of the spiritual wolves, she may not go outside the monastery to the time of her death, nor when she is in the basilica, where a door can be seen.

4. Therefore, she who by God's inspiration enters the monastic life shall not be permitted to receive the religious garb right away, not until her will has been proved in many tests; rather, entrusted to one of the older women for a full year, let her keep on wearing that clothing in which she came. Moreover, on the subject of changing clothes or of

[19]Text: *Regula Sanctarum Virginum*, ed. G. Morin (Bonn, 1933), 5.

having a bed in the dormitory, she shall be under the authority of this older woman, and as the latter sees her character or devotion, let her thus take pains to regulate her either quickly or slowly.

5. Moreover, those who come to the monastery as widows, or who have left their husbands, or who have changed their garb, may not be welcomed unless beforehand they make over all their property to whomever they choose, either by deed, by gift, or by sale, so that they retain nothing in their own power, so as to seem either to dispose of property or to possess it as their own, on account of the Lord's saying, "If you would be perfect, go, sell all that you possess" (Mk. 10:21 = Mt. 19:21 = Lk. 18:22). "If anyone does not leave everything and follow me, he cannot be my disciple" (Lk. 14:26, 27, 33). For this reason I speak to you, venerable daughters, because consecrated women who have possessions cannot attain perfection. On this point, if even those who have entered the religious life do not wish to carry out this rule, either they shall not be welcomed or they certainly shall not be permitted to receive religious garb until they free themselves from all the hindrances of this world.

6. Indeed, those who cannot have their resources in their own power because their parents are still living, or those who are still minors, are required to deed them over when they come into possession of their parents' property or when they reach legal age. Therefore we enjoin this upon your holy souls, fearing the example of Ananias and Sapphira, who, when they said they had bestowed all on the apostles, brought part and faithlessly kept part for themselves (Acts 5:1-11), which is neither seemly, lawful, nor advantageous.

7. No one may be allowed to have her own maid for her service, not even the abbess; but if the women need it, let them receive relief from the younger women. And if it is possible, never let any little girls be admitted to the monas-

tery unless they are six or seven years old, have already learned their letters, and can submit to obedience (or let them be admitted only with difficulty). The daughters of either the nobility or the common people may not be admitted for their upbringing or for their higher education.

27. And because the Mother Superior of the monastery must rule so that she has concern for the salvation of souls and must think continually about the monastery's resources, about the need for bodily sustenance, and also be on hand to greet people warmly, and to reply to letters from whomsoever of the faithful, all concern about the woolwork, from which clothing is furnished for the holy sisters, shall belong to the charge of the prioress or to the woman in charge of spinning. Thus by their diligence, whatever clothes are necessary are faithfully prepared, with zeal and with the love of God, so that as often as the holy sisters have need, she shall distribute clothes to them with holy discretion.

36. Before all else, for the sake of protecting your reputation, let no man enter the private part of the monastery and oratories, except bishops, the provisor and the priest, the deacon, the subdeacon, and one or two lectors whose years and way of life recommend them, who at different times are needed to say the Mass. When indeed the roofs are to be repaired, or doors and windows constructed, or something of this kind fixed, such workmen and servants for this kind of work may come in with the provisor, if necessity demands, but not without the knowledge or permission of the Mother Superior. Indeed, the provisor himself should never enter the inner part of the monastery except for those services which we recounted above, and never, or only with difficulty, should he enter without the abbess or some credible witness, so that the holy women may have their privacy, as is seemly and expedient.

37. Likewise, secular matrons or girls, or the rest of

women still in lay clothes, are in the same way forbidden to enter.

> Organized monastic life became the favored pattern for women and men who wished to adopt Christian asceticism. However, from the early years of Christianity, long before the rise of communal monasticism in the fourth century, the practice of a man and a woman dedicated to Christian asceticism sharing a house had been popular. The Church frowned on the practice, called "spiritual marriage," and attempted to abolish it, without notable success. It still posed grave problems in John Chrysostom's time. In the late fourth or early fifth century, Chrysostom wrote two treatises on the subject, one addressed to men and the other to women. He argued that "spiritual marriage" subjected its practitioners to sexual temptation and allowed outsiders to slander the Church. In his treatise to women, *On the Necessity of Guarding Virginity,* Chrysostom vividly portrays an imaginary situation that might arise if a man and a woman lived together in "spiritual marriage."

10.[20] ...Since it is not the Unsleeping Eye they fear, but rather it is the eyes of men that produce this anxiety in them, well then, let us rob them of this consolation by bringing these matters which the walls had kept hidden and in the shadows into public view and open the doors to those eager to see—after we have first routed them from their beds. Or rather, if you prefer, let us first closely examine what goes on inside the house. Let us grant that they are separated by walls and sleep in separate rooms, for no man, I think, even if he chose to behave in an extremely disgraceful fashion, would go so far in making an example of himself as to sleep in the same room with a virgin. Then let them be separated

---

[20]Text: *Saint Jean Chrysostome: Les Cohabitations suspectes; Comment observer la virginité,* ed. Jean Dumortier (Paris, 1955), 130.

by walls—so what? That concession is not sufficient to free them of suspicion! However, let us not talk about suspicion at the present, not even if a thousand maidens were living with him, but rather examine meanwhile the other form of disgrace.

Perchance they arise at the same time, not to observe the night vigils (for no reverence can ever come from souls such as these), and pass by each other as they are lying down, conversing with one another at night. Could there be anything more disgraceful? And if it happened that the woman suddenly took ill, the walls would not henceforth serve as any protection, but the man, having arisen before the others, comes in beside the recumbent virgin and uses her sickness as his excuse. Since servant girls are often disposed to be quite sluggish, he sits down next to her and takes charge of all her needs, needs which usually only women ought to serve. She is not ashamed, either, but even feels proud, nor does he blush, but rejoices mightly, and the more shameful the servitude he displays, the more mightily he rejoices. The apostolic verse which goes, "Their glory is in their shame" (Phil. 3:19), is here manifested through their deeds. And when the maids have arisen, the disgrace is greater. For they run into his presence with uncovered head, bare-armed, wearing only a tunic, since they were thrown into confusion by being roused at night; or rather, picture him shuffling and scurrying in their midst, while they are required to perform all the tasks. What could be more disgraceful? Even if a nurse is in attendance, he is not ashamed; far from it, he is full of conceit when the maidens from outside the household arrive. For he sees only one thing, how he can demonstrate his service to the sick woman, unaware that the more he evidences this concern, the more he rather disgraces both himself and her. What wonder if he does not blush in the presence of the nurse? For often in the middle of the night these men do not hesitate to do the work of common maids, running to the nurse's dwelling. But now after she arrives, they drive him out, even if he, truly shameless, is unwilling to go; at the next moment she permits him to come back in and sit beside her. Even if someone invented a thousand ways to disgrace him, what could he devise which would be as shameful as the things these men construct for themselves?

11. When day breaks and both must arise from bed, watch out! Be on guard! She cannot set foot into the outer room without trepidation, for often when she enters she runs the risk of rushing headlong into the naked body of the man. And he himself, anticipating this, sometimes comes in after he has announced himself beforehand, yet sometimes he enters incautiously and becomes the butt of uproarious laughter. I do not wish to say any more. These things, even if they are trivial, are likely to furnish the tinder for a smoldering licentiousness. These incidents and even worse than these take place in the household.

But when he must return home after he has hurried to the marketplace, here again we meet with even greater unseemliness. For inasmuch as he is entering his own house, he is not obliged to give previous announcement; he finds the virgin sitting with women and is put to shame, and often she experiences the same sentiment as well. The woman considers it a disgrace to receive women, the man, to receive men, but they do not refuse to live with one another although they refuse each other the privilege of entertaining guests of the same sex. What could be worse than this? It is when they find him seated beside a woman who is weaving and grasping the distaff.

Why should anyone speak of the outrages, the daily battles? For even if there is firm friendship between them, it is still probable that such upsets occur. I for my part have heard that some of them even give way to jealousy, for where there is no spiritual love, this result necessarily comes to pass as well. Hence there are continual calamities, hence there are corruptions, hence the virgins become vile and impudent; even if their bodies are undamaged, their morals are. When a virgin learns to discuss things frankly with a man, to sit by him, to look at him, to laugh in his presence, to disgrace herself in many other ways, and does not think this is dreadful, the veil of virginity is destroyed, the flower trampled underfoot. Hence they shrink from nothing, there is nothing they avoid. To the contrary, they become the bulwarks of marriage and peddlers in shoddy merchandise; they hinder many women who wish to be part of the order of widows, imagining that they have found this defense for their own shortcomings.

Hence they are despised by everyone. Hence even married women are not shamed by these virgins, inasmuch as the former comport themselves better in all respects than the latter do. For it is far preferable to unite in a single marriage, or even in a second one, than to behave in such an unseemly fashion and have everybody suspect them of prostitution and procurement....

> The Christian exaltation of asceticism also carried with it a strong denunciation of second marriage. For Tertullian, writing about 200 A.D., second marriage is simply a capitulation to lust and is unworthy of Christians who should rather be thinking of the impending Kingdom and the possibility of their own martyrdoms. In his *Exhortation to Chastity,* Tertullian writes these stinging words on the subject of second marriage:

IX.[21] If we completely understand Paul's meaning, second marriage must be said to be nothing else than a kind of fornication. For when he says that married people have this as a concern, "how to please one another" (I Cor.

[21]Text: CSEL 70.141.

7:32-34)—he doesn't mean this in an ethical sense, however, for he wouldn't revile an honorable concern—he wishes his words to be understood as meaning that married people are concerned with dress, ornamentation, and every attention to beauty in an attempt to be alluring. For it is the genius of fleshly lust to please by beauty and clothing, and lust is indeed the cause of fornication. Does not some aspect of fornication seem to you to be implicated in marriage, since the same acts are found in both?

The Lord himself said, "Whoever looks on a woman with lust has already committed adultery with her in his heart" (Mt. 5:28). Does the man who looks on her with the intent of marriage do so with less lust or with more? What if he has even married her? He would not have done so unless he desired to marry her and looked on her with lustful intent—unless it is possible to take a wife whom you have neither seen nor desired!

Of course, there's a big difference whether it is a husband who desires his own wife, or an unmarried man who desires another woman (besides, to the unmarried man, every woman is an "other" woman inasmuch as she is another's)—nor does he become a husband in any different way than he becomes an adulterer!

"But the laws seem to differentiate between marriage and fornication," someone objects. Obviously! The two are distinguished by the difference between illegality and legality, not by the nature of the act itself. What otherwise is it that both men and women do when they engage in marriage and fornication? Plainly, it is bodily union, the lust of which the Lord equated with fornication.

Someone asks, "Are you then tearing down even first, that is, monogamous marriages as well?" Yes, and not without good reason, because even they rest on that same shamefulness as does fornication. Therefore, "It is best for a man not to touch a woman" (I Cor. 7:1), and for this reason the holiness of the virgin is pre-eminent, because it is free from any connection with fornication. And since these points can be raised as an inducement to continence even in the cases of first and monogamous marriage, how much more will they predispose us to refuse a second marriage? Feel favored if God has allowed you to marry once and for all! You will, however, deserve favor if you know that he has not indulged you a second time. Otherwise you will abuse his indulgence, since you use marriage without moderation. "Moderation" is understood to come from *modus*, a measure or limit.

Is it not enough for you to have fallen from the highest rank of immaculate virginity to a lower one by marrying? Doubtless you will tumble down still further to a third marriage or a fourth, or maybe even more, after you were not continent in the second stage (of first marriage), because a man who did not refrain from appealing for second marriages, was not unwilling to make even more marriages. Therefore let us marry daily—and marrying, let us be caught by the Last Day, like Sodom and Gomorrah (Gen. 19:24-25), by that day when the "Woe!" pronounced on those who are pregnant and nursing (Mk. 13:17 = Mt. 24:19 = Lk. 21:23) shall be fulfilled, i.e., the "Woe!" pronounced on the married and the unchaste, for from marriages come wombs and breasts and babies! And when will there be an end of marrying? I believe it will be after the end of living!

XII. I know with what pretexts we color the insatiable desire of the flesh. We allege as an excuse the needs of assistance: a home to be managed, a household to be run, coffers and keys to be guarded, the woolwork to be distributed, food to be arranged for, worries to be shared. Would anyone really say that only in the houses of married men things are well-off, that the households of celibates, the property of eunuchs, the fortunes of soldiers or those who travel without wives, have perished? Are we not in fact also soldiers? Indeed, we are under a tighter discipline, since we serve under so great a Commander. And are we not also wayfarers in this world? But why indeed, O Christian, are you thus disposed to think that you cannot travel without a wife?

Now a partner in domestic labors may be indispensable to you. Then take one! Take some spiritual wife from among the widows, one beautiful by her faith, dowered with poverty, adorned with age: you will make a good marriage! Even having several wives of *this* sort is pleasing to God!

But Christians think about posterity—Christians, for whom there is no tomorrow! The servant of God, who has disinherited himself from the world, desires heirs! And for that reason indeed does he repeat marriage, he who has no children from the first one. Thus he will have this first benefit, that he will want to live a longer time than that Apostle who hastens to the Lord (Phil. 1:23)! Surely this man will be most unencumbered in persecution, most resolute in martyrdom, most ready to share his property, most moderate in acquiring possessions; finally he will die free from care... perhaps leaving sons to bring funeral sacrifices in his honor!

Surely such things are not done with the commonwealth in mind, are they? Are they done lest cities fail, if there are no progeny? Or lest the rights of law not be exercised? Lest commerce fade away? Lest the temples be deserted? Lest there will be none to shout, "Christians to the lion"? For this is what they want to hear, those who seek offspring.

The inconvenience of having children, particularly in our time, should be sufficient recommendation for widowhood. Men must be compelled by laws to beget children, because no wise man would ever voluntarily want sons! Then what will you do if you, unwillingly and with your scruples, impregnate your wife? Will you terminate her pregnancy with the help of drugs? I think that for us it is no more permissible to kill a fetus before birth than the child after it is born. But perhaps at the time of your wife's pregnancy you will have the audacity to beg a remedy for such a great anxiety from God, although you refused God's assistance when it was available to you? I imagine that you'll cast about for some woman who is already barren, or who is of an age to feel the chill of years. That's shrewd enough, an excellent approach for a Christian! For we don't believe, do we, that when God willed it, a barren or an aged woman gave birth? Such is more likely to happen when a man challenges God to a competition by the presumption of his own present prudence! In fact, we know a man, one of the brethren, who took a barren woman in a second marriage on account of his daughter; he became a father again, just as for the second time he became a husband!

> Tertullian further drove home his case against remarriage in *On Monogamy*. Here he attempted to shame his audience by pointing out that even chaste pagan women behaved better on the issue of single marriage than did their Christian counterparts.

17.[22] ... Pagans are likely to be appointed as our judges. A queen of Carthage will arise and pass judgment on Christians. A refugee, alone in a foreign land and at the very time of founding such a strong state, although she ought of her own accord to have desired marriage with a king, yet lest she experience a second marriage, chose on the contrary "to burn rather than to marry."[23] And that Roman matron will be classed with her who, even though it was by an assault at night, had nonetheless known another man. She washed

[22]Text: CSEL 76.77.
[23]Dido, queen of Carthage. In Virgil's *Aeneid*, Dido rejected a North African king as a suitor after her husband's murder. Tertullian twists the story: Dido actually wanted to marry Aeneas, but he deserted her. Tertullian puns on Paul's words that "it is better to marry than to burn"(I Cor. 7:9) in his reference to Dido's suicide by immolation.

away the stain on her flesh with her own blood, that she might vindicate monogamy in her own person.[24] There have also been those women who preferred to die for their husbands rather than marry after their husbands' deaths. Indeed, both monogamy and widowhood serve idols. No one but a once-married woman places a wreath on Fortuna Muliebris or likewise on Mother Matuta.[25] Only once do the Pontifex Maximus and the wife of a Flamen marry.[26] The priestesses of Ceres, even while their husbands live and with their consent, are "widowed" in friendly separation.

There are also those who may judge us as far as absolute continence goes: the Vestal Virgins, and those of Achaian Juno, of Scythian Diana, and of Pythian Apollo. Even the priests of that Egyptian bull[27] will pass judgment on Christians for their weakness in matters of continence.

Blush, O flesh, that has "put on Christ" (Rom. 13:14)! Let it be enough for you to marry only once: let monogamy, in which you were created from the beginning and to which you are being recalled at the end, be enough for you. Return, even to the first Adam, if you cannot return to the last Adam, that is, Christ. Once for all did the first Adam taste of the tree, once for all did he lust, once for all did he cover his shameful parts, once for all did he blush before God, once for all did he hide his disgrace, once for all was he exiled from the paradise of holiness—once for all henceforth did he marry. If you were in him, you have your model; if you have passed over into Christ, you will have to be better. Show us a "third Adam," one who is twice-married, and you will then be able to be what you cannot be with these two Adams as your exemplars!

[24]Lucretia, whose story (probably legendary) is told by Livy and Ovid.
[25]Fortuna Muliebris: a Roman goddess associated with fertility and women. Mother Matuta was the Roman goddess of growth.
[26]The Pontifex Maximus was the head of Roman priests. The Flamen Dialis was the chief priest of Jupiter.
[27]The Egyptian god Apis, popular in Rome.

Lastly, John Chrysostom in his treatise *On Not Marrying Again,* probably composed in the 380s, expressed his astonishment that women who had been through the tribulations of marriage once would wish to risk them a second time. He appeals to the practical advantages of remaining a widow.

1.[28] It is not astonishing that women who are inexperienced in relations with men, birth pangs, and all the other things marriage entails when it enters human households, seek husbands. For so the proverb runs, "The excruciating business of battle is sweet to the raw recruits." But for women who have suffered myriad evils, who often are convinced by the force of events that those females are blessed who have been released by death from the difficulties of the world, who thousands of times have cursed themselves, the matchmakers, and the day on which bridal chambers were devised—for these women, after such despair, to desire the same things again seems to be absolutely astounding and puts me at a loss. I wonder why women who have been delivered from those very things now pursue them again as desirable, when in the very midst of the situation they considered them something from which to flee?

Having turned the matter over in my mind, ever with difficulty, I am convinced that I have discovered the reason for their behavior. Or rather, there is not only one reason, nor even just two, but many. On the one hand, some women are betrayed by the passage of time into forgetting the past. Mindful only of the things at hand, they approach marriage as a release from the evils of widowhood. However, they find many more difficulties in the second than in the first marriage, with the result that their voices utter the same complaints they previously expressed. Others, once more agape at the things of the world, clinging to the glory of this

<hr />

[28]Text: SC 138.160.

present life and considering widowhood a shameful estate, choose the sufferings of marriage out of a desire for empty glory and extravagant conceit. And there are also widowed women who are in neither of these categories, but who are ruled by sexual incontinence alone; they return anew to their earlier state and try to hide their true motive under the aforesaid pretexts.

I do not have the effrontery to blame these women and condemn them because of their second marriages, nor do I advise anyone else to do so, since this approach seemed inappropriate to the blessed Paul, or rather, to the Holy Spirit. When he had said, "A woman is bound by the law for as long a time as her husband lives. But if her husband dies she is free to marry whom she will, only in the Lord" (I Cor. 7:39), and having assented that the widow might marry again if she wished, he also said, "But she is happier if she remains as she is." Lest anyone imagine the injunction to be a human one, Paul added, "And I believe that I have the Spirit of God" (I Cor. 7:40), showing that the Spirit wrote these words. . . .

For in making this comparison, we do not thrust second marriage into the ranks of evil things. Rather, we concede that it is lawful, and a voluntary matter, but we honor foremost, indeed we marvel at, the estate far superior to this. Why in the world do we do this? Because for a woman to have one husband is not the same thing as for her to have two. For the woman who rests content with one husband shows that she would not have even chosen him at the beginning if she had rightly known the experience of marriage. But she who leads a second husband to the bed of the first furnishes a not insignificant proof of her great love of the world and her identification with earthly things. The first woman, while living with her husband, did not flutter with excitement over any other man, but the second woman, even if she did not actually sin with others while she lived with her husband, nonetheless admired many other men more than him.

5. . . . Tell me, what is the profit in choosing slavery rather than freedom? What is the benefit of having much money, if you are not able to use it for the things you desire? Is it not in many ways better to have few possessions, but ones under your control, than to have everything in the world and be subjected yourself, along with them, to another person? For the moment I pass over the cares, the affronts, the abuses, the jealousies, the heedless suspicions, the labor pains, and all the other problems. In discussing these matters with a virgin, it would be reasonable to speak of them, for she is inexperienced, ignorant of these affairs. But a person will only annoy a widow by running through these difficulties: she has been quite pointedly instructed by these experiences, so that it is superfluous to attempt to teach her through discussion.

Nonetheless, it is good to add this much more: the woman who was a virgin when she married will relate to her husband in more frankness and freedom than the woman who marries as a widow. For even if a man accepts a widow as his wife, it is not as if he had taken her as a virgin, for his amorous desires are more violent and frenzied with the virgin than with the widow—a point, I suppose, that is obvious to everybody. A husband does not embrace and love a widow with his whole heart, for she is practiced with another man.

> Thus by appealing both to the divine origins of virgin-ity and to the practical advantages celibacy might offer women, the Church Fathers advanced their case. What Eve had lost through the Fall, Christian women might regain by their adoption of the celibate life.

Chapter Four

WOMEN IN THE WIDER WORLD

The often repeated assertion that the coming of Christianity benefited women in general is not borne out in our evidence from the period. For women willing to undertake a life of Christian asceticism, some new avenues were opened. The majority of women, however, were bound not only by the traditional roles assigned them; their activities were further curtailed by the Fathers' appeal to Scripture.

> One of the chief New Testament prohibitions concerned women as teachers. I Timothy 2:11-15 set the tone for later theologians on this point: women were forbidden to teach and a theological rationale was given for the prohibition. John Chrysostom's commentary on these verses is found in his *Homily 9 on I Timothy*.

1.[1] ... "But I do not permit a woman to teach." "I do not permit," Paul says. What importance does the sequence of argument have here? Indeed, a great one. He was discoursing on quietness, on seemliness, on modesty. He said, "I do not want you to speak." Wishing now to cut off from every side the pretext for conversation, he adds, "Let them not teach, but let them join the rank of the learners." Thus they will show their submissiveness by their silence, for the sex is

[1] Text: PG 62.544.

in a certain way loquacious. Therefore he hems them in on every side. "For Adam," he says, "was formed first, then Eve. And Adam was not deceived, but the woman was deceived and came into sin." What, then, do these things have to do with the present? Truly, Paul says, the male sex enjoyed the greater honor, for he was formed first. And elsewhere he showed that men were greater. Thus, he says, "For the man was not created for the woman, but the woman for the man" (I Cor. 11:9). Why does he say this? He wishes the man to be pre-eminent in every way. Let him have pre-eminence first from these things, from the created order, he says, and secondly, from the event that transpired shortly thereafter. She taught the man once, upset everything, and made him liable to disobedience. Therefore God subjected her, since she used her rule, or rather, her equality of honor, badly. "Your inclination shall be for your husband,"[2] he says (Gen. 3:16). Before this event, these words had not been said.

But how was Adam not deceived? Then did Adam not sin, if he was not deceived? Pay close attention. The woman said, "The serpent deceived me" (Gen. 3:13). But Adam did *not* say, "The woman deceived me." Rather he said, "She gave me and I ate" (Gen. 3:12). Now it is not the same thing to be deceived by a fellow human being, of the same kind as we, as to be deceived by an animal, a servant, one who has been subordinated. For the latter is what deception is. Thus, in comparison with the woman, he says that the man was "not deceived," because she was deceived by a servant, a thing in subjection, whereas he was lured by his wife. Again, it is not said of Adam that "he saw the tree, that it was good for eating," but that was said about the woman. He says that "she ate and gave to her husband" (Gen. 3:6), so that he sinned not because he was blinded by desire, but merely by his wife's persuasion.

[2]"and he shall rule over you."

The woman taught once and for all, and upset everything. Therefore he says, "Let her not teach." Then does it mean something for the rest of womankind, that Eve suffered this judgment? It certainly does concern other women! For the female sex is weak and vain, and here this is said of the whole sex. For he does not say, "*Eve* was deceived," but "the woman," which is the common name of the sex, not her particular name. What then? Did the whole female sex come into sin through her? As he said concerning Adam, "In the likeness of Adam's sin who is a type of him who is to come" (Rom. 5:14). Thus also here, the female sex sinned, not the male. What then? Do women not have salvation? Most certainly, he said. And how is that? Through having children.

> Yet I Timothy 2:12 seemed to contradict other Biblical passages, such as Acts 18:24-28, an account of the Christian matron Priscilla's instruction of the male convert, Apollos. Chrysostom attempted to explain why Priscilla's teaching was praiseworthy while female instruction in general was not. The following selection is from his homily, *Greet Priscilla and Aquila,* on Romans 16:3.

I,3.[3] ... It is worth looking into the reason why, when Paul greets them, he places Priscilla's name before her husband's. For he did not say, "Greet Aquila and Priscilla," but "Priscilla and Aquila." Now he did not do this unwittingly, for it seems to me that he knew she was more pious than her husband. And that interpretation is not just a guess, one can learn it from the Acts of the Apostles. Apollos was an eloquent man, skilled in the Scriptures, but he knew only the baptism of John. This woman took him, instructed him in the way of God, and made him a perfect teacher (Acts 18:24-28). The women who lived at the time of the apostles did not participate in the things women do

[3]Text: PG 51.191.

today, so as to clothe themselves in splendid garments, beautify their faces with paint and eye makeup, urge on their husbands to make them buy more extravagant dresses than their neighbor's wife and their peers have, and white mules, gold-spangled bridles, the service of eunuchs, a great swarm of maidservants, and all the other ridiculous things you can imagine.

Those women of earlier times discarded all these things. They rejected worldly vanity and sought one thing only, namely to become companions of the apostles and to share in their pursuits. Thus Priscilla was not the only woman of this sort; all the rest were like this, too. Indeed, concerning a certain Persis, Paul said, "She has toiled much for us" (Rom. 16:12).[4] He also marvels over these labors of Mary and Tryphaena (Rom. 16:6, 12), because they worked along with the apostles and stripped themselves for the same contests.

But why then, when he writes to Timothy, does he say, "I do not permit a woman to teach, nor to have authority over a man" (I Tim. 2:12)? This is the case whenever the man is reverent, holds the same faith, shares in the same wisdom. But if the man is an unbeliever, wandering in error, Paul does not deprive her of the power of a teacher. At any rate, he writes to the Corinthians, "If a woman has an unbeliever as a husband, let her not leave him. For how do you know, wife, if you will save your husband?" (I Cor. 7:13-16). But how can a believing woman save an unbelieving husband? Quite clearly, through her instructing, teaching, and leading him to the faith, just as Priscilla did for Apollos. In a word, then, when Paul says, "I do not permit a woman to teach," he is talking about public instruction that involves arguing in front of people and about the teaching that befits the priesthood. But he does not rule out her exhorting and

---

[4]Chrysostom obviously thinks this is a female, not a male.

giving advice in private. For if this had been ruled out, he would not have applauded Priscilla for her actions.

Chrysostom could also recommend that women give "private instruction" within the household as a way to shame men, to set wayward husbands straight. An example of women's instruction to husbands is given in his *Homily 7 on Matthew,* in which Chrysostom criticizes men who flock to the theatre to watch prostitutes swim naked in tanks of water.

6.[5] . . . But lest we only cast blame, come, let us also invent a means to set these men straight. What then will the means be? I want to hand you over to your own wives so that they may instruct you. According to the law of Paul, *you* ought to be the teachers, but since the order is overturned by sin and the body is above while the head is below,[6] let us take even this other route. If you are ashamed to have a woman as a teacher, however, then flee sin and you will quickly be able to ascend the throne given you by God. As long as you err, Scripture sends you not only to a woman, but also to the irrational animals of the lower kind; it is not even ashamed to send you, you who have been honored with reason, to the ant as a student (Prov. 6:6). Indeed, this is no accusation of Scripture, but of those who thus desert their noble descent. Well, then, we'll do it! For now, we'll pack you off to the academy of the animals and show you how many birds, fish, four-footed beasts and creeping things appear more decent and chaste than you. . . .

Why were the Fathers so wary of women as teachers? One answer they gave was that women inclined to heresy and might lead others astray by their heretical teaching. Various Gnostic sects had allowed female teachers, and the charismatic Montanists of the second century had

[5]Text: PG 57. 80.
[6]For man as the "head" of the woman, see I Cor. 11:3.

two celebrated female prophetesses: such examples stood as warnings against women's teaching. In the following selection from the *Refutation of All Heresies,* the third-century Christian writer Hippolytus reports the honor given the prophetesses in the Montanist sect.

VIII, 19.[7] ... They have been deceived by women, a certain one named Priscilla and one named Maximilla, whom they consider to be prophetesses, into whom they say the Comforter, the Holy Spirit, has come. And before these, they similarly believed a certain Montanus to be a prophet .... They also glorify these women above the apostles and every spiritual gift, so that some among them have come so far as to dare to say that there is something more in them than in Christ. These people confess, as does the Church, that God is the Father of the universe and the Creator of everything, and they confess everything that the Gospel testifies about Christ, but they bring in new observances by way of fasts and holidays, diets of dry food and radishes, alleging that they have been taught to do so by these women.

In *Epistle 133,* dated 415 A.D., Jerome describes the supposed proclivity women show for heresy. Leaders of the earlier Gnostic sects as well as fourth-century heretics are singled out for special mention.

4.[8] Since this is the way things are, what do they want with "wretched women, burdened with sins, carried about by every wind of doctrine, always learning and never reaching knowledge of the truth" (cf. Eph. 4:14; II Tim. 3:6-7)? And what do they want with those men who are companions of the females, who have itching ears, who do not know how to listen or how to speak? They accept the oldest dirt as if it had been newly composed, and likewise, as Ezekiel puts it, they do their covering without tempering the materials; when the shower of truth comes unexpectedly, it is destroyed (cf. Ezek. 13:10-16).

Simon Magus founded his sect assisted by the help of Helena, a prostitute. Nicolaus of Antioch, inventor of all impurities, led a crowd of women. Marcion sent a woman ahead of him to Rome, to prepare the people's minds to be deceived by him. Apelles had in Philumena a comrade in his doctrines. Montanus, the eulogist of an impure spirit, first corrupted with gold and later defiled with heresy many churches through the agency of Prisca and Maximilla, women who were rich and of noble birth. I leave the old examples and pass on to ones nearer our time.

Arius, in order to take possession of the world, deceived the emperor's sister beforehand. Donatus was helped by the wealth of Lucilla to pollute with stinking waters all the unfortunates throughout Africa. In Spain, Agape, a blind woman who was somebody's wife, led a blind man Elpidius to a ditch; and he had as his successor Priscillian, most devoted to the Zoroastrian magi and himself formerly a magus, who became a bishop. To him was joined Galla, who left as a successor a sister not by birth but by name, who spurred on another and closely related heresy. Now, too, the mystery of iniquity is at work; both sexes in turn trip each other up so that we are driven to adopt that prophetic verse, "The partridge calls, she gathers those whom she has not borne; she makes riches for herself and not with justice; in the midst of her days she shall forsake them, and at her end she shall be foolish" (Jer. 17:11).

Yet Jerome was known to praise women who refuted heretics, even when their refutations took place in the public arena. His friend Marcella, for example, led an attack in about 400 A.D. against the revival of Origen's teaching in Rome. Because he approved her position and disliked the scholars responsible for translating and promoting Origen's work, Jerome found nothing

unseemly about her public refutation of Origenism. In
Epistle 127 he praised her as follows:

10.[9] ...She was in the front line in condemning the
heretics; she brought forth witnesses who earlier had been
taught by them and later were set straight from their heretical error. She showed how many of them had been deceived;
she hurled at them the impious book, *On First Principles,*
that was being taught after having been "corrected" by the
hand of the scorpion.[10] She called upon the heretics in
frequent letters to defend themselves, but they preferred to
be condemned while absent rather than be proved false
while present. The source of this so glorious victory was
Marcella; she was the beginning and cause of these blessings, about which you know me to report the truth....

> That all Christian women suffered from "weak intel-
> lects," as the Fathers sometimes suggested, is flatly con-
> tradicted by references to the scholarly activities in which
> some of them engaged. Education in the late Latin world
> was tied to class, and girls of the aristocracy apparently
> received the same general literary education as their
> brothers, even if they did not enjoy higher formal training
> in law, philosophy, and other specialized subjects.
> Numerous early Christian texts suggest that some
> females took much interest in the study of the Bible and in
> theology. Here is Jerome's commentary on Paula's zeal
> for Old Testament study in his *Epistle 108,* written in 404
> A.D., shortly after her death:

26.[11] I will describe what I began to report: no talent was
ever more tractable than hers. She was slow at speaking, and
quick at listening, remembering that precept, "Hear, Israel,

---

[9]Text: CSEL 56.153.
[10]Rufinus of Aquileia, who had translated several of Origen's works into Latin.
He was accused of having toned down the heretical import of the original Greek
text of Origen's *On First Principles.*
[11]Text: CSEL 55.344.

and keep silent"(Deut. 27:9). She had memorized the Scriptures. She loved the history in them and said it was the foundation of truth, but even more she followed the spiritual understanding of Scripture, and by this coping-stone protected the edifice in her soul. At last she urged me that she, along with her daughter, might read through the Old and New Testaments, guided by my discussion. I declined out of modesty, but because of her persistence and her frequent requests I agreed, so that I might teach her what I had learned not by myself—for conceit is the worst teacher—but from the illustrious men of the Church. If at any passage I was at a loss and frankly confessed that I was ignorant, she by no means wanted to rest content with my reply, but by fresh questions would force me to say which of the many possible meanings seemed to me the most likely. And I will say something else here that perhaps will seem unbelievable to malicious people: from the time of my youth, I have learned the Hebrew language to some extent, through much effort and sweat, and I study it indefatigably so that if I do not forsake it, it will not forsake me. When Paula wanted to learn it, she pursued the project to the point that she chanted the Psalms in Hebrew and her diction echoed no trace of the distinctive character of the Latin language. We notice in her holy daughter Eustochium, even today, the same ability....

> Melania the Elder may well take the prize for being the most learned early Christian woman about whom we know. Scholars now think the following chapter from Palladius' *Lausiac History* refers to Melania the Elder.

55.[12] She was very learned and a lover of literature. She turned night into day by going through every writing of the ancient commentators, three million lines of Origen, and

---

[12]Text: *The Lausiac History of Palladius*, ed. C. Butler (Cambridge, 1898; rp. Hildesheim, 1967), 149.

two hundred fifty thousand lines of Gregory, Stephen, Pierius, Basil, and other excellent men. And she did not merely glance through them casually, but laboring over them, she read each work seven or eight times. Therefore she was able to be freed from "knowledge falsely called" (I Tim. 6:20) and to take flight by the influence of the books, making herself a spiritual bird, passing over to Christ in good hopes.

Unfortunately, we have almost no materials remaining from ancient Christianity that were composed by women. Thus it is interesting to find as an early contribution to Christian literature a poem written about 360 A.D. by the aristocratic Roman matron, Faltonia Betitia Proba, on the creation of the world and the life of Jesus. The most startling feature of Proba's poem is its form: it is a *cento*,[13] a poem composed entirely from verses and half-verses of earlier poetry, in this case Virgil's. Although all the Virgilian references for the following lines of Proba's *Cento* cannot be listed below, the poem is indeed composed from lines borrowed from the *Aeneid*, the *Eclogues*, and the *Georgics*, with the exception of Biblical names. The fact that Proba could undertake such a venture demonstrates that she must have known Virgil's work almost by heart. Proba here writes on the creation of Adam and Eve:

He pulled the plump clay and gave it shape   116
By kneading on the spot the fertile ground,
Its soil quickened from the year's first months.
And now—so suddenly—the image of
Such holiness! Man's new shape went forth
Handsome at first beyond comparison,
Resembling God in countenance and shoulders—
                                                        120

13Text: CSEL 16. 576.

Man, whose mind and intellect a greater God
Influences, and so sends forth to greater tasks.
For Man a match is sought; but from so large
A throng none dared approach the Man; none dared
Be named helpmeet to his new realm.
Without delay, at once God gave untroubled
Rest throughout the young man's limbs,
And made his eyes close in pleasant sleep.   125
And now in the middle course of shady night,
The Almighty Sire laid the ribs and entrails bare.
One of these ribs he plucked apart from
The well-knit joints of youthful Adam's side,
And suddenly arose a wondrous gift—
Imposing proof—and shone in brilliant light: 130
Woman, a virgin she, unparalleled
In figure and in comely breasts, now ready
For a husband, ready now for wedlock.
For him, a boundless quaking breaks his sleep;
He calls his bones and limbs his wedded wife.
Dazed by the Will divine he took and clasped
Her hand in his, folded his arms around her.   135

   (Proba describes the birth of Christ and the mas-
sacre of the innocents:)

The promised day arrived, the day when first   346
He showed his holy face, the founder of
A godly race, sent for dominion;
And virtue, mixed with God, came in his person.
His cherished Father's image came upon him.
Just then, at once, in Heaven's peaceful space,   350
And trailing brilliant fiery trains of light,
A star came on the move. The nobles recognized
A deity, spontaneously with every gift
Increased him, and worshiped his holy star
With adoration. Then truly faith was plain,
And bright the name of his paternal worth;   355

Themselves, they recognized the countenance
Of dazzling God, the signs of divine grace.
Straightway the news took wing and swiftly reached
The king; the runners had given the task their all.
The tale kindled his wrath, inflamed his heart
With loud opinion—also glided to His
Mother's ears. She, much aware of these

Events, early divined his schemes and dire   360
Wickedness, realized the gathering storm,
She first. And knowing what would come to pass,
She had commissioned that the babe be reared
In secret, while the king's concern was
Indecisive, while his mind was boiling
Hot with wrath. But overwrought, the ruler
Gave the command to cast the scion down
And all his future race, to burn him up   365
With flames banked underneath; he ordered men
Dispatched who would report the facts.
They did as told, and on the double went
And terrorized the city, filled it full
Of panic. Then shouts and strident squalling,
The sobbing breath of babes in arms
crescendoed.   370
Corpses of sons lay strewn before their parents'
Eyes, flung at the doorway. But the mother,
With good reason spurred to terror at
Such plaintive sobs, ferrying her child
Upon her breast, escaped the violent mob,
And made her way again to the full mangers.
And here, beneath the pitching, lowly roof,   375
She began to nurse her son, her full paps
Milking to his tender lips. Here, child,
Your cradle will be the first to pour
Out blossoms in profusion, just for you;
And mixed with cheerful sow's bread everywhere

Will be the earth; and bit by bit the Egyptian bean
Will overflow with delicate acanthus.[14]

Although letters and treatises on how to raise sons
were common, Jerome stands out among the Church
Fathers for his words on the education of daughters. In
Epistle 128, Jerome advises a father on the upbringing of
his infant daughter. His introduction, given below, is a
charming acknowledgment of how difficult it is to write
pedagogic treatises for babies. Here, as elsewhere, he
owes much to Quintilian.

1.[15] It is a hard business to write to a little girl who does
not comprehend what you are saying, whose mind you do
not know, and whose inclination you vow with peril: to
follow a famous orator's speech, the promise is more to be
praised in her than the reality.[16] For how will you exhort a
girl to self-restraint who wants cakes, who stammers in a
babbling voice upon her mother's lap, to whom honey is
sweeter than words? Will she listen to the deep sayings of the
Apostle when she delights more in old women's tales? Will
she perceive the enigmas of the prophets, when a nurse's
scowl disturbs her? Will she understand the majesty of the
Gospel when its brilliance dims the consciousness of every
mortal being? Shall I urge her to subject herself to her
parents, she who with childish hand thumps her smiling
mother? For these reasons our Pacatula will receive this
letter, but will read it later on. In the meantime, let her learn
the alphabet, form words, learn the names of things, and
connect words into phrases. So that she may practice these
things in her tinkling voice, promise her a reward of little
cakes, mead, whatever is sweet to the taste; she will hurry if

---

[14]The last lines were taken from Virgil's Fourth *Eclogue* and describe the
wondrous child who would soon appear. Christians came to interpret the child as
Jesus.

[15]Text: CSEL 56.156.

[16]Cicero, *On the Commonwealth,* frag. 5.

she expects to receive spring-like flowers, shining gems, alluring dolls. Meanwhile she should also try to spin, even if she often breaks the threads, so that at some later point she will not break them. After her work, let her have some play, dangle from her mother's neck, snatch kisses from relatives. Let her sing Psalms for a reward so that she may love what she is forced to repeat, so that it will not be work, but pleasure, not a necessity, but a desire.

> A similar work is Jerome's *Epistle 107,* addressed to Paula's daughter-in-law Laeta, suggesting to her and her husband Toxotius how they might raise their daughter (named after her grandmother), who had already been dedicated to the virginal life. Notable is his advice that girls should learn Greek, just as boys did, and that small bribes, as well as friendly competition, could spur a child's learning.

4.[17] Such should be the education of a soul that is to be a temple of the Lord. She should learn to hear and speak nothing other than what relates to the fear of God. She should not understand filthy words, not know worldly songs, and in addition, her tender tongue should get accustomed to sweet Psalms. She should be kept away from lustful boys; her very maidservants and women-in-waiting should be kept at a distance from worldly relationships, lest when they have learned something wicked, they may more wickedly teach. Have made for her letters out of boxwood or ivory, and call each by its proper name. Let her play with these so that her play may also be instruction. And let her keep the letters in order in her mind, so that in her memory she may go over the names in a rhyme. However, often change the internal order and mix up the letters so that the last ones are in the middle and the middle ones at the beginning: thus she may know them not only by sound, but

[17]Text: CSEL 55.293.

also by sight. When indeed she begins to draw the stylus over the wax with shaky hand, either guide her tender fingers by putting your hand on top of hers, or carve the letters of the alphabet on a tablet so that her marks may be kept enclosed within the margins cut for her and cannot wander outside.

Have rewards for spelling and let her be lured with little presents in which those of her age can take pleasure. Let friends be instructed along with her whom she may envy when she is stung by their receiving praise. She is not to be scolded if she is a bit slower, but her talent should be stimulated by praises; let her rejoice when she surpasses others and be sorry when she is surpassed. Above all, guard against her hating her studies, lest a bitterness toward them learned early in childhood penetrate beyond her young years. The very names through which she becomes gradually accustomed to build up words should not be by chance, but should be intentionally fixed and increased—for example, those of the prophets and the apostles, or the list of the patriarchs descended from Adam, as in Matthew and Luke, so that while she engages in the other enterprise, her memory is being prepared for the future.

Choose a teacher of goodly years, life, and learning. I do not think that a learned man will be embarrassed to do for a relative or for a high-born virgin what Aristotle did for the son of Philip;[18] so that he might teach him the beginnings of his letters, he descended to the lowly position of an elementary school teacher. Things should not be scorned as trifling when without them great things cannot be established. The very sound of the alphabet and the rudiments of learning brought forth from the mouth of a learned man differ from those that issue from the mouth of a boor. Whence also you should take care lest the girl, under the foolish blandishments of women, gets accustomed to clipping short her

[18]Aristotle tutored the young Alexander the Great.

words and to playing in gold and purple clothing: of these, one will damage her speech and the other her character. Let her not learn in her tender years what later on she will have to unlearn. . . .

(As little Paula grows older, her education progresses:)

9. Daily let her recite back to you a set amount from the Scriptures. Let her learn by heart a number of verses in Greek—but let Latin learning follow it at once, because if from the start the tender mouth is not placed in a certain way, the tongue is spoiled by a foreign accent and the native language is rendered contemptible by foreign imperfections. Let her have you as a teacher, let her untutored childhood be in admiration of you. Let her see nothing in you or in her father that, if she should do it, she would sin. Both of you remember that you are parents of a virgin and teach her more by example than by voice. Flowers quickly wither; quickly are violets, lilies, and crocus spoiled by an injurious wind. Never let her go out in public without you; let her not visit the basilicas of the martyrs and the churches without her mother. Let no young man, no curly-haired youth, joke with her. Let our little virgin celebrate the days of vigils and solemn night-long services in such a way that she is not separated from her mother's side even by a finger's breadth. . . .

12. Let her love codices of the divine books above jewels or silk, and in these, let her place her confidence not in gilding, Babylonian parchment, and inlaid pictures, but in a correct and learned arrangement. Let her learn first the Psalter, let her divert herself with these songs and be educated for life by the Proverbs of Solomon. From Ecclesiastes she should get used to trampling underfoot the things of the world. Let her eagerly follow the examples of virtue and patience in Job. Let her continue on the Gospels, never to be put down from her hand, and imbibe the Acts of the Apostles and the Epistles with her whole heart, of her own

free will. When she has enriched the storehouse of her heart with these treasures, let her commit to memory the prophets, the Heptateuch, the books of Kings and Chronicles, and the writings of Ezra and Esther. Only then may she finally without danger learn the Song of Songs, for if she were to read it at the beginning, she would be injured, not comprehending that under the fleshly words, it is a wedding song of a spiritual marriage.

Let her avoid all apocryphal writings; if she wants to read them, not because of the truth of their teachings, but out of respect for the miracles contained in them, let her know that the apocryphal writings are not composed by those people to whom they have been ascribed and that many defective things have been mixed in, so that there must be great discretion to seek the gold in the mire.

Always let her keep Cyprian's[19] works in her hand, and let her run through the letters of Athanasius[20] and the books of Hilary[21] without stumbling. Let her take pleasure in those words and talents of men in whose books reverence for the faith does not waver. If she reads the works of others, let it be so that she may judge rather than follow them.

> (Jerome argues that the best way for little Paula to receive a correct education would be for Laeta and Toxotius to send the child to Bethlehem, to her grandmother and Jerome. He compares his role in little Paula's education to that Aristotle had in the education of Alexander the Great:)

13. . . . If you will send Paula, I myself promise to be both teacher and nurse. I will carry her about on my shoulders; old as I am, I will fashion her stammering words much more gloriously than did the worldly philosopher: the one I shall

[19]Bishop of Carthage in the mid-third century.
[20]Bishop of Alexandria in the fourth century.
[21]Bishop of Poitiers in the fourth century.

teach is not a Macedonian king who would die in Babylon by poison,[22] but a handmaid and bride of Christ, who will be offered to the Ruler of Heaven.

> If women were shut out from a teaching role, whatever their educations and talents, so also were they excluded from the priesthood. The Church Fathers argued that the practices of the heretical sects in this regard set no precedent for mainstream orthodox Christianity. Nor should Christian women appeal to the example of Thecla as a justification for women's baptizing. Tertullian in his treatise *On Baptism* inveighs against counting an episode from the *Acts of Paul and Thecla*[23] as a legitimation for women being allowed to baptize.

17.[24] ...In fact, concerning the *Acts of Paul,* wrongly attributed to him, they appeal to the example of Thecla as giving women the right to teach and to baptize. Let them know that a priest in Asia constructed this document, as if he were heaping up glory for Paul by his own effort; when he was convicted and confessed that he had done it out of love for Paul, he lost his position. For how credible will it seem that Paul gave a woman the power of teaching and baptizing, when he firmly prohibited a woman from learning? He said, "Let them be silent and question their husbands at home" (I Cor. 14:34-35).

> John Chrysostom also reproved women who wanted to assume a priestly role in his treatise *On the Priesthood.*

II,2.[25] ...Those duties that I mentioned above could be carried out easily by many who are subject to authority, not only men, but also women. But when there is a need for

[22]Alexander the Great died at Babylon in 323 B.C. It was suspected that he was poisoned.
[23]See above p. 78.
[24]Text: CSEL 20.215
[25]Text: PG 48.633.

someone to be set over the church and to be entrusted with the care of so many souls, let the whole female sex step aside from the greatness of the matter, and most men as well....

III,9. ...The divine law has shut women out from the ministerial office but they use force to get inside. Since they do not prevail on their own, they do everything through the agency of others. They have invested themselves with such power that they admit and depose men from the priesthood as they choose. Everything is topsy-turvy, so that we see the realization of the proverb, "The ruled lead the rulers." And were it men!—but it is those who have not been entrusted to teach. Why do I say "teach"? The blessed Paul did not assent to have them speak in church (I Cor. 14:34). I heard someone say that they have helped themselves to freedom of speech to the extent that they even find fault with the church authorities and upbraid them more sharply than masters do their own servants.

> Although Chrysostom did not allow women to claim the priestly office in actuality, he could rhetorically call a woman a "priest" who had led her two daughters to "baptism" through drowning during a time of persecution. In his homily on *Saints Bernice and Prosdoce,* Chrysostom praises the valiant mother in these words:

6.[26] ...They entered the midst of the river and gave themselves up to those currents. The mother entered with her two daughters. Let mothers and virgins listen: let the latter thus obey their mothers, and let the former thus raise their daughters, thus love their children. Accordingly, the mother entered in the midst of her daughters, one on either side: the married woman in the midst of the unmarried ones, marriage in the midst of virginity, Christ in their midst. Just as a tree's root has two shoots rising up on either side, thus also that blessed woman then entered with the virgins on

[26]Text: PG 50.638.

each side of her; she gave them up to the waters and so they drowned. Or rather, they were not drowned, but were baptized with a new and incredible baptism. If you wish to learn whether the baptism that then took place was a true one, listen to how Christ speaks with the sons of Zebedee: "You will drink from my cup," he said, "and you will be baptized with the baptism with which I am baptized" (Mk. 10:39). And what sort of baptism did Christ receive after the baptism of John, except death on the cross? Thus just as James was baptized with the baptism of Christ, not by being crucified, but by having his head cut off with a sword (Acts 12:2), so also these women, although they were not crucified but met their end by the water, were baptized with the baptism of Christ.

It was the mother who baptized them. "What are you saying? That a woman baptizes?" Yes, such baptism women also administer; just so, this woman also then baptized and became a priest. Indeed, she brought spiritual offerings and her resolution substituted in her case for the laying on of hands. Indeed this was a miracle: she did not need an altar for the sacrifice, nor wood, nor fire, nor a sword. For the river became all these things, the altar, the wood, the sword, the fire, the sacrifice, and a baptism that was by far a truer baptism than this. On this point, Paul said, "We have grown into the likeness of his death" (Rom. 6:5). Concerning the baptism of martyrs, he does not still say "a likeness of his death," but that we are "conformed to his death" (Phil. 3: 10). . . .

> Although excluded from the priesthood, women could join the order of widows if they met the qualifications. And in the fourth century, we have evidence concerning female deaconesses who helped with various liturgical functions that pertained to women. Some fourth- and fifth-century church councils also refer to deaconesses:

Nicaea (325 A.D.), Canon 19: About the Paulianists[27] who have fled from that sect to the Catholic Church, a rule has been established that they must certainly be rebaptized. If any who in the past were reckoned among their clergy are seen to be free from guilt and reproach, let them be rebaptized and ordained by the bishop of the Catholic Church. If indeed their examination should detect that they are unfit, it is right for them to be deposed. Let the same form be observed likewise in regard to the deaconesses, and, generally speaking, about those who are numbered among their clergy. Let us have in mind as deaconesses those who have taken on monastic garb, but since they have no imposition of hands, they are certainly to be counted as among the laity.

Chalcedon (451 A.D.), Canon 15: It is resolved that deaconesses are not to be ordained before they are forty years old, and this with careful scrutiny. If indeed after she has received the veil and for a certain time has kept her ministry, she gives herself in marriage, to the insult of God's grace, such a woman shall be anathematized along with him who married her.

The roles allowed to women as widows and deaconesses—but not as priests or public teachers—are further elaborated in the *Apostolic Constitutions,* a fourth-century document, probably of Syrian origin,that lists various church laws. It is noteworthy that, according to the eastern tradition represented by the *Apostolic Constitutions,* deaconesses were ordained, a practice not followed by the western church. The order of deaconesses was short-lived, however; from the early Middle Ages on, their role seems to have been subsumed under that of the nun. The following selection from the *Apostolic Constitutions* provides evidence about the orders open to women in eastern Christendom.

---

[27]Followers of the third-century schismatic, Paul of Samosata.

II,26,6.[28] And let the deaconess be honored by you as an image of the Holy Spirit. She should do or say nothing without the deacon, as the Comforter does not act or speak on its own, but glorifies Christ and awaits his will. And as we do not believe in Christ apart from the teaching of the Spirit, so let no woman approach the deacon or the bishop without the deaconess. . . . Let your widows and orphans be reckoned by you as an image of a sacrificial altar. Let the virgins be honored as an image of the altar of incense and of the incense, in addition.

III,1. Let widows assume their positions when they are not less than sixty years old (I Tim 5:9), so that, to some extent, because of their age, there may be certainty not marred by suspicion about second marriages. But if you let a younger woman be assumed into the order of widows, and if she should marry, not being able to bear widowhood in her youth, she will bring indecorum into people's estimation of the order of widows. Moreover, she shall give an account to God, not because she bound herself in a second marriage, but because she did not keep her promise and behaved wantonly toward Christ (I Tim 5:11). Therefore it is necessary when one makes a promise, to make it firmly, not recklessly. "For it is better for her not to vow, than to vow and not pay" (Eccl. 5:5). But if a younger woman who lived with a husband for a short time and lost him through death or by an occasion of some other sort, and stays by herself, having the gift of widowhood, she will be found blessed, resembling the widow Sarepta of Sidon, with whom the holy prophet Elias stayed (I Kings 17:9). A woman like this can be likened to "Anna, the daughter of Phanuel of the tribe of Aser, who did not leave the Temple, but continued in prayers and entreaties night and day, who being eighty years old, had lived with a husband seven years from her

[28]Text: *Didascalia et Constitutiones Apostolorum*, ed. F.X. Funk (Paderborn, 1905), 105.

virginity, who gloried in the coming of Christ and gave thanks to the Lord and spoke about him to all those who awaited redemption in Israel" (Lk. 2:36, 37). Such a woman will be honored, since she has been proved; she is both famed among men on earth and has eternal praise with God in heaven.

III,2. Let not the younger widows, however, be placed in the order of widows, lest under the pretext of incapacity to control themselves in their prime, they undertake a second marriage and make trouble. Let them be aided and assisted, lest under the excuse of having been deserted they come to a second marriage, entangled in unseemly business. For you should know this, that marrying once in accordance with the law is righteous and is in congruence with God's purpose, but second marriage, after a woman has made the promise for widowhood, is illegal, not because of the union but because of the falsehood involved. Third marriages are a sign of incontinence, and marriages beyond the third are open fornication and unambiguous licentiousness. For God at creation gave one woman to one man, for the "two shall be one flesh" (Gen. 2:24). However, let the younger widows after the deaths of their first husbands be conceded second ones, lest they fall under the Devil's judgment, many snares, and irrational passions so harmful to souls, that bring punishment upon them rather than indulgence.

III,3. True widows are those who had only one husband and are attested by many people for their good works. They are real widows, temperate, pure, faithful, pious, who have raised children well, and have blamelessly offered hospitality to strangers (cf. I Tim. 5:3-10), and ought also to be assisted as one dedicated to God. . . .

III,5. Let each widow be gentle, quiet, kind, incapable of anger, guileless, not talkative, not clamorous, not hasty to speak, not an evil-speaker, not a hunter after words, not double-tongued, not meddlesome. Should she see or hear anything unjust, let her be as one not seeing and not hearing. And let the widow care for nothing else than to pray on behalf of those who give and the whole Church. When someone asks her something, let her not reply readily, except for things pertaining to faith and righteousness and hope in God, sending those who wish to be instructed about the teachings of piety to the leaders. Let her answer only in order to overthrow the error of polytheism, proving the doctrine of God's unity. But concerning the things that follow after these doctrines, let her not answer recklessly, lest by uttering something unlearned, she might inflict blasphemy on the word. . . . For when unbelievers hear the doctrine about Christ (above all the points about his Incarnation and Passion) taught inadequately, not as it ought to be, they will mock and sneer at it as false rather than offer praise, and the old woman will be responsible for indiscretion and for blasphemy, and will inherit woe. "For woe," he says, "to the person by whom my name is blasphemed among the Gentiles" (Is. 52:5 LXX).

III,6. Thus we do not permit women to teach in the Church, but only to pray and listen to those who teach. Indeed, even our Teacher himself, the Lord Jesus Christ, who sent us the twelve to teach the people and the nations, nowhere did he send out women for preaching, yet he was not at a loss for such women. For there were with us the mother of the Lord and his sisters; in addition, Mary Magdalene and Mary the mother of James, and Martha and Mary the sisters of Lazarus, and Salome, and some others. For if it had been necessary for women to teach, he would first have commanded even those women who were with us to teach the people. . . .

III,8. Widows, then, ought to be solemn, obeying the bishops, the presbyters, and the deacons, moreover, truly also the deaconess, behaving with reverence, respect, and fear, not rising up against them nor wanting to do anything contrary to the ordinance except with the assent of the deacon....

III,9. And about a woman's baptizing, we are informing you that there is no small danger to the women who attempt it. Therefore we do not advise it. For it is dangerous, or rather, it is illegal and impious. For if "the man is the head of the woman" (I Cor. 11:3), he was chosen for priesthood; it is not right to set aside the order of creation and leave what is chief to descend to the lowest part of the body. For woman is the body of the man, being from his side and subjected to him, from whom also she was separated for the sake of the production of children. He said, "For he shall rule over you" (Gen. 3:16). For the man is the ruler of the woman, since he is also her head.

And if in what came earlier we did not allow women to teach, how can we assent to their being priests, which is contrary to nature? For this is an error of Gentile atheism to ordain women as priests to the goddesses; it is not in the dispensation of Christ. And also, had it been necessary for women to baptize, certainly the Lord would have also been baptized by his own mother, not by John, or when he sent us to baptize, he would have sent women with us as well for this purpose. But now, nowhere, neither by command nor in writing did he transmit this, since he knew the order of nature and the fittingness of things, being the Creator of nature and the Legislator of the arrangement.

III,16. ... Ordain also a deaconess, faithful and holy, for the services pertaining to women, for whenever the bishop cannot send a male deacon to certain women's households because of the unbelievers, you shall thus send a woman deaconess, because of the suspicions of wicked people. For we require a woman as deaconess for many needs. First of all, in the baptism of women, the deacon shall anoint only their foreheads with holy oil and after him the deaconess shall anoint them, for there is no need for the women to be observed by men....

(Prayer for the ordination of a deaconess: the bishop lays on his hands and says,)

VIII,20. "O eternal God,the Father of our Lord Jesus Christ, the Creator of man and of woman, who did fill with the Spirit Miriam, Deborah, Anna and, Huldah,[29] who did not deem unworthy that your only-begotten Son should be born of a woman, who also in the tent of witness and in the Temple ordained women as keepers of your holy gates[30]: now look upon this your servant who is being ordained as a deaconess, and give her the Holy Spirit, and purify her from any defilement of the flesh and spirit (II Cor. 7:1), so that she may worthily accomplish the work entrusted to her and to your glory and the praise of your Christ, with whom to you and to the Holy Spirit be glory and adoration forever. Amen!"

VIII,24,2. A virgin is not ordained, for we do not have a command from the Lord. For the advantage of virginity is not so that marriage is slandered, but in order to provide time for piety.

VIII,25,2. A widow is not ordained, but if she lost her husband a long time ago, has lived temperately and without blame, and has cared most excellently for her household, like Judith and Anna,[31] those most reverend women, let her be appointed to the order of the widows. But if she lost her husband recently, let her not be trusted; rather, let her youth be judged by time. For emotions, too, sometimes grow old with humans, if they are not restrained by a better bridle.

Some few Christian women of substantial means might undertake works of charity on a larger scale in the public world. In *Epistle 77,* Jerome recounts how his friend Fabiola founded a hospital in Rome. Jerome is particularly sensitive to people's criticism of Fabiola: she

[29]Ex. 15:20-21; Judg. 5; Lk. 2:36-38; II Kings 22:14-20.
[30]E.g., Ex. 38:8; I Sam 2:22.
[31]Judith 8:2 ff.; Lk. 2:36-38.

had divorced an adulterous first husband and remarried while the first husband still lived. After the death of her second husband, she repented her supposed sins and devoted her considerable fortune to works of Christian charity. Jerome's account of her establishing a hospital and tending the sick with her own hands illuminates one way a woman could manifest her Christian concern through active work in the larger world, rather than by retreat and contemplation.

6.[32] We have lingered so long on her penitence, we have bogged down again in the shallows, so to speak, that a larger field, one without impediment, might open up for her praises. When under the eyes of the whole church she was restored to communion, what did she do? Is it likely that, in a better day, she was forgetful of evils? Did she again wish to attempt the dangers of sailing after shipwreck? No, in fact, she rather gave away and sold all of the property which she could manage (it was extensive, however, corresponding to her rank) and in her wealth, she prepared an association for the poor to use.

And first of all she established a hospital, into which she gathered the sick off the streets, where she might restore the limbs of the wretched that were wasted with weakness and starvation. Shall I now describe the diverse misfortunes of human beings: noses mutilated, eyes gouged out, feet half-burnt, ghostly hands, bloated bellies, meager legs, swollen shins, flesh eaten away and putrid, welling up with worms? How often did she not carry on her own shoulders those who were consumed by jaundice and filth? How often did she wash the corruption and bloody pus from wounds which some other man did not dare to glimpse? She used to supply food by her own hand and refresh with drops of water those who were in fact just breathing cadavers. I know many rich

[32]Text: CSEL 55.42.

and religious persons who because of weak stomachs do works of mercy of this sort by the agency of others, and show their mercy through money, not by their own hand. Certainly I do not condemn them and by no means would I construe their squeamishness as a lack of faith. But just as I bestow indulgence on their weak stomachs, I praise to the skies the zeal of an excellent character. A strong faith makes light of such nasty details. It knows with what kind of retribution the proud mind of the rich man was condemned, the rich man clad in purple who did nothing for Lazarus (Lk. 16:19-31). That man on whom we cannot look, at whose sight we disgorge vomit, he is like unto us, formed from the same clay, constructed from the same elements. Whatever he suffers, we also may suffer. Let us count his wounds as our own, and all hardness of mind toward our fellow-creature will be shattered by our merciful consideration for ourselves.

> Not if I had one hundred tongues or one hundred
> mouths, a voice of iron,
> Could I run through the names of all diseases,[33]

which Fabiola changed into refreshment for such numbers of wretched people, so that many of the healthy begrudged the poor their weakness.

And yet she acted with similar liberality toward clergy and monks. What monastery was not sustained by her wealth? What naked or bed-ridden person did not have clothes woven by Fabiola? To what needy person did she not quickly pour forth a speedy donation? Rome was too narrow for her pity: thus she travelled through the islands, she made the rounds of the Etruscan Sea and the province of the Volscians[34] with her bounty, and also the winding and secluded shores on which crowds of monks stay; she did this

[33]Virgil, *Aeneid* VI, 625-627.
[34]An ancient people in Italy.

either in her own person or had her gifts conveyed by trustworthy, holy men.

Another way in which Christianity opened a wider world to women was through its encouragement of pilgrimage. The fourth century saw a flowering of Christian interest in the Holy Places of Palestine and in the Egyptian ascetics. The emperor Constantine's mother Helena was credited with raising interest in pilgrimages by her own journey to Palestine and her lavish contributions for the building of churches there. Helena is also said to have found the True Cross, that is, the cross on which Jesus had been put to death. The fifth-century Christian historian Socrates Scholasticus reports on Helena's activities in the following selection from his *Church History*.

I,17.[35] The mother of the emperor, Helena (after whom the emperor named the city, Helenopolis, formerly the town of Drepanes), enjoined by God through dreams, went to Jerusalem. Discovering that which formerly was Jerusalem to be "desolate as a crop-watcher's hut," according to the prophet (Is. 1:8 LXX), she diligently sought the tomb of Christ, the location of the grave from which he arose. And she found it with God's help, albeit with some trouble. What the cause of the trouble was, I shall briefly report. People who were inclined to Christianity honored the tomb after the time of Christ's Passion, but those who rejected Christianity heaped up earth on the spot, built a temple to Aphrodite,[36] and erected her statue, not preserving the memory of the place. This situation lasted a long time and the emperor's mother heard about it. Thus when she had the statue taken down, the soil that had been heaped up on the spot removed, and the area opened up, she found three crosses in the tomb.

[35]Text: Socrates Scholasticus, *Ecclesiastica Historia*, ed. R. Hussey (Oxford, 1853), I, 104.
[36]The Greek goddess of love.

One was the blessed cross on which Christ had been out-
stretched and the others were those on which the two thieves
were put to death by crucifixion. With these was also found
the tablet of Pilate on which he had written that the crucified
Christ was the King of the Jews, this title being proclaimed
in various alphabets. The emperor's mother was in a state of
some distress since it was unclear which cross they were
seeking. The bishop of Jerusalem, named Macarius, soon
alleviated her anxiety; by his faith he dismissed her doubt.
For he asked God for a sign and received it. The sign was
this: a certain woman of the area who suffered from a
chronic disease had just come to the point of death. The
bishop arranged for each of the crosses to be brought to the
dying woman, believing that she would regain her strength if
she touched the honored cross. Nor was he mistaken in his
hope, for when the two crosses that were not the Lord's were
brought near, she remained no less in her dying condition,
but when the third, the genuine cross, was brought near her,
the dying woman immediately was healed and regained her
health. This, then, was the way in which the wood of the
cross was found.

The emperor's mother built on the spot of the sepulchre a
sumptuous church and named it the "New Jerusalem," plac-
ing it opposite that old and forsaken city. She left on the
very spot a piece of the cross enclosed in a silver chest as a
remembrance for those wanting to inquire after it. The other
part she sent to the emperor, who, when he received it,
believing that the city where it was kept would be made
completely safe, concealed it in his own statue that was set
on a great column of porphyry, placed in the forum that is
called Constantine's in Constantinople. Although I have
written this from hearsay, nearly all the residents of the city
of Constantinople say it is true. In addition, Constantine
took the nails with which the hands of Christ were fixed to
the cross (indeed, his mother had found them, too, in the
tomb and had sent them) and made them into bridle-bits

and a helmet that he used in his battles. The emperor defrayed the cost of all the supplies for the construction of the churches. He also wrote to bishop Macarius to hasten the construction of these buildings. And when the emperor's mother had finished the "New Jerusalem," she constructed another church, not inferior, at the cave in Bethlehem where the birth of Christ according to the flesh took place.[37] But this wasn't all: she built another church on the mountain of the Ascension. She was so pious in these matters that she prayed in the company of women. She invited the virgins who were listed on the rolls of the church to a banquet and served them herself, carrying the food to the tables. She also gave a great deal to the churches and to the poor. And when she had piously completed her life, she died at about eighty years of age. Her corpse was transported to the capital city, New Rome,[38] and placed in the imperial tomb.

> Once Helena set an example of travel to the Holy Land, a veritable swarm of female as well as male pilgims followed. One famous eyewitness account is that composed by Egeria, a nun who journeyed from western Europe to Palestine in the late fourth century and wrote a travel diary for her sisters back home. Her travelogue reveals her deep interest in exploring the Biblical sites, in venerating the memory of Thecla[39] (then believed to have been an historical person), and in observing the rituals and customs of the Christian Church in Palestine. The Latin style of *The Pilgrimage of Egeria* does not conform to the classical standards of elegance upheld by such Christian writers as Jerome and Paulinus of Nola.

3,1.[40] Thus on Saturday evening we reached the mountain

[37]The early church preserved a tradition that Jesus had been born in a cave. See the apocryphal *Protevangelium of James*, 18.
[38]Constantinople.
[39]See above, pp. 78-88.
[40]Text CCL 175.39.

and arrived at some monastic cells. The monks who lived there received us very courteously, showing us every kindness, for there is a church there with a priest. Thus we stayed the night there and then early on Sunday, with that priest and the monks who lived there, we began to climb the mountains one at a time. These mountains are climbed with extreme difficulty, because you do not approach them going around in a spiral, as we say, but you go straight up each one, as if you were ascending a wall, and then you have to go straight down each one of the mountains until you reach the very foot of that one in the middle, the particular one called Sinai.

3,2. So here, by the will of Christ our God, and aided by the prayers of the holy men who came with us, we thus ascended with enormous effort, because it was necessary for me to ascend on foot, as it was absolutely impossible to ascend in the saddle. Nonetheless, you did not feel the effort, and why I didn't feel the effort was because by God's will I was seeing fulfilled the wish I had. Thus we reached the top of the mountain of God, holy Sinai, at 10 a.m. This is the place where the Law was given, that is, the place where the majesty of the Lord descended on the day when the mountain smoked (Ex. 19:18).

3,3. Thus in this place there is now a church, not large, because the place itself, that is, the top of the mountain, is not very large. Nonetheless, this church has a great charm of its own.

3,4. When by God's will we had climbed to the very summit and had arrived at the door of this church, lo, there was the priest assigned to the church coming from his monastic cell, hastening to meet us. He was a blameless old man, a monk from the early years of his life, and as they say here, an "ascetic" and (what more could be said?) a man such as was worthy to be in this place. Then there came the other priests and all the monks who lived near the mountain, that is, those who were not yet prevented either by age or by feebleness.

3,5. Indeed, no one dwells on the top of the central mountain, for nothing is there except the church alone and the cave where the holy Moses was.

3,6. Then when the whole passage from the book of Moses was read at the very spot and the sacrifice was made in the prescribed manner, we received communion. As we were leaving the church, the priests gave us "blessings" of the place, i.e., fruit that grows on this mountain. For this holy mountain, Sinai, is completely rock, so that it doesn't have even a bush. Nonetheless, down at the foot of these mountains, i.e., either around this one that is in the middle or around those encircling it, there is a little ground. Steadfastly the holy monks in their diligence plant shrubs and start orchards or plots near their cells, and they seem to take the fruit as if it were from the soil of the mountain itself, fruit that they, notwithstanding, have produced by their own hands.

3,7. After we had received communion and the holy men had given us the "blessings," and we had come out of the church door, then I began to ask them to show us each place. Immediately the holy men agreed to point out each one. For they showed us the cave where the holy Moses was when he went up onto the mountain of God the second time and received the tablets again, after he had broken the first ones when the people sinned (Ex. 34:1-28), and they agreed to show us other places that we wanted to see and that they knew very well.

3,8. I want you to know, venerable ladies and sisters, that in this place where we stood, at the church, when we looked down from the top of the central mountain at the mountains surrounding us, that at first we could scarcely climb, near the central one on which we stood, they seemed like little hills. But they were nonetheless so high that I thought I had

never seen any higher, except for the central one that surpasses them by far. From there we could see Egypt, Palestine, the Red Sea, the Parthenian Sea that leads to
Alexandria, in addition to the endless boundaries of the
Saracens, although it can scarcely be believed, which nonetheless the holy men showed us each of these things.

> (From Mt. Nebo, Egeria looks in the direction of the
> Dead Sea.)

12,5. Indeed, from here you can see the greater part of
Palestine, which is the Promised Land, and everything in
the land of Jordan, at least as far as the eye can see. On the
left we saw all the lands of the Sodomites as well as Zoar, but
Zoar is the only one left of those five cities.

12,6. And there is a memorial there, but of the other cities
nothing can be seen except the overturned ruins, just as they
were turned into ashes (Gen. 19:24). We were even shown
the spot, which indeed you read about in Scripture, where
there was a token of Lot's wife (Gen. 19:26).

12,7. But believe me, venerable ladies, the pillar itself
cannot now be seen, although the place where it was is
shown, but the pillar itself is said to have met its end in the
Dead Sea which covered it over. Indeed, we saw the place,
but we saw no pillar, and therefore on this point I cannot
lead you astray. For the bishop of that place, i.e., Zoar, told
us that it was already now some years that the pillar was not
visible. For where the pillar stood, now completely covered
by water, is perhaps six miles from Zoar.

17,1. After some time had passed, when it was already
three full years since I had come to Jerusalem and had seen
all the holy places to which I had been drawn to pray, I
thought I should thus now, in God's name, return to my own
country. By the will of God, I wanted also to go to Syrian
Mesopotamia in order to see the holy monks, who are said
to be numerous there and of such an exceptional way of life

that it can scarcely be reported. Also I wanted to offer prayers at the martyrium of St. Thomas the Apostle, where his uncorrupted body was placed, that is, at Edessa, where he was to be sent after Jesus' ascension into heaven, as Jesus, our God, testifies in a letter that he sent to Abgar the king by the messenger Ananias.[41] This letter is kept in great reverence at the city of Edessa, where this martyrium is.

17,2. And I want you to believe, my dear ones, that there is no Christian who having come all the way to the holy places, that is, those in Jerusalem, does not go on to there to pray. And this place is twenty-five stopping places from Jerusalem.

17,3. And because Antioch is closer to Mesopotamia, there was a good opportunity for me, by the command of God, as I returned from Constantinople, because the road went through Antioch, from whence I went to Mesopotamia, and that, at God's bidding, is what was done.

(Egeria hears read the supposed correspondence between Jesus and King Abgar.)

19,16. Then after the holy bishop reported all these things, he said to me, "Let us now go to the gate, through which Ananias the bearer of that letter entered, the letter we were talking about." When we had gone to the gate, the bishop, standing, gave a prayer and read to us there the letters themselves and again blessing us, he said another prayer.

19,17. This holy man also told us that from the day Ananias the messenger entered through that gate with the Lord's letter, up to the present day, an observance is kept that no unclean man nor anyone in mourning should cross through this gate, nor has any dead body been removed through this gate.

---

[41]See the Abgar legend in the apocrypha of the New Testament; also Eusebius, *Church History* I, 13.

19,18. Then the holy bishop showed us the tomb of Abgar and of his whole family—very beautiful, but fashioned in an old style. Then he led us to the older palace where king Abgar had lived before, and he pointed out to us what further palaces there were.

19,19. And this pleased me a lot, that the letters both of Abgar to the Lord, and of the Lord to Abgar, letters the holy bishop read to us there, I received from this holy man. And granted that I have copies of them at home, nonetheless it seemed more pleasing to me to receive them there from this man, lest by chance the copy that came to us at home was lacking something, for indeed the one I received here is fuller. If Jesus our God wills it and I return home, you will read them, ladies dear to me.

(Egeria goes to the shrine of Thecla.)

22,1. When I had returned to Antioch, I spent a week there, until the time when everything necessary for our journey was prepared. Then, leaving Antioch, and on the road for several stopping places, I came to the province called Cilicia, which has Tarsus for its capital city, where I had already been when I was going to Jerusalem.

22,2. Since the martyrium of St. Thecla is three days from Tarsus, that is, in Isauria, it pleased me much to go on there, especially since it was so close by.

23,1. Leaving Tarsus, I came to a certain city by the sea called Pompeiopolis, still in Cilicia. And from there I entered Isaurian territory and stayed in a city called Corycus. On the third day I came to a city called Seleucia of Isauria. When I arrived there, I went to the bishop, a truly holy man and a former monk. I also saw there a very beautiful church in the same city.

23,2. Since St. Thecla's shrine is placed above the city on a flat hill, perhaps fifteen hundred feet from the city, I chose to go out there to make the lodging that had to be made. At the holy church there is nothing else except innumerable monastic cells for men and women.

23,3. For I found there one of my dearest friends, a person to whose way of life everybody in the east bears witness, the holy deaconess named Marthana, whom I had met in Jerusalem where she had come up to pray. She governs there monastic cells of "apotactites" or virgins. Would I be able to describe her joy or mine when she saw me?

23,4. But I should return to my subject. There are a great many monastic cells there on that hill and in the middle is an immense wall that encloses the church in which is the martyrium, for the martyrium is very beautiful. Therefore the wall was put there to guard the church against the Isaurians who are evil and often steal, lest they try to do something against the monastery placed there.

23,5. When I had arrived there in the name of God, a prayer was given at the martyrium and the entire *Acts of St. Thecla* were read. I gave boundless thanks to Christ our God who counted me worthy, though I was unworthy and undeserving, to fulfill my desires in all things.

23,6. I stayed there for two days, seeing the holy monastics or "apotactites," men as well as women, who were there, and after praying and receiving communion, I returned to Tarsus to continue on my route....

(Egeria describes the rituals connected with the celebration of Pentecost in Jerusalem.)

43,1. The fiftieth day after Easter is a Sunday, a day of great exertion for the people. Everything is done according to custom from the time of the first cock-crow. They keep vigil in the Anastasis, so that the bishop may read the Gospel passage that is always read on Sunday, that is, the one about the Lord's resurrection, and afterwards they do in the Anastasis what they are accustomed to do during the whole year.

43,2. When morning comes, all the people go into the Great Church, that is, the Martyrium, and they do everything that they are accustomed to do; the priests give sermons, and afterwards the bishop. All the proper things are done, that is, the Offering is made in the way customary on Sunday, but on this day the Dismissal at the Martyrium is moved up so that it takes place before 9 a.m. Right after the Dismissal has been given at the Martyrium, all the people, every one, lead the bishop to Zion with hymns, so that they are at Zion by 9 a.m.

43,3. When they have come there, that passage is read from the Acts of the Apostles where the Spirit descends so that all the languages that were spoken were understood (Acts 2:1-11); afterwards the service is held in due order. For the priests there read this passage that is read because this is the spot on Zion (another church is there now) where once, after the Passion of the Lord, a multitude was gathered with the apostles, where there was done what I said above. Afterwards the service is performed in the appropriate way and the Offering made. There and now when the people are dismissed the archdeacon raises his voice and says, "Today, just after noon, let us all be ready at the Imbonon on the Mount of Olives."

43,4. Thus all the people return home, each to renew himself in his own house, and immediately after lunch, they climb the Mount of Olives, i.e., the Eleona, each one as he can, for not everyone hastens, so that not a Christian remains inside the city.

43,5. Once they have climbed the Mount of Olives, i.e., the Eleona, they go first to the Imbonon, that is, to that place from which the Lord ascended into heaven (Acts 1:9-12). The bishop sits here and the priests, and all the people. There they have Scriptural readings, interspersed with the singing of hymns, and they also say the antiphons appropriate to this day. Even the prayers that are

interspersed are such as have subject matter that fit the day
and place. That passage from the Gospel is read that tells of
the Lord's Ascension and again they read from the Acts of
the Apostles, where it speaks of the Lord's Ascension into
heaven after the resurrection (Acts 1:9-11).

43,6. When this is finished, the catechumens are blessed,
then the faithful. And it now being 3 p.m., they descend
from there and go with hymns to that church which is also
on the Mount of Olives, that is, the church which is the cave
in which the Lord used to sit and teach the apostles. By the
time they get there it is already past 4.p.m. There they have
Vespers, a prayer is said, the catechumens are blessed and
then the faithful. Then they descend with hymns and antiphons appropriate to that day. Thus they come slowly and
calmly to the Martyrium.

43,7. When they arrive at the gate of the city, it is already
night and the people are brought church lamps for leading
them. From the gate it is quite a long way to the Great
Church, that is, the Martyrium, and they arrive there at
perhaps 8 p.m., because they go slowly the whole route lest
people get tired from walking. The great doors which face
the market are opened and all the people enter the Martyrium with the bishop, singing hymns. When they have
entered the church, hymns are sung, a prayer is said, the
catechumens are blessed and then the faithful. And from
there they go again, singing hymns, to the Anastasis.

43,8. In like manner, when they have come to the Anastasis, hymns and antiphons are sung, a prayer is said, the
catechumens are blessed, and then the faithful; the same
thing is done at the Cross. And from there, once again, all
the Christian people, each and every one, lead the bishop to
Zion with hymns.

43,9. When they arrive, suitable Scriptural passages are
read, Psalms and antiphons are sung, a prayer is said, the
catechumens are blessed and then the faithful, and the

Dismissal is given. When the Dismissal has taken place, everyone comes near to kiss the bishop's hand and thus everyone returns to his home about midnight. Much effort is thus expended on this day, since they have never stopped this whole day from the vigil at first cock-crow at the Anastasis. And everything that is celebrated has been so prolonged that it is after the Dismissal has been given in Zion, at midnight, that all return to their homes.

> (Egeria reports on the instruction of catechumens in Jerusalem.)

45,1. And I ought also to write about how they instruct those who are to be baptized at Easter. For the person must register his name before Lent begins, and the priest notes all the names before those eight weeks of Lent (as it lasts here), as I have said.

45,2. When the priest has written down all the names, then on the next day of Lent, i.e., the day on which the eight weeks begin, the bishop's chair is placed in the center of the Great Church, i.e., the Martyrium. The priests sit on chairs on both sides and all the clergy stand. And thus one by one those seeking baptism are led up; if they are men, they come with their fathers, if they are women, with their mothers.[42]

45,3. Then the bishop asks the neighbors of each one who comes in, "Does this person lead a good life? Does he respect his parents? Is he a drunkard or a liar?" And he inquires about the vices that are more serious in human beings.

45,5. And if the person is shown to be without fault in all these things about which the bishop has asked the witnesses present, he writes down the person's name in his own hand. If, however, he is accused on some point, the bishop orders him to go out, saying, "Let him correct his ways and when he has corrected them, then let him come to the font." He

---

[42]Perhaps those who present them as candidates for baptism.

investigates the men and the women in the same way. However, if someone is a stranger, it is not so easy for him to come forth for baptism, unless he has witnesses who know him.

46,1. Ladies and sisters, I ought to write this down lest you think that this is done without explanation. For such is the custom here that those who are coming up for baptism, during the forty days, which is a fast, are exorcised by the clergy early in the morning, right after the Dismissal has been given at the morning service at the Anastasis. Right away the bishop's chair is placed in the Martyrium, the Great Church, and all who are to be baptized, both men and women, sit around the bishop in a circle. The fathers and mothers, and also whoever of all the people who want to hear, enter and sit down, but they must belong to the faithful.

46,2. A catechumen can not come in there when the bishop is teaching them the Law, which he does as follows: beginning with Genesis, he runs through all of Scripture in those forty days, setting forth its literal meaning and then interpreting its spiritual meaning. Also they are taught about the resurrection and likewise everything about the faith during those days. And this is called "catechetics."

46,3. After they have finished their five weeks of instruction, then they receive the Creed. Just as he set forth the meaning of all Scripture, so likewise he explains the Creed, going through each phrase first in its literal meaning and then in its spiritual sense. And thus it is in those places that all the faithful can follow the Scriptures when they are read in church because they all have been taught for the forty days, that is, from 6 to 9 a.m., since instruction is given for three hours.

46,4. God knows, ladies and sisters, that the voices of the faithful are louder when they come in to hear the bishop give instruction or expound on points than when he sits and preaches in the church on each of the points that are explained in such a way. They are dismissed from catechetics at 9 a.m. and the bishop is led straightway from there to the Anastasis with hymns, and the Dismissal is made at 9 a.m.; thus they are taught for three hours a day throughout the seven weeks. For in the eighth week, that is called the Great Week, there is no more free time for them to be taught so that they can carry out those things that I have written about above.

46,5. When already seven weeks have passed and there remains only Easter Week, which is here called the Great Week, then the bishop comes down to the Great Church, the Martyrium. The bishop's chair is placed at the back of the apse, behind the altar, and one by one they go there, a man with his father, a woman with her mother, and each recites the Creed for the bishop.

46,6. When they have recited the Creed for the bishop, the bishop addresses them all and says, "For these seven weeks you have been instructed in all Scriptural law and you have also heard about the faith, and even further, you have heard about the resurrection of the flesh, but about the whole meaning of the Creed, only what you as catechumens were able to hear. But the teachings about things that are the higher mysteries, that is, about baptism itself, you cannot hear because you are still catechumens. But lest you imagine that anything is being done without explanation, when you have been baptized in the name of God, you will hear about these things during the eight days of Easter, after the Dismissal from church is given. Because you are yet catechumens, the more hidden of God's mysteries cannot be told to you."

Jerome, too, gives an account of a pilgrimage: Paula's voyage to Egypt and the Holy Land. Paula set out from Rome in 385 A.D., never to return. She became so enam-

ored of the Holy Land that she decided to spend the rest
of her life there and built monasteries for both men and
women at Bethlehem. Jerome includes the following description of her trip in his eulogy of Paula, *Epistle 108.*

(Paula has sailed from the port of Rome.)

7.[43] Brought to the Pontiae islands, once made famous by
the illustrious memory of a woman, Flavia Domitilla,
whom the emperor Domitian exiled for confessing to the
name of Christian, Paula saw the cells in which she had
spent her long martyrdom, and setting sail, she desired to
see Jerusalem and the Holy Places. The winds were too slow
for her, any speed sluggish. Sailing between Scylla and
Charybdis[44] she entrusted herself to the Adriatic Sea as
through calm water she came to Methone where she revived
her body for a while,

> placing limbs dripping with sea water on the shore
> through Malea and Cythera, through the sea
> and the scattered Cyclades, and seas linking the crowded
> lands.[45]

Then, after Rhodes and Lycia, she saw Cyprus. There she
fell at the knees of the holy and venerable Epiphanius,[46] and
was detained for ten days, not for her restoration, as he
imagined, but in order to do the work of God, as events
demonstrated. For passing through all the monasteries in
that region, as far as she could, she left funds for the refreshment of the brothers whom love of the holy man had led
here from the entire world. Then sailing through the shallows, they crossed the sea to Seleucia. From there, going up
to Antioch, she was detained for a while by the love of the
holy confessor Paulinus. In the middle of winter, this lady,

---

[43]Text: CSEL 55.312.
[44]Identified (probably falsely) with the Straits of Messina.
[45]Virgil, *Aeneid* I, 173; III, 126-127.
[46]Bishop of Salamis in Cyprus, 367-403 A.D.

by the glowing zeal of her faith gained ground while sitting upon an ass, she who in former times used to be carried by the hands of eunuchs.

8. I leave out her trip through Lebanon and Phoenicia, for I am not disposed to write down her itinerary—I will list as many places as are contained in the sacred books. After departing from Berytus, a Roman colony, and the ancient city of Sidon, she entered the little tower of Elijah on the shore at Zarephath (I Kings 17:9), where she adored her Lord and Savior. She went over the sands of Tyre, on which Paul had placed his knee (Acts 21:5), came to Accho, now called Ptolemais, and through the fields of Megiddo that knew the guilt of Josiah's murder (II Kings 23:29); she entered the land of the Philistines. She admired the ruins of Dor, once a very powerful city, and Strato's Tower, whose fortunes had changed, and which was called by Herod, king of Judea, Caesarea in honor of Caesar Augustus. In this town she saw the house of Cornelius (Acts 10:1), a little church of Christ, and the small house of Philip and the rooms of the four virgins who prophesied (Acts 21:8-9). Next she went to Antipatris, a small, half-ruined town, which Herod had named after his father, and Lydda, changed to Diospolis, famous for the resurrection and recovery of Dorcas and Aeneas (Acts 9:32-41). By no means far away from this are Arimathea, the village of Joseph, who buried the Lord (Mk. 15:43; Mt. 27:57; Lk. 23:50-52) and Nob, once a priestly city (I Sam. 22:19), now a tomb for the dead; also Joppa, the port of the fleeing Jonah (Jonah 1:3), that —if I may briefly relate something from a poetic tale— beheld Andromeda bound to a rock.[47] Starting on her way again, Paula came to Nicopolis, that formerly was called Emmaus, near where the Lord was recognized in the breaking of the bread, and by which he dedicated the house of

---

[47]Andromeda: a mythological princess fastened to a rock by her father as an offering to a sea-monster; she was rescued by Perseus

Cleopas as a church (Lk. 24:30). Advancing from there, she ascended to lower and higher Bethoron, cities founded by Solomon and annihilated by many attacks of war afterwards.

To her right she saw Ajalon and Gibeon, where Joshua, son of Nun, commanded the sun and the moon when he fought against the five kings (Josh. 10:12), and where he condemned the Gibeonites, who by deceit and treachery had obtained a covenant to be "hewers of wood and drawers of water" (Josh. 9). At the city of Gibeah, destroyed right down to its foundation, she stood for a little while, pondering its sin, the hacking to bits of the concubine, and the three hundred men of the tribe of Benjamin who were saved (Judg. 19-20) for the sake of Paul the apostle (Rom. 11:1; Phil. 3:5).

9. Why delay any more? Leaving behind on the left the mausoleum of Helena, the queen of Adiabenorum who had assisted the people with grain during a famine, Paula entered Jerusalem, the city of three names: Jebus, Salem, Jerusalem, that was called Aelia after Hadrian restored the city from ruins and ashes. And when the proconsul of Palestine, who knew her family very well, sent his deputies and ordered the praetorian place readied for her, she chose instead a humble cell. She went around to all the places with such eagerness and zeal that she could not have left the first unless she were hastening to the others. Throwing herself down before the Cross, she worshipped as if she saw the Lord hanging there. Entering the tomb of the resurrection, she kissed the stone that the angels rolled away from the door of the sepulchre (Mk. 16:3-5; Mt. 28:2), and the spot where the body of the Lord himself had lain she licked with her mouth, like one thirsting for the water desired by faith. All Jerusalem was witness to what tears she shed there, what groans of grief she poured forth—the Lord himself, whom she continually implored, was witness.

From there she left to climb Mt. Zion, which is translated

either as "fortress" or "watchtower." This was the city that David once captured and built. Of its capture is written, "Woe to you, city of Ariel"—that is, "the lion of God," for once it was very strong— "the city that David captures" (Is. 29:1 Vg.), and about its rebuilding is written, "His foundations are in the holy mountains; the Lord loves the gates of Zion more than all the tents of Jacob" (Ps. 87:1,2)—not those gates that today we see crumbled into embers and ashes, but the gates against which Hell does not prevail and through which enter the multitude of those faithful to Christ. In that place was shown to her the column tinged with blood that upholds the portico of a church; to the column Jesus is said to have been bound during his flagellation (Mk. 15:15; Mt. 27:26; Jn. 19:1). The place was pointed out where the Holy Spirit descended on the one hundred and twenty souls, thus fulfilling the prophesy of Joel (Acts 1:15; 2:4).

10. Next, having distributed money to the poor and to her fellow servants, as she had the means, she went straight on to Bethlehem. Stopping on the right side of the road at the tomb of Rachel, where Rachel gave birth to a son who was not called as his dying mother wished, "Benoni," i.e., "son of my grief," but as his father had prophesied in the spirit, "Benjamin," "the son of my right hand" (Gen. 35:18-19). And from there she entered the cave of the Savior.[48] As soon as she saw the inn and stable sacred to the Virgin, in which the "ox knew its owner, the ass his master's crib" (cf. Is. 1:3), that what was written by the same prophet might be fulfilled, "Blessed is the man who sows beside the waters, where ox and ass tread" (Is. 32:20), she swore in my hearing that she saw with the eyes of faith the Christ child wrapped in swaddling clothes, crying in the manger, the Magi worshipping God, the star gleaming from on high, the Virgin Mother, the solicitous man who would bring him up, the

[48]See note 37 above.

shepherds coming by night to see the word that had come to be (Mt. 2; Lk. 2), and even then they inscribed the opening of the Gospel of John, "In the beginning was the Word," and "the Word was made flesh" (John 1:1, 14). She swore she saw the slaughtered innocents, violent Herod, Joseph and Mary fleeing to Egypt (Mt. 2). She said, joy mixed with tears, "Hail, Bethlehem, house of bread," in whom was born that Bread who descended from Heaven (John 6:33). . . .

14. I will pass on now to Egypt, halting for a short while in Succoth and at the fountain of Samson which he made by the jawbone (Judg. 15:15-19), and I wet my parched lips so that refreshed I might see Moresheth, once the tomb of the prophet Micah, now a church (Micah 1:1). Then passing by the side of the land of the Horites and Gittites, Marisa, Idumea, and Lachish, and through the most yielding sands that carry off the traveller's footprints and through the vast desert wastes, let me come to the river of Egypt, Sihor,[49] which means "muddy," and go through the five cities of Egypt, where they speak the language of Canaan, and the land of Goshen and the plains of Zoan, in which God worked a miracle, and the city of No, later changed to Alexandria, and Nitria, the Lord's town, in which the filth of many people is daily washed with the most pure soap of virtue.[50]

As soon as we saw the city, the holy and venerable man, bishop Isidore the Confessor, ran to meet her with a countless mob of monks, of whom many were raised to priestly and levitical rank; she was made glad at the glory of the Lord but confessed herself unworthy of such honor. What should I report about the Macarii, Arsetes, Sarapion, and the other names of the pillars of Christ? Was there a cell she did not enter? Any to whose feet she did not hasten? In each of the holy men she believed she saw Christ himself, and whatever

[49]The Nile.
[50]Nitria was famous for natron (hydrated sodium carbonate) pits.

she conferred on them, she rejoiced that she conferred on the Lord. Her zeal was amazing, and her endurance scarcely believable in a woman! Forgetting her sex and her bodily weakness, she desired to settle down amid so many thousands of monks with the girls accompanying her. Since all received her, she might perhaps have done it, if it were not the greater wish for the Holy Places drew her back. And on account of the blistering heat, she came by boat from Pelusium to Maiouma, returning with such speed that you would think her a bird. After a short time, intending to remain forever in Bethlehem, she lived for three years in a cramped hospice until she could construct the little cells and monasteries and build a lodge for travellers next to the road, because Mary and Joseph had not found an inn (Lk. 2:7). Let this here be the narrative of her journey, which she made in the company of many virgins and her daughter.

Although debarred by the Church from public teaching and from the priesthood, early Christian women found ways to develop their scholarly skills, to utilize their funds and their talents in monastic development, and to enter the stimulating world of travel that was sanctioned as pilgrimage.

Chapter Five

WOMEN AS MODELS
AND MENTORS

Despite the many restrictions the Church Fathers placed on women, despite their many denigrations of female intellect and character, they also composed laudatory letters and treatises about the important women in their lives. The changed tone of these accounts is startling. Here women are upheld as glorious exemplars of Christian devotion, so outstanding in their faith, their generosity, and their intellectual powers that they deserve to be ranked above most Christian men. From a later viewpoint, we can readily perceive that the authors' passion for rhetorical speech, when coupled with their intense devotion to the women involved, sometimes worked against a sober presentation of their subjects' qualities. Yet the selections that follow give illuminating insights into the lives of women in the upper strata of Roman society in the fourth and fifth centuries. By no means can we take them as representative of women in the lower social classes: concerning the latter, we find little or nothing in the "high" literary texts and must depend on legal documents, grave inscriptions, and other such evidence. Yet our age, with its more democratic interests, should not scorn these accounts for their non-typicality: they are the single strongest evidence that male patristic writers could, and did, overcome their prejudices and see women as worthy bearers of the new religious ideals. Most of these women at some point renounced worldly society for a life of Christian asceticism. John Chrysostom and Augustine leave portraits of their mothers, thus providing us with insight into the problems and lifestyles of Christian matrons and widows.

The first selection is Jerome's eulogy of the Roman widow Marcella, written to her young friend and companion, Principia. Principia had shared Marcella's devotion to Christian chastity, as well as her house. *Epistle 127* was written in 412 A.D., two years after the Goths sacked Rome, the event that apparently brought on Marcella's death. Especially noteworthy is Jerome's reference to the circumstances that led Marcella to her ascetic resolution: the visit to Rome in 340 A.D. of Egyptian religious men, who brought to the western capital perhaps the first accounts of the desert fathers. If Jerome's chronology is accurate, Marcella must have been one of the very first female ascetics in Rome; she died there at a ripe old age, since Jerome never convinced her to come settle in Bethlehem with him and Paula.

2.[1]Bereaved by her father's death, she also lost her husband after seven months of marriage. Cerealis, whose name was illustrious among consuls, eagerly sought her hand because of her age, the antiquity of her family line, her sober behavior, and her remarkable physical beauty—usually very pleasing to men. Since he was an old man, he offered her his wealth and wanted to transfer his gift to her, not as if she were his wife, but as if she were his daughter. When her mother Albina grasped at a chance to have so eminent a guardian for the widow beyond the family circle, Marcella

[1]Text: CSEL 56.146.

replied, "If I wished to marry rather than to dedicate myself to perpetual chastity, I would seek a husband, not an inheritance." And when he confided that it was possible for an old man to live a long time and for a young man to die speedily, she neatly rallied, "Certainly a young man can die soon, but an old man cannot live long"....

4. . . . Marcella fasted in moderation, abstained from eating meat, and knew the smell of wine more than its taste, taking it for the sake of her stomach and for her frequent sicknesses (cf. I Tim. 5:23). She rarely used to go out in public and scrupulously shunned the houses of noble ladies, lest she be forced to see that which she had disdained. She frequently visited the basilicas of the apostles and martyrs for private prayers, and avoided the crowded assemblies of the people. She was so obedient to her mother that she sometimes did what she herself did not wish. When her mother, loving her own blood relation, wanted to transfer all her goods from her children and grandchildren to her brother's children, Marcella preferred the poor instead, but nevertheless could not oppose her mother; she yielded her necklaces and whatever there was of household furnishings to those already rich, wishing to lose her money rather than to sadden her mother's spirit.

5. At that time, none of the noble women in Rome had resolved on the monastic profession, or had dared to do so—for then it was thought a strange and disgraceful business to appropriate the lowly name in public. From some Alexandrian priests, bishop Athanasius, and afterwards Peter, who fled for refuge to Rome to avoid persecution by the Arian heretics, as if it were the safest haven for their communion, Marcella now learned of the life of the blessed Antony, then still living, of the Pachomian monasteries in the Thebaid,[2] and of the discipline for virgins and widows. Nor was she ashamed to make her profession, because she

[2]See pp. 133-134 above.

understood how to please Christ. Many years later she was imitated by Sophronia and other women. . . . The venerable Paula delighted in Marcella's friendship, and it was in her cell that Eustochium, the glory of virgins, was trained; hence it is easy to judge the teacher's caliber where there are pupils such as these.

An unbelieving reader might perhaps laugh at me for laboring so long over the praises of the ladies. He will rather condemn himself for pride than us for foolishness if he will ponder how the holy women who were companions of our Lord and Savior ministered to him from their own substance (Lk. 8:1-3), and how the three Marys stood before the cross (John 19:25) and how especially Mary Magdalene, who received the name "tower" (Magdala) from the zeal and ardor of her faith, was first worthy to see Christ rising, even before the apostles (John 20:11-18). For we judge moral excellences not by people's sex, but by their quality of spirit. . . .

7. When at last the Church's need had drawn me to Rome, along with the holy bishops Paulinus and Epiphanius (of whom the first ruled the church in Syrian Antioch, while the other ruled that in Salamis, on Cyprus), I modestly avoided the eyes of noble women, but she thus pressed on, in the Apostle's words, "in season and out of season" (II Tim. 4:2), so that her diligence conquered my modesty. And because my name was then especially esteemed in the study of the Scriptures, she never came without asking something about Scripture, nor did she immediately accept my explanation as satisfactory, but she proposed questions from the opposite viewpoint, not for the sake of being contentious, but so that by asking, she might learn solutions for points she perceived could be raised in objection. What virtue I found in her, what cleverness, what holiness, what purity, I am afraid to say, lest I exceed what belief finds credible and excite you to greater grief by calling to mind of how great a

good you have been deprived. I will say only this, that whatever in us was gathered by long study and by lengthy meditation was almost changed into nature; this she tasted, this she learned, this she possessed. Thus after my departure, if an argument arose about some evidence from Scripture, the question was pursued with her as the judge. And because she was so discreet and knew about what the philosophers call in Greek "*to prepon*," that is "how to behave appropriately," when she was thus questioned, she used to reply as if what she said was not her own, even if the views were her own, but came either from me or from another man, in order to confess that about the matters she was teaching, she herself had been a pupil. For she knew the saying of the Apostle, "I do not, however, permit a woman to teach" (I Tim. 2:12), lest she seem to inflict an injury on the male sex and on those priests who were inquiring about obscure and doubtful points.

(The Goths have invaded Rome.)

13. Meanwhile, as happens in situations of such great confusion, a bloodstained victor also entered Marcella's house. Let it be right for me to repeat what I heard, rather to report what was seen by holy men who were present; they say that you also were her companion in danger. She is said, when they entered, to have received them with an undaunted look, and when they demanded gold, she by her cheap tunic absolved herself from the assumption that she had buried wealth. Nonetheless, they did not believe her voluntary poverty. They say that she felt no pain when they struck her with clubs or whips, but that she prostrated herself at their feet in tears, begging that you not be separated from her company, that you as a young woman would not have to endure acts that she as an old woman did not have to fear. Christ softened their hard hearts, and familial respect found a place among the bloody swords. And when the barbarians escorted both her and you to the basilica of the

blessed apostle Paul, that they might show you either safety or a sepulchre, she is said to have burst forth in such joy and to have given thanks to God because he had preserved you virginal, because the capture of the city had not made her poor, but had found her so, because lacking daily bread, she was filled by Christ so that she did not feel hunger, because she could say that both in word and in deed, "Naked came I forth from my mother's womb, and naked I shall return. If it seemed best to the Lord, so it was done. Blessed be the name of the Lord" (Job 1:21 Vg.).

14. After several days, she fell asleep in the Lord, sound of mind, whole and vigorous in body. She left you as the heir of her poverty, or rather, the poor through you. Closing her eyes, she was in your arms; breathing her last, it was onto your lips; amid your tears, she smiled, conscious of a good life and future rewards. I have dictated this as the work of one brief night for you, venerable Marcella, and for you, my daughter Principia, seeking to please both God and my readers, not by a love of eloquence, but by a bequest of my most kindly feeling for you.

> Jerome's closest female friend, Paula, spent the end of her life in Palestine with Jerome. It was largely her wealth that had made possible the construction of monasteries for men and women in Bethlehem, described in Chapter Three. Jerome was completely crushed by her death in 404 A.D., and wrote the following memorial of Paula (*Epistle 108*) to her daughter Eustochium. Eustochium as an adolescent had come with her mother to Bethlehem and now took over the management of the women's monastery.[3]

3.[4] ... Others may trace her descent from the past, even from her swaddling clothes, from her very rattles, if I may

---

[3]For more on Paula's scholarly interest and her pilgrimage through the Holy Land and Egypt, see pp. 163-64, 197-203 above.
[4]Text: CSEL 55.308.

put it thus. They may mention her mother, Blesilla, and her father, Rogatus—of these, the first was an offspring of the Scipios and the Gracchi, while the second derived from a line rich and noble throughout all Greece until this day (he was said to have had the blood of Agamemnon, who destroyed Troy in a ten-year siege). We will praise nothing except what is her own, what is brought forth from the most pure fount of her holy mind. . . .

4. Thus derived from such a family, she was joined to Toxotius as her husband, who bore the high-born blood of Aeneas and the Julii, whence indeed the virgin of Christ, his daughter Eustochium, is named Julia, and he is "Julius, a name from great Julius descended."[5] I mention these things because they are wonderful in those who scorn them. Worldly men respect those who are strong in prerogatives. *We* praise those who for the sake of the Savior despise these things; astonishing in its way, we lightly esteem those who have them and we commend those who do not long to have them. She, I say, by her excellent birth, fecundity, and modesty was deemed excellent by her husband first of all, then by her relatives, and by the testimony of the entire city. She bore five children: Blesilla, on whose death I consoled her at Rome; Paulina, who left her holy and admirable husband Pammachius as heir to both her profession and her possessions (I produced a little book about her death for him); Eustochium, who now is at the Holy Places, a very precious necklace of virginity and of the Church; Rufina, whose premature burial spread confusion through her mother's reverent mind; and Toxotius, after whom she ceased to bear children. You can thus understand that for a long time she no longer wanted to observe the duty of a wife, but discharged it because of her husband's wish to have male children.

[5]Virgil, *Aeneid* I, 288.

(Upon her husband's death, Paula devoted herself to acts of charity, but began to think of more serious ascetic renunciations.)

6. ...Not mindful of home, of children, of servants, of possessions, of anything that pertains to the world, she was eager to proceed alone (if it is possible to say that) and without a retinue to the desert of the Antonys and the Pauls.[6] At last, when winter was gone and the sea open, when the bishops[7] were returning to their churches, she sailed with them by prayer and by her wish. Why do I delay further? She went down to the port accompanied by her brother, relatives, in-laws, and what is more important, her children. Now the sails were stretched and the ship was drawn into the deep by the rowing of the crewmen. Little Toxotius on the shore was extending supplicating hands; Rufina, now a young woman, implored her mother with silent tears that she wait until her marriage. Nonetheless, Paula raised dry eyes to Heaven, overcoming her devotion to her children by her devotion to God. She did not know herself as a mother that she might prove herself worthy as a handmaid of God. Her inward parts were churning; she was battling with grief as if she were being torn apart limb from limb, and in this seemed more admirable to all, because she conquered great love. Among the harsh fates of captivity, of being in the hands of enemies, none is more cruel than parents being separated from their children. She endured this with full confidence, though it is against the law of nature; yes, she sought it with a rejoicing spirit, and making little of the love of her children by her greater love for God, she took comfort in Eustochium alone, who was her companion both in her purpose and of her journey. Meanwhile, the ship was cutting through the sea and all who were being

---

[6]Jerome wrote a life of the hermit Paul, who he claimed was the first of the desert fathers.
[7]Bishops who had visited Paula in Rome.

conveyed with her looked back at the shore; she was averting her eyes lest she see what she could not view without torment. I confess that no woman loved her children like this; before she departed, she disinherited herself of earthly things and bestowed all on them, so she might find an inheritance in Heaven.

(When Paula died at the age of 56 in 404 A.D., Jerome composed a poem for her tombstone:)

33. Farewell, Paula, and with your prayers assist the ripe old age of your friend. Your faith and works unite you with Christ, in whose presence you will more easily receive what you ask. "I have raised a monument more lasting than bronze"[8] which no longer passage of time can destroy. I cut an epitaph on your sepulchre, which I append to this work, so that wherever my letter may go, the reader may know that you were buried in Bethlehem, and lauded there.

The inscription on the tomb:

Scipio begot her, she who was of Pauline stock
A shoot of the Gracchi, famed offspring of Agamemnon,
She whose parents called her Paula
Lies here in this tomb.
Her daughter Eustochium,
First of Roman senatorial rank,
Received as an inheritance
The poverty of Christ and the boorishness of Bethlehem.

And on the doors of the cave:

Do you see a narrow tomb cut in the rock?
It is the resting place of Paula,
Who possesses the heavenly realms.
Leaving brother, kin, Roman homeland, riches,
And offspring, she lies buried in a Bethlehem cave.

[8]Horace, *Odes* III, 30, 1.

Here was your manger, Christ,
And here, the kings bearing mystic gifts
To a mortal man, surrendered them to God as well.[9]

> Years before Paula and Jerome arrived in Palestine,
> Melania the Elder had renounced the aristocratic life in
> Rome and journeyed to Palestine where she founded
> monasteries for men and women in Jerusalem. The fol-
> lowing two selections illuminate the life and times of this
> learned[10] and determined woman. The first is from Palla-
> dius' *Lausiac History*.

46.[11] The thrice-blessed Melania was of Spanish origin
and later was a Roman. She was a daughter of Marcellinus,
one of the consuls, and wife of a certain high-ranking man (I
am not remembering well which one). When she was
widowed at twenty-two, she was deemed worthy of divine
love. She told no one her plan, because she would have been
prohibited at the time, since Valens held rule in the empire.[12]
She arranged to name a guardian for her son, and taking all
her movable property, she had it loaded on a ship and sailed
off at full speed to Alexandria, along with illustrious women
and children. There, having sold her things and turned
possessions into money, she departed for the mountain of
Nitria and met with the Fathers, with Pambo, Arisisus,
Serapion the Great, Paphnutius of Scete, Isidore the Confessor, and Dioscorus, bishop of Hermopolis. And she spent
up to half a year with them, going around the desert and
seeking out all the holy men.

Later the Augustan prefect banished Isidore, Pisimius,
Adelphius, Paphnutius, and Pambo, among whom also was

[9]Mt. 2:11.
[10]See pp. 164-65 above.
[11]Text: *The Lausiac History of Palladius*, ed. C. Butler (Cambridge, 1898; repr.
Hildesheim, 1967), 134.
[12]Emperor of the east from 364-378 A.D. and a sympathizer with Arian heretics.

Ammonius Parotes, and twelve bishops and priests, to
Palestine, around Diocaesarea. She followed them and ministered to them from her private wealth. Since servants were
prohibited, so it was reported (for I happened to meet the
holy Pisimius, Isidore, Paphnutius, and Ammonius), she
donned a slave's hood and in the evenings used to bring
them the things they needed. When the consul of Palestine
learned about this, he wished to fill his own pocket and
thought he would blacken her reputation.[13] He seized her
and threw her into prison, unaware that she was a free
woman. But she disclosed her identity to him in this way: "I
am the daughter of thus-and-such a person, and so-and-so's
wife—but I am the slave of Christ. Do not despise my vile
appearance, for I can exalt myself if I so choose. You do not
have the means to blacken me in this matter nor to take
anything from me. I have thus made this clear to you lest
you unknowingly become liable to charges." It is necessary
in dealing with insensitive people to use conceit like a hawk!
The judge then comprehended the situation; he apologized,
revered her, and ordered that she might meet with the holy
men unhindered.

After their recall, she built a monastery in Jerusalem and
stayed there for twenty-seven years, having a group of fifty
virgins. Near Melania lived the most noble, sturdy Rufinus,
of similar habits to hers. He was from the city of Aquileia in
Italy and later he was judged worthy of the priesthood.
Among men there was not to be found a more reasonable
and capable person. During the twenty-seven years, both of
them received those who turned up in Jerusalem for the sake
of a vow, bishops, monks, and virgins; at their own expense,
they edified all those who passed through. They united the
four hundred monks involved in the schism over Paulinus,[14]
and having convinced every heretic who fought against the

[13]A pun: "blackness" in Greek is *melania.*
[14]A schism that tore apart the church at Antioch from the 360s until the 380s.

divinity of the Holy Spirit, they led them back to the Church. They bestowed honors on the clergy of the area with gifts and food, and thus completed their lives without offending anyone.

54. I have reported above in a superficial way about the marvellous and holy Melania. Not less important, I shall now finish weaving into the story the remaining items. She lavished so much wealth in her godly zeal, as if she were ablaze with fire, that the residents of Persia, not I, should do the reporting. No one in either the east or the west, the north or the south, failed to benefit from her good works.

For twenty-seven years she offered hospitality; at her own expense, she assisted churches, monasteries, guests, and prisons. Her family, her son, and her own trustees supplied her with money. She persevered in her hospitality to such an extent that she did not keep a span of earth, nor pulled by longing for her son, did she separate herself from love of Christ. But through her prayers, the young man pressed on to a height of education and character, married, as was expected by worldly judgments, and became honored. He also had two children. Then after a long time, she heard about the situation of her granddaughter,[15] that she had married and had decided to renounce the world. Fearing lest they be destroyed by evil teaching or by heresy or by evil living, she, although an old woman of sixty years, embarked on a boat and departed from Caesarea, arriving at Rome after twenty days.

There she met a very blessed and noteworthy man, Apronianus, a Greek; she taught him and made him a Christian, persuading him to practice sexual continence with his own wife, named Abita, who was Melania's niece. She strengthened her granddaughter Melania along with the latter's husband, Pinian, and taught her daughter-in-law, Albina,

---

[15]Melania the Younger.

her son's wife. She got them ready to sell publicly all their possessions, led them out of Rome, and steered them to the harbor of a decent and calm life. Thus in reference to all these things, she was fighting the beasts—the senators and their wives, who would have prevented her from renouncing the remaining houses. But she said to them, "It was written four hundred years ago, 'Little children, it is the last hour' (I John 2:18). Why do you love the vain things of life, lest the days of the Antichrist overtake you and you not enjoy your wealth and your forefathers' property?"

And when she had freed all these relatives, she led them to a monastic life. She also taught the younger son of Publicola and led him to Sicily. She sold everything of hers that remained and went to Jerusalem, taking the proceeds. She distributed her money within forty days and fell asleep at a good old age, in the most profound gentleness, leaving also a monastery in Jerusalem and the funds for its upkeep.

And when all of them were far away from Rome, a barbarian hurricane of a kind that had long ago been predicted in prophecy fell on Rome.[16] Not even the bronze statues in the Forum were left intact, but everything was delivered up to destruction by the barbarian madness. Thus Rome, beautifully decorated for twelve hundred years, became a ruin. Then those whom Melania had instructed and those who had opposed her instruction praised God, who persuaded the unbelievers through the revolutionary events, because when all the others were taken captive, only those houses were saved that had become a burnt offering for the Lord through Melania's zeal.

> Another partisan of Melania the Elder, and perhaps her cousin, was Paulinus of Nola. In *Epistle 29* to Sulpicius Severus, Paulinus takes the occasion of Melania's return from Palestine to Italy in about 400 A.D. and her visit to Nola to discourse on her life and character.

[16]The Goths' capture of Rome, 410 A.D.

6.[17] Moreover, the Lord conferred this additional grace by reason of your gifts and letters: our brother Victor presented himself during these very special days in which we welcomed that holy lady from Jerusalem after her twenty-five year sojourn there. What a woman she is, if it is permissible to call such a manly Christian a woman! What shall I do in this situation? Fear of being unbearably sickening keeps me from adding to the volumes already written about her, but the greatness of her person, or rather, of God's grace, seems to require that I do not in haste omit a passing mention of so great a soul. I shall briefly report to you about her. Just as those who are sailing, should they glimpse some noteworthy spot on the shore, do not pass on by, but for a short while pull in the sails or suspend the oars, so that by delaying they can gaze and so delight their eyes, thus shall I redirect the course of my disquisition. In this I may yet be seen to pay you back some recompense for your book, brilliant in content and in eloquence, if I will honor this woman, a member of the weaker sex, with the virtues of Martin, for she is a soldier of Christ:[18] a noblewoman, she gave herself a greater nobility than her consular grandfathers by her disdain for physical nobility.

7. ...A woman of more elevated rank, she loftily cast herself down to a humble way of life, so that as a strong member of the weak sex she might censure indolent men, so that as a rich person appropriating poverty, and as a noble person adopting humility, she might confound people of both sexes.

8. Thus because Marcellinus the consul was her grandfather, because her family strove for honor and had magnificent wealth, she was married when she was still young. Shortly she became a mother, but she did not possess that mortal happiness for long, lest she for long would prize

---

[17]Text: CSEL 29.251.
[18]Paulinus was writing to Sulpicius Severus, author of a *Life of St. Martin of Tours.* Paulinus told Sulpicius how much Melania had enjoyed the *Life.*

218 Women as Models and Mentors

earthly things. Besides the other bereavements that she bewailed in the company of her husband when her suffering was rendered useless by premature births, her troubles only increased: within a year's time she lost two sons and a husband. Only an infant son was left as a remembrance of, not a compensation for, her loved ones.... Thus as an attendant to these funerals in sorrowful procession, at once widowed and deprived of her children, she came to Rome with her one son who was an incitement to, rather than a solace for, her tears. As a baby, he either sensed these woes before he had any experience of his own, and already knew to lament the death of another when he was as yet unable to comprehend his own life; or, cruelly unaware and cheerful in his childhood, he laughed in his pitiable play amidst his mother's moans.

9. Taught by these proofs not to be bound by the perishable world and to place great hope in God, whom alone we cannot unwillingly lose, she clothed herself and her son with salutary knowledge, so that she loved her little boy by paying him no heed and kept him by leaving him behind; she would have him, absent, whom she had entrusted to the Lord, more than she could have possessed him in person, more than if she had consigned herself to him....

10. She had many contests against the hateful dragon[19] in the first rounds of her warfare, for the envy of the spiteful enemy did not allow her to make an easy and peaceful departure. By exerting heavy pressure on her noble kinsfolk, arming them to detain her, he tried to obstruct her plan and thwart her leaving. But then she was strengthened beyond the force of the attacks; while everybody wept, she cheerfully unfettered the chains of human familial regard along with the chains of the ship. She resolutely contested with the waves of the sea; off she sailed, that she might conquer the great waves of the world. And as soon as by a

[19]Satan.

spiritual gift she chose to exchange the worldly life for the city of Jerusalem, where she might be a pilgrim from her body, she brought it to pass that she was an exile from her fellow-citizens and a citizen among the saints. She wanted to serve with prudence and holiness in that place in which she did serve, so that she could reign in the realm in which there is freedom.

> (Paulinus describes some of her activities in Palestine, covering the same events as Palladius. Paulinus then reports her return to Italy, where she was greeted by her son Publicola and her granddaughter, Melania the Younger, among others.)

12. I shall now skip over the rest of her affairs and her times; I shall cross the sea on which she, returning, sailed, thus emulating her own journey, that I may limit my discourse more quickly by relating her arrival here, in which I witnessed the great grace of God. She was brought to the city of Naples, a short distance from Nola, where we live. At Naples she was met and welcomed by her children and grandchildren, then soon hurried on to Nola, to our humble hospitality, and came to us surrounded by an honored escort of her extremely wealthy children. I saw there the glory of the Lord in that journey of mother and children, although they were very dissimilar in attire. She was seated on an emaciated little horse, worth less than a donkey, and they accompanied her with all the pomp of this world, all the pomp with which honored and rich senators can be surrounded. The Appian Way both groaned and glittered with swaying wagons, decorated horses, golden chariots for the ladies, and many two-wheeled carriages—but the grace of Christian humility outshone such empty magnificence. We saw a confusion in this world worthy of God, purple silk and gilded apparatus in the service of old black rags. We blessed the Lord who "makes the humble lofty and wise"(cf. I Sam.

2:7) and "fills them with good things and sends the rich away empty" (Lk. 1:53).

13. Indeed, we have a cottage, raised above the ground, that stretches quite a way from the dining hall. It has a covered walkway positioned between it and the guest rooms. It was as if this cottage were enlarged by God in his grace, for it furnished a narrow but not unmanageable space, not only for the many holy women with Melania, but also for the crowds of rich people. The roofs of the nearby buildings of our patron Felix[20] were reverberating from the choruses of boys and virgins in the cottage. . . . Now know that there is such power of God in that member of the weak sex, that woman who finds restoration in fasting, repose in prayer, bread in the Word, clothing in rags. Her hard couch (it is a cloak and a patchwork quilt on the ground) is made soft by her scholarly work, because her delight in reading mitigates the insult of the inflexible bed, and it is rest to her holy soul to keep vigil in the Lord. . . .

> The behavior of women like Paula and Melania the Elder was considered scandalous by other members of their social class, even by Christians, as Jerome reveals in *Epistle 45.*[21]

4. O envy, from the beginning so given to biting you! O craftiness of Satan that forever hunts down holy things! No other women in the city of Rome afforded gossip except Paula and Melania who, despising their wealth and deserting their love-pledges, (i.e., their children), raised the Lord's cross, one might say, as a standard of the faith. Had they hastened to Baiae,[22] had they selected perfumes, had they used their riches and widowhood as incitements to luxurious living and freedom, they would have been called proper

---

[20]Paulinus was patron of a shrine to St. Felix at Nola.
[21]Text: CSEL 54.325.
[22]A fashionable resort on the Bay of Naples.

ladies, holy women. Now they are willing to appear beautiful in sackcloth and ashes, and with fasting and lice to sink to the fires of Hell! As if they were not permitted to perish with the mob, while the masses applaud! If it were Gentiles or Jews who slandered this way of life, they would have the comfort of not pleasing those with whom Christ was displeased. Now, in truth—for shame!—it is those with the name of Christian who let slip the care of their own households, who, neglecting the beam in their own eye, seek a straw in their neighbor's (Mt. 7:3 = Lk. 6:41). They rip to shreds a holy profession and fancy that they have a remedy for their own punishment if no one can be thought holy, if they can slander everyone, if they can show that the masses perish and that sinners are a multitude.

> Melania the Elder had a granddaughter and namesake who became nearly as famous an ascetic as she. Among the wealthier woman in early fifth-century Rome, Melania the Younger and her husband Pinian (with whom she took a vow of chastity after the deaths of their children) fled Rome as the invading Goths pressed close, and after a North African sojourn, settled in Jerusalem. She later built monasteries for men and women on the Mount of Olives, as her grandmother had done before her. Palladius in the *Lausiac History* reports some details of her life.

61.[23] Since above I promised that I would relate to you things about the daughter of Melania the Elder, I am paying my debt, as is necessary. For it would be wrong for us to overlook her physical youth and cast down such virtue uncommemorated, when she actually surpassed by far even zealous old women. Her parents forced her to be married to one of the leading Romans. Since she was constantly

[23]Text: *The Lausiac History of Palladius*, ed. C. Butler (Cambridge, 1898; repr. Hildesheim, 1967), 155.

pricked by tales of her grandmother, she was goaded to the point where she would not cooperate in the marriage. When two children were born to her but both died, she pushed on to such a hatred of marriage that she said to her husband, "If you choose to practice asceticism with me according to the teaching of chastity, I will recognize you as the ruler and lord of my life. But if this appears too difficult for you, since you are a young man, you may take all my possessions, but leave my body free so that I may fulfill my yearning for God and inherit the zeal of my grandmother, as I also have her name. For if God willed us to bear children, he would not have taken my children at an untimely hour."

Thus for quite a while they fought against the yoke, but God at last had mercy on the young man and laid on him also an ardor for renunciation, so for them was fulfilled what is written, "How do you know, wife, if you will save your husband?" (I Cor. 7:16). She had thus been married at thirteen years of age and had lived with her husband for seven years; at twenty she made her renunciation. First she gave her silk dresses at the altars; this the holy Olympias had also done. Entrusting her silver and gold to a certain priest, a Dalmatian monk named Paul, she sent eastward across the sea ten thousand pieces of money to Egypt and the Thebaid, ten thousand to Antioch and the area around it, fifteen thousand to Palestine, ten thousand to the churches in the islands and the areas beyond, and in like manner she defrayed the costs of the western churches by herself.

All these things and four times more did she snatch "from the mouth of the lion" (Amos 3:12), I mean Alaric,[24] because of her own faith. She freed eight thousand of her slaves who wished to be freed. As for the rest who did not wish their freedom but who chose to serve her brother, she let him take all of them for three pieces of money. She sold publicly her property in Spain, Aquitania, Taraconia, and Gaul, leaving

[24]Chief of the Goths who sacked Rome in 410 A.D.

for herself only that in Sicily, Campania, and Africa; she held it to provide for monasteries. This was her wisdom about the burden of wealth.

And this was her ascetic practice: she ate every other day—and in the beginning, she ate only once in five days or more; she also arranged to work during the day with her slaves who had become ascetics along with her. She had with her Albina, her mother, who similarly lived an ascetic life, and who in turn privately scattered her own wealth abroad. Thus they dwell in the country, sometimes in Sicily, at other times in Campania, with fifteen eunuchs and sixty virgins, both free women and slaves. And similarly her husband Pinian lives with thirty monks, reading, tending a garden, and participating in holy events. They greatly honored us when several of us came to Rome on behalf of the blessed John the bishop. They refreshed us both by entertaining us as strangers and by providing abundant travel supplies, with much joy reaping the fruit of eternal life by their God-given works of the finest mode of life.

> Melania the Elder was also an inspiration to Olympias, a wealthy young widow of Constantinople who became the close friend of John Chrysostom. Olympias used some of her fortune to build a monastery for women in Constantinople, which she oversaw. She was also ordained as a deaconess. Palladius in the *Lausiac History* gives a brief account of Olympias.

56.[25] The most holy and admirable Olympias came to follow Melania the Elder's resolution in her reverence and in her footsteps. She was the daughter of Seleucus, one of the ex-counts, the granddaughter of Ablabius, an ex-prefect, and bride for a few days of Nebridius, an ex-prefect of the city, yet she was the wife of no one—for they say she died a

---

[25]Text: *The Lausiac History of Palladius*, ed. C. Butler (Cambridge, 1898; repr. Hildesheim, 1967), 149.

virgin, though partner of the Word of truth. Distributing all her possessions, she gave them to the poor. She contended eagerly in no minor contests for the sake of the truth, taught many women, held solemn conversations with priests, honored the bishops, and was deemed worthy to be a confessor on behalf of truth, for those who reside in Constantinople judge her life to be among those of the confessors.[26] When she had thus completed her life, she journeyed on her way to the Lord amidst her contests for God.

> A longer version of Olympias' life and times is found in an anonymous fifth-century document, apparently composed by someone who knew her. From Olympias' *Life* we learn more about this woman who was Chrysostom's confidante, to whom he poured out his heart in seventeen letters he wrote from his exile. The following selection is from the *Life of Olympias, Deaconess.*

2.[27] She was daughter according to the flesh of Seleucus, one of the imperial officers, but according to the spirit, she was the true child of God. It is said that she was descended from Ablabius, who was governor, and she was bride for a few days of Nebridius, the prefect of the city of Constantinople, but in truth she did not grace the bed of anyone. For it is said that she died an undefiled virgin, having become a partner of the divine Word, a consort of every true humility, a companion and servant of the holy, catholic and apostolic Church of God. Left an orphan, she was joined in marriage to a husband, but by the goodness of God she was preserved uncorrupted in flesh and in spirit. For God, who watches over everything, who foresees the outcome of humans, did not deem it worthy for the one who was briefly her husband to live with her for a year. The debt of nature was shortly demanded of him, and she was preserved a blameless virgin until the end.

[26]Those willing to give themselves as martyrs at the time of the persecutions.
[27]Text: SC 13bis. 408.

3. Again she could have used the apostolic rule which says, "I wish young widows to marry, run a household" (I Tim. 5:14), but she did not agree to this, although she had birth, wealth, a very expensive education, a naturally good disposition, and was adorned with the bloom of youth; like a gazelle, she leaped over the insufferable snare of a second marriage. "For the law was not laid down for the righteous man, but for the unruly, the impure, and the insatiable" (I Tim. 1:9). Through a certain demonic jealousy, it transpired that her untimely widowhood became the subject of mischief. She was falsely accused before the emperor Theodosius of having dispensed her goods in a disorderly fashion. Since indeed she was his relation, he took pains to unite her in marriage with a certain Elpidius, a Spaniard, one of his own relatives. He directed many persistent entreaties to her and when he failed to achieve his goal, he was annoyed. The pious Olympias, however, explained her position to the emperor Theodosius: "If my King, the Lord Jesus Christ, wanted me to be joined with a man, he would not have taken away my first husband immediately. Since he knew that I was unsuited for the conjugal life and was not able to please a man, he freed him, Nebridius, from the bond and delivered me of this very burdensome yoke and servitude to a husband, having placed upon my mind the happy yoke of continence."

4. She clarified these things to the emperor Theodosius in this manner, before the plot against the most holy John, patriarch of Constantinople. The emperor, when he had heard the testimony against the pious Olympias, commanded the man then prefect of the city, Clementinus, to keep her possessions under guard until she reached her thirtieth year, that is, her physical prime. And the prefect, having received the guardianship from the emperor, oppressed her to such a degree at Elpidius' urging (she did not have the right either to meet with notable bishops or to come near the church) so that groaning under the strain, she

would meekly bear the option of marriage. But she, even more grateful to God, responded to these events by proclaiming, "You have shown toward my humble person, O sovereign master, a goodness befitting a king and suited to a bishop, when you commanded my very heavy burden to be put under careful guard, for the administration of it caused me anxiety. But you will do even better if you order that it be distributed to the poor and to the churches, for I prayed much to avoid the vainglory arising from the apportionment, lest I neglect true riches for those pertaining to material things."

5. The emperor, upon his return from the battle against Maximus,[28] gave the order that she could exercise control over her own possessions, since he had heard of the intensity of her ascetic discipline. But she distributed all of her unlimited and immense wealth and assisted everyone, simply and without distinction. For the sake of many she surpassed that Samaritan of whom an account is given in the holy Gospels (Lk. 10:29-37). Once upon a time, he found on the road down to Jericho a man who was crushed half-dead by robbers; he raised him onto his own beast, carried him as far as the inn, and having mixed the oil of generosity with strong wine, he healed his wounds.

Then straightway after the distribution and sealing up of all her goods, there was rekindled in her the divine love, and she took refuge in the haven of salvation, the great, catholic, and apostolic church of this royal city. She followed to the letter with intelligence the divinely-inspired teachings of the most holy archbishop of this sacred church, John, and gave to him for his holy church (imitating also in this act those ardent lovers and disciples of Christ who in the beginning of salvation's proclamation brought to the feet of the apostles their possessions [Acts 4:32-5:11]), ten thousand pounds of

---

[28]Theodosius put down the revolt of Maximus in 388, but did not return to Constantinople until 391.

gold, twenty thousand of silver and all of her real estate situated in the provinces of Thrace, Galatia, Cappadocia Prima, and Bithynia; and more, the houses belonging to her in the capital city, the one situated near the most holy cathedral, which is called "the house of Olympias"; together with the house of the tribune, complete with baths, and all the buildings near it; a mill; and a house that belonged to her in which she lived near the public baths of Constantinople; and another house of hers which was called the "house of Evander"; as well as all of her suburban properties.

6. Then by the divine will she was ordained deaconess of this holy cathedral of God and she built a monastery at an angle south of it. All the houses lying near the holy church and all the shops which were at the southern angle mentioned belonged to her. She constructed a path from the monastery up to the narthex of the holy church, and in the first quarter she enclosed her own chambermaids, numbering fifty, all of whom lived in purity and virginity. Next, Elisanthia, her relative who had seen the good work pleasing to God, that God gave to her to carry out, also herself a virgin, emulating the divine zeal, bade farewell to the ephemeral and empty things of life with her sisters Martyria and Palladia, also virgins. Then the three entered with all the others, having made over in advance all of their possessions to the same holy monastery. Likewise also Olympia, the niece of the aforesaid holy Olympias, with many other women of senatorial families, chose the Kingdom of Heaven and disdained these lowly things below which drag us down, in accordance with the grace and good favor of God who wishes all to be saved and who fosters the divine love in them. They entered also with the rest, so that all those who gathered together according to the grace of God in that holy fold of Christ numbered two hundred and fifty, all adorned with the crown of virginity and practicing the most exalted life which befits the saints.

7. When these events had transpired in this manner by divine assistance, the noble servant of God, Olympias, again brought to the above-mentioned hallowed church through the most holy patriarch John the entire remainder of all her real estate, situated in all the provinces, and her interest in the public bread supply. And he also ordained as deaconesses of the holy church and her three relatives, Elisanthia, Martyria, and Palladia, so that the four deaconesses would be able to be together without interruption in the most sacred monastery founded by her.

8. One was struck with amazement at seeing certain things in the holy chorus and angelic institution of these holy women: their incessant continence and sleeplessness, the constancy of their praise and thanksgiving to God, their "charity which is the bond of perfection" (Col 3:14), their stillness. For no one from the outside, neither man nor woman, was permitted to come upon them, the only exception being the most holy patriarch John, who visited continuously and sustained them with his most wise teachings. Thus fortified each day by his divinely-inspired instruction, they kindled in themselves the divine love so that their great and holy love streamed forth to him. The pious and blessed Olympias (who in these matters too imitated the women disciples of Christ who served him from their possessions [Lk. 8:1-3]) prepared for the holy John his daily provisions and sent them to the bishop, for there was not much separation between the episcopal residence and the monastery, only a wall. And she did this not only before the plots against him, but also after he was banished; up to the end of his life, she provided for all his expenses as well as for those who were with him in his exile.

13. Let these things be said. I have deemed it necessary and entirely useful for the profit of many to run over in the narrative one by one the holy virtues of the noble servant of God, Olympias, who is among the saints. For no place, no

country, no desert, no island, no distant setting, remained without a share in the benevolence of this famous woman; rather, she furnished the churches with liturgical offerings and helped the monasteries and convents, the beggars, the prisoners, and those in exile; quite simply, she distributed her alms over the entire inhabited world. And the blessed Olympias herself burst the supreme limit in her almsgiving and her humility, so that nothing can be found greater than what she did. She had a life without vanity, an appearance without pretence, character without affectation, a face without adornment; she kept watch without sleeping, she had an immaterial body, a mind without vainglory, intelligence without conceit, an untroubled heart, an artless spirit, charity without limits, unbounded generosity, contemptible clothing, immeasurable self-control, rectitude of thought, undying hope in God, ineffable almsgiving; she was the ornament of all the humble and was in addition worthily honored by the most holy patriarch John. For she abstained from eating meat and for the most part she went without bathing. And if a need for a bath arose through sickness (for she suffered constantly in her stomach), she came down to the waters with her shift on, out of modesty even for herself, so they said.

14. And she looked after the needs of many fathers, as I have said, and of those of the most blessed John the archbishop, proving herself worthy of his virtue. For when he had been plotted against and exiled, as has already been explained, the pious woman provided without distraction for his need and for those with him. This is no small thing for the workers of Christ who are anxious both night and day for Christ's affairs. As Paul greeted Persis, Tryphaena, and Tryphosa (Rom. 16:12), the pious Olympias, imitator of God, perhaps received the same greeting.

And I know that this completely virtuous and divinely-inspired Olympias provided also for the blessed Nectarius,

the archbishop of Constantinople, who was completely persuaded by her even in the affairs of the church, and for
Amphilochius, bishop of Iconium, and Optimus, and Peter,
and Gregory, the brother of the holy Basil, and Epiphanius
the archbishop of Constantia in Cyprus, and many others of
the saints and inspired fathers who lived in the capital city.
Why is it necessary to say that she also bestowed upon them
property in the country and money? And when the aforesaid
Optimus died in Constantinople at this time, she shut the
eyes of the great man with her own hands. In addition, she
relieved the piteous without measure in all ways. She sustained Antiochus of Ptolemais, and Acacius, the bishop of
Beroea, and the holy Severian, the bishop of Gabala, and in
a word, all the priests residing there, in addition to innumerable ascetics and virgins.

15. And due to her sympathy for them, she endured many
trials by the actions of a willfully evil and vulgar person;
contending eagerly in not a few contests on behalf of the
truth of God, she lived faultlessly in unmeasured tears night
and day, "submitting to every human being for the sake of
the Lord" (I Pet. 2:13), full of every reverence, bowing
before the saints, venerating the bishops, honoring the
presbyters, respecting the priests, welcoming the ascetics,
being anxious for the virgins, supplying the widows, raising
the orphans, shielding the elderly, looking after the weak,
having compassion on sinners, guiding the lost, having pity
on all, pity without stinting anything on the poor. Engaging
in much catechizing of unbelieving women and making
provision for all the necessary things of life, she left a
reputation for goodness throughout her whole life, which is
ever to be remembered. Having called from slavery to freedom her myriad household servants, she proclaimed them
to be of the same honor as her own nobility. Or rather, if it is
necessary to speak truthfully, they appeared more noble in
their way of dress than that holy woman. For there could be

found nothing cheaper than her clothing; the most ragged items were coverings unworthy of her manly courage. And she cultivated in herself a gentleness so that she surpassed even the simplicity of children themselves. Never any blame, not even from her neighbors, was incurred by that image of Christ, but her whole intolerable life was spent in penitence and in a great flood of tears. One was more likely to see the fount run dry in the trenches than her eyes, lowered, always gazing on Christ, leave off crying for awhile. Why go on? For to whatever extent I might provide leisure for my mind to recount the contests and virtues of this ardent soul, one will find many and poor the descriptions of the deeds. And does anyone not believe that I speak with restraint concerning the steadfast Olympias, who besides was an entirely precious vessel of the Holy Spirit? There was an eyewitness who also viewed the life of this blessed woman, her angelic regime; since he was her true spiritual friend and related to her family, much was distributed by him in accordance with her intent.

The exaltation of young women who opted for the ascetic life was a special passion with Jerome. He even wrote to girls he had never met, congratulating them on their decision for ascetic renunciation. One such letter, *Epistle 130,* Jerome wrote to a young adolescent, Demetrias, who with her family had fled to North Africa at the time of the Gothic invasion of Rome in 410 A.D. Four years later, Jerome pictures her summoning up courage (and appealing to the example of Agnes)[29] to refuse an impending marriage. That Demetrias was the great-great-granddaughter of Faltonia Betitia Proba, who composed the Virgilian *Cento* discussed in Chapter Four, is another example of the familial links among notable female Christians of this era.

[29]See pp. 106-14 above.

5.[30] ... When her wedding day was already close and a bridal chamber was being prepared for the upcoming marriage, people say that she, in secret and without witnesses, having only the night for a solace, armed herself with such sentiments as these: "What is to become of you, Demetrias? Why do you tremble so to defend your chastity? This situation demands candor and courage! If in a time of peace you are so afraid, what would you do if you were suffering martyrdom? If you cannot endure a scowl from your family, how could you bear the persecutors' tribunals? If the examples of men do not challenge you, be encouraged and take confidence from the blessed martyr Agnes[31] who overcame both youth and tyranny, who by her martyrdom won the victor's crown for the name of chastity. You do not know, wretched girl, you simply do not know, to whom you owe your virginity!

"A short while ago you trembled at the hands of barbarians; you have sought protection in the bosoms and mantles of your mother and grandmother; you have seen yourself a captive and your chastity not in your own power; you have shuddered at the enemies' savage look; you have viewed the rape of God's virgins with secret pain. Your city, once the capital of the world, is the tomb of the Roman people, and you are an exile on the Libyan shore: will you accept an exiled man as a husband? What matron of honor will attend you? What retinue will lead you to the bridegroom's house? A harsh Punic tongue[32] will sing the shameless Fescennine songs[33] to you. Stop procrastinating! 'Perfect love casts out fear' (I John 4:18). Take to yourself the shield of faith, the breastplate of righteousness, the helmet of salvation (cf. Eph. 6:16, 14, 17): march forth to battle. The preservation of your virginity carries a martyrdom of its own. Why do you

---

[30]Text: CSEL 56.179.
[31]See pp. 106-14 above.
[32]Punic was a native language of North Africa.
[33]Coarse songs of ridicule sung at weddings.

fear your grandmother? Why are you frightened of your mother? Perhaps they themselves wish something that they do not believe you wish."

When she had worked herself up by such goads, she cast off all her bodily adornment and her worldly garments as impediments to her profession of virginity. She returned her precious necklaces, expensive pearls, and glowing gems to their cases. She donned a cheap tunic, covered herself with an even cheaper cloak, and at an unexpected moment, suddenly threw herself down at her grandmother's knees with many tears and lamentations, showing who she really was. That holy and dignified woman was dumbfounded to see such strange garments on her granddaughter; her mother stood stunned by joy. Both women did not believe that what they had wanted to be true, was indeed true. Their voices stuck in their throats. They were moved to diverse emotions; between blushing and blanching, they felt apprehension and joy.

6. At this point I must surrender, I must not attempt to report that which I diminish by expressing. The stream of Cicero's genius would dry up and the opinions Demosthenes brandished and hurled would prove too slow and dull if faced with expressing the greatness of that unbelievable joy. Whatever the mind can think yet speech cannot explain, we heard was done at that time. Eagerly they rushed to kiss their granddaughter and daughter. Weeping copious tears of joy, they raised the prostrate girl by the hand and embraced her trembling form. In her profession they recognized their decision and rejoiced that a virgin had made a noble family yet more noble by her virginity. She had discovered how to make her family distinguished, how to assuage the ruins of the city of Rome. Good Jesus, what rejoicing was there throughout the entire household! At once many virgins shot up as from a fertile root, and the example of their patron and mistress was followed by a mob

of clients and domestic servants. The profession of virginity glowed throughout all households; if those who professed were inferior to Demetrias in worldly circumstance, their reward was one with hers, chastity.

I speak inadequately. All the churches throughout Africa rejoiced, so to speak, with exultation. The rumor, much-repeated, reached not only the cities, the towns, the villages, but even the nomads' hovels. All the islands between Africa and Italy were full of this report and the joy ran further with unrestrained foot. Then Italy changed her mourning garments and the half-ruined walls of Rome regained in part their previous splendor, believing that by the complete conversion of their foster-child, God was favorably inclined toward them.

You would think the power of the Goths was annihilated and that the rabble of deserters and slaves had been struck from on high by God's lightning and thunder! Not thus did the people of Rome cheer when Marcellus first won his battle at Nola, after thousands of Roman soldiers had been killed at Turbia, Thrasyminus, and Cannae![34] Even earlier than that, there was less joy when the nobles who had been redeemed with gold, the seed of the Roman race, learned in their imprisonment that the armies of the Gauls had been overthrown![35] The news about Demetrias penetrated the eastern shores and the triumph of Christian glory was heard in the inland cities as well. What Christian virgin did not boast that she was in her company? What mother, Juliana, did not proclaim your womb blessed? Among unbelievers there may be doubt as to future rewards: in the meantime, O virgin, you have received more than you offered. Had you become the bride of a man, just one province would have known you, but as a virgin of Christ, the entire world has heard of you.

[34]A Roman victory over Hannibal, 216 B.C.
[35]390 B.C.

Pitiable parents, incomplete in the Christian faith, are apt to dedicate daughters to virginity who are deformed or weak in some bodily part because they can find no suitable husbands for them—as the saying goes, glass beads are worth as much as pearls.[36] Without doubt there are those who, wishing to appear more pious to themselves, give to their virgin daughters amounts so small that they scarcely suffice for basic provisions, while their worldly children of both sexes are given all the property. Recently in this city a certain rich man who was a presbyter left his two daughters who had made virginal professions without funds, while he provided his other children with abundant means for luxurious living and pleasures. Many of our women who have made their professions have done the same thing, I am sorry to report. Would that they were rare examples! Yet the more numerous they are, so much more blessed are those women who do not follow the example of the majority.

7. It is reported and loudly praised by all Christians that Christ's holy yokefellows[37] gave her everything that had been set aside for her marriage, lest they injure her Bridegroom—no, rather, that richly dowered, she might come to her Bridegroom with all her previous wealth, that it might not be lost on worldly things, but sustain the needs of God's servants. . . .

> All the above selections were composed by men who wrote of women not members of their immediate families. The next three selections were composed by a brother and two sons of the women described. The first is from Gregory of Nyssa's *Life of St. Macrina.* Gregory writes that he composed the treatise for a fellow ecclesiastic who wanted more information about his remarkable sister. Notable in the account is Gregory's insistence that it was Macrina who led their brother, the famous Cappadocian theologian Basil of Caesarea, to renounce

---

[36]Cf. Tertullian, *To the Martyrs* 4.
[37]Demetrias' mother and grandmother.

worldly glory for a life of Christian asceticism, and that Macrina engaged in elevated "philosophical" conversations even on her deathbed. Gregory's encomium dates to the 380s A.D.

1.[38] The form of the work, based on the general character of its heading, appears to be a letter, but it has been stretched beyond the limits of a letter into a lengthy prose work. But I defend myself with the excuse that the subject on which you directed me to write is greater than is commensurate to a letter. In any case, you have not forgotten our meeting that took place when I was about to revisit Jerusalem in accordance with a vow, that I might see the tokens of the Lord's fleshly sojourn in those places: I ran across you near the city of Antioch. We discoursed back and forth on all kinds of topics (you brought forward many subjects for our conversation, so that it was not likely to be a silent meeting), and as is usual, as happens many times in these conversations, the flow of talk proceeded to the memory of a certain honored person's life.

It was a woman who was the subject of our discourse, if indeed you can say "a woman," for I do not know if it is appropriate to call her by a name taken from nature when she surpassed that nature. Our conversation did not receive its credibility from our having heard the reports of others; since experience was our teacher, our words went through the tale in precise detail, not at all relying on the testimony of another person's hearsay.

The virgin whom we recalled was no stranger to our family, so I did not need to learn the marvellous things about her from others. We were born from the same parents; she was, so to speak, a kind of first-fruits offering, the first offshoot of our mother's womb. Thus because you thought a history of her good deeds would bring a certain

[38]Text: SC 178.136.

benefit, because such a life ought not to be neglected, ought not to escape notice in the time to come, nor the highest summit of human virtue to which she raised herself through philosophy be concealed through silence, I thought it would be good to comply with your wish and to report her story in as few words as I could, simply and without artifice.

2. This virgin was named Macrina. There was an esteemed Macrina earlier in our family, our father's mother, who in the time of the persecutions had contended as a confessor on behalf of Christ, and this is why the little girl was so named by her parents. But though this was her acknowledged name used by acquaintances, another had been given her in secret, given by a kind of epiphany before she came to light at birth. For her mother was of such virtue that she was led by the divine will in all things, embracing an especially pure and spotless way of life, so that had she been left to her own devices, she would have chosen not to marry. But as she was orphaned of both father and mother and was blooming in her physical prime, the fame of her beauty attracted men as suitors. There was a risk that if she were not voluntarily joined to a man, she might suffer some unwanted abuse, since those driven mad by her beauty were preparing to seize her. For this reason she chose a man known and attested for the seemliness of his life; thus she acquired a guardian for her own life. Straightway at her first pregnancy she became the mother of Macrina.

And when the time came in which she should be freed from the pain of childbirth, she fell asleep and seemed to carry in her hands that which was still embraced in her womb. Someone more magnificent in form and appearance than a human manifested himself, addressing that child she was carrying by the name "Thecla," for there was a Thecla considered important among the virgins.[39] Having done this

[39]See pp. 78-88 above.

three times, he disappeared from before her eyes and eased the pain, so that she awoke from her sleep and saw her dream become reality. Thus "Thecla" was her secret name. But it seems to me that the apparition addressed her as this not so much as a guide to the mother in the choice of name, but to foretell the life of the infant and to show the similarity of her choice of life by the identity of her name with that of the other Thecla.

3. Thus the child grew. Although she had her own nurse, she was mostly raised by her own mother's hands. Once she grew out of infancy, she quickly learned that which children comprehend, and to whatever learning her parents' judgment led, in that regard the little girl's nature showed through. Her mother was eager to have the girl educated, not indeed in the educational curriculum of the secular world, in which the first years of study are taught mostly through the poets. For she believed that it was shameful and totally inappropriate to teach a tender and malleable nature either the sentiments of tragedy, which concern women and give the poets their inspiration and subject matter, or the indecencies of comedy, or the reasons for Troy's evils, in a way defiling the child with unseemly stories about women. But whatever of inspired Scripture seemed reducible to the level of the early years, this was the child's instructional material, especially the Wisdom of Solomon, and beyond this, mostly whatever led to the moral life. She was not ignorant on any point at all about chanting Scripture's Psalms. She went through each part of the Psalm at its special time, when getting up, when engaging in work, when resting, when she took her meals, when she arose from the table, when she went to bed or arose for prayers; always she had the Psalms with her like a good travelling companion, not forsaking them for a moment.

4. Having grown up with these practices and ones like them, and having especially practiced her hand at wool-

working, she reached her twelfth year, in which the flower of youth especially begins to shine forth. Here it is worthy of wonder how, although the beauty of the young girl had been kept hidden, it did not escape notice, nor did anything in that whole country seem similarly wondrous in comparison to her beauty and graceful form, so that the hands of painters could not match its beauty. The skill that contrives all things and dares the largest projects, so as by imitation to impress again the forms of the elements themselves, was not powerful enough to copy closely the felicity of her form. Because of this beauty, a great swarm of suitors who desired marriage surrounded her parents. Her father (indeed, a sensible man and one observant in judging the good) picked out from the rest a certain distinguished young man of the family, known for his moderation, just now returned from his schooling. To him our father decided to betroth his daughter when she should come of age. Meanwhile, the young man was of the most promising hopes and as a gratifying wedding present, he offered the young woman's father his good reputation as an orator, manifesting his oratorical ability in trials on behalf of the victims of injustice. But envy cut down those promising hopes by snatching him away from life at a pitifully young age.

5. The maiden was not ignorant of what her father had decided, but when his resolution regarding her was cut off by the young man's death, she called her father's decision a marriage, as if it had been actualized. She thought it right to remain unmarried for the rest of her life, and her decision was more fixed than one would have thought for someone her age. Frequently her parents had conversations with her about marriage, for many men wanted to be suitors on account of the fame of her beauty. She used to say that it was inappropriate and unlawful not to be content once and for all with a marriage decided by her father, and to be forced to seek another, since by nature marriage is unique, just as

birth and death are. She confidently affirmed that the man joined to her by her parents' decision was not dead, but was living in God; because of the hope of the resurrection, she judged him to be away, not dead, and thought it unnatural not to keep faith with a husband who was away on a journey.

By such arguments she disregarded those who tried to convince her. She decided that she had one safeguard for her good resolution: not ever to be separated from her mother, not even for a moment's time. Thus her mother often said to her that she had been pregnant with and carried the rest of her children for the usual time, but that this daughter she carried within her always, embracing her in her womb, so to speak. Living with her daughter was by no means burdensome or without advantage for the mother, for the care she received from her daughter took the place of the service of many maidservants to her, and there was a certain good exchange between them by which they replenished themselves. The mother cared for the soul of the young woman, and the daughter cared for her mother's body, satisfying her every desired need. Frequently with her own hands she made bread for her mother. This was not her primary occupation, but after she had lent her hands to the mystic services, she thought it appropriate for her way of life to so use her remaining time; in her zeal for this task, she furnished her mother with food by her own labors. Not only this, she was a co-administrator in all of her mother's pressing concerns. For her mother had four sons and five daughters, and paid taxes to three governors for property that was distributed over that many provinces. Thus in many ways her mother was for this reason distracted by cares, for the father had already departed from life. In all these things, Macrina was a partner in her mother's burdens, dividing with her the concerns and lightening the weight of her sufferings. Just as by her mother's rearing she had kept her own life blameless under the maternal eyes and was constantly guided and witnessed, so she also gave her mother great direction toward the same goal, I mean that of philosophy, by her own life, gradually attracting her to the simple, immaterial way of life.

6. After the mother had decorously arranged the sisters' affairs, in accordance with what seemed suitable for each one, the great Basil,[40] brother of the aforesaid woman, returned from school where he had been trained in rhetoric for a long time. She indeed detected that he was enormously puffed up with pride over his rhetorical abilities; he despised all the worthy people and exalted himself in self-importance above the illustrious men of the province. Yet she drew him with such speed to the goal of philosophy that he renounced worldly renown. He expressed contempt at being an object of marvel on account of his rhetoric. He deserted to this laborious life of manual labor to prepare himself by complete poverty and unfettered life directed toward virtue. But his life and his later pursuits, by which he became famous everwhere under the sun and obscured the glory of all those illustrious for their virtue, would require a thick book and much time. Let my discourse take itself back to the proposed topic.

7. Since any reason for worldly living had already been taken from them, she persuaded her mother to renounce her usual style of life and her more vainglorious pastimes, and the services of the persons under her command to which she had grown accustomed in earlier times, and to become in her mind like the masses, to mingle in the same way of life as the virgins with her who had been transformed from the slaves and servants they were into her sisters and equals. . . .

> (Macrina after her mother's death continued to live the ascetic life in the company of other virgins. When Gregory was on a church mission, he visited his sister nearby

---

[40]Later bishop of Caesarea.

at Annisa. He found her Superior of the convent, but near to death.)

15. ...A certain man led me to the house in which the great Macrina was, opened the door, and I entered that holy place. She was already greatly oppressed by illness, yet she was not resting on a bed or mattress, but on the ground, on a plank covered with sackcloth; another board whose function was to replace a pillow propped up her head, supporting the sinews in an inclined fashion, thus satisfactorily holding up her neck.

17. When she saw me come near the door, she raised herself on an elbow, not able to come towards me, for already the fever had consumed her strength. But fixing her hands on the floor and stretching out from the pallet as far as she could, she paid me the honor of a bow. I ran to her and with my hands raised her head that was bending toward the ground, set her straight again, and returned her to her customary reclining position. She stretched out her hand to God and said, "You have fulfilled this favor for me, O God, and have not deprived me of my wish, for you have moved your servant to visit your handmaid." So as not to bring melancholy to my soul, she tried to muffle her groans, somehow to hide the constraint on her breathing, and by all means to dispose the situation toward cheerfulness. She introduced topics on her mind and by asking questions, gave me a chance to talk. The memory of the great Basil[41] crept into the course of the conversation and my heart sank. I cast down my face and tears welled up in my eyes. But she, far from also being dejected by our emotion, made the recollection of the saint a starting point for the higher philosophy. She went through such arguments in detailed manner, speaking about natural phenomena, recounting the divine plan hidden in sad events, revealing things about

[41]Basil of Caesarea died in 379 A.D.

the future life, as if she were possessed by the Holy Spirit. As a result my soul seemed to lack little from being lifted outside human nature by her words, and with the guidance of her speech, to stand inside the heavenly sanctuaries.

(Gregory recounts in detail Macrina's death, funeral, and burial, and ends his account with a few miracle stories.)

39. I do not think it convincing to add to my discourse all the other things of this sort we heard from those who lived with her and knew the details about her. For most men judge the trustworthiness of what is told them by the measure of their own experience, and what is beyond the capacity of the listener, they assault with suspicions of falsity, as being beyond the truth. Therefore I am omitting that unbelievable incident connected with agriculture: at the time of famine, the grain that had been distributed in accordance with the need gave the impression that it had not been at all diminished, but remained the same in amount as before it was given out to supply the need of those who begged for it. And there were other such incidents, even more incredible, cures of diseases, expulsion of demons, true prophecies of things to come, all of which are believed to be true by those who knew about these things in detail, even if they are beyond belief; they are deemed outside the realm of what can be accepted to those who are very carnal. They do not know that "in proportion to faith" (Rom. 12:6) the distribution of spiritual gifts comes about, small for those of little faith, but great for those who have within themselves a great capacity for faith. Thus, lest I hinder the unbelievers who have no faith in the gifts of God, I refrain for this reason from reporting next the greater miracles. I think that what has been said suffices to round out my narrative about Macrina.

In the next selection, John Chrysostom briefly reports on his mother Anthusa's life, especially on the difficulties she faced when left a widow at the age of twenty with two children. Upon reaching young manhood, Chrysostom was pressed by his best friend Basil to leave his mother's home and share a residence with him. Chrysostom was prepared to act upon the proposal, when his mother pleaded with him not to abandon her, as Chrysostom describes in the following selection from *On the Priesthood*. The plan was in any case aborted by Basil's sudden elevation to the priesthood.

1,5.[42] But my mother's constant pleas prevented me from granting Basil this favor, or rather, prevented me from receiving it from his hands. For when my mother became aware of this scheme, she took me by the hand, led me into the part of the house reserved exclusively for her, and sat next to me on the bed on which she had borne us. She unleashed streams of tears and added words more pathetic than the tears, making a bitter lament to me in this manner: "My child," she said, "I was not permitted to enjoy your father's virtue for long, since that was the plan that seemed good to God. Your father's death followed on the birth pangs with which I bore you, designating you to be an untimely orphan and me an untimely widow, to learn the dreadful events of widowhood that only those women who have experienced them can rightly understand. For no word can match the storm and billow that the maiden is up against who has recently left her father's home and is inexperienced at business matters, but who is suddenly hurled into unrestrained grief and must necessarily bear cares beyond her years and sex. She must, I think, pay attention to the servants' sluggishness and carefully note their evil deeds, fend off the schemes of relatives, bear nobly the abuses of those who exact the public taxes and the harshness

[42]Text: PG 48.624.

of the tax payments themselves. Should the dead man depart leaving behind a child and should it be a daughter, the mother will also be afforded a great concern, but nonetheless she escapes the outlay of funds, she escapes the fears. A son, in contrast will fill her with myriad fears each day and with many anxieties. I made allowance for the expenses I had to bear for necessary goods if I wished to bring up my son as befits a free man. Yet all the same, none of these difficulties convinced me to enter into the union of a second marriage, nor to bring another bridegroom into your father's house. I remained in the midst of the stress and the confusion and did not flee the iron furnace of widowhood, aided chiefly by grace from above. Yet it brought me great comfort amid those horrors to gaze constantly at your face and to cherish for myself a living image of the departed, an image that was almost exactly like him.

"Thus while you were still a child and had not yet learned to talk, when you were at an age when children are an enormous delight to their parents, you furnished me with much comfort. I bore my widowhood nobly and you cannot say to censure me that I lessened your patrimony, something I know that many with the misfortune of being orphans have experienced. Indeed, I kept your patrimony completely intact and defrayed all expenses necessary for your honored reputation; omitting nothing, I paid for them out of my own money, money that came from my own home. Don't imagine that I say these things as a reproach! As a return for all these things, however, I ask one favor from you, that you do not invest me with widowhood a second time nor again kindle the grief already laid to rest: wait for my death. I shall perhaps depart after a short time."

The last selection is Augustine's tribute to his mother, Monica, found in his *Confessions*. The character of that book, Augustine's revelation of his youthful spiritual and psychological development, makes it an especially rich source for perceiving the emotional bond that linked mother and son. Monica's mother, we gather, was a Christian, yet Monica was given in marriage to a pagan, Patricius, whom she converted only as he approached death. Monica's ordeals as a wife are here frankly described by Augustine, who does not seem to think that his father's treatment of his mother was unusual. Monica spent years of her life suffering over her sexually and religiously wayward son[43] until he finally arrived safe within the Catholic fold. The mystical experience Augustine and his mother shared at Ostia shortly before her death is one of the most famous sections of the *Confessions*. Augustine's devotion to Monica is especially evident in the closing lines of this selection, in which he begs his readers to pray for his mother in Heaven. The book is written as a confession or prayer to God, the "You" addressed in the text.

I,11.[44] In fact, as a boy I had heard about the eternal life that had been promised to us through the humility of the Lord our God's lowering himself to our pride, and already I was stamped with the sign of his cross, already seasoned with his salt from the womb of my mother, who put great hope in You. You saw, O Lord, how once when I was a boy, I was suddenly feverish with stomach pains, almost about to die. Since You were my guardian, You saw, my God, with what agitation of spirit and with what faith I demanded the baptism of Your Christ, my God and my Lord, from the piety of my mother and of the mother of us all, Your Church. My fleshly mother was disturbed, because she more lovingly brooded over my eternal salvation, with a pure heart in Your faith. Had I not at once been restored, she would rapidly have arranged for me to be initiated and

---

[43]Augustine kept a mistress for fifteen years and was a Manichean for nine or ten years.
[44]Text: CSEL 33.15.

bathed in the health-giving sacraments, confessing You, Lord Jesus, for the forgiveness of sins. And so my cleansing was delayed, almost as if it were thus necessary that if I should live, I would become still more unclean, because obviously after baptism the guilt from the uncleanness of sins would be greater and more dangerous.

Thus already I believed, as did my mother and all the household, my father alone excepted, who nonetheless did not drive out the authority of my mother's piety so that I did not believe in Christ, inasmuch as he did not yet believe. For my mother busied herself in order that You might be my Father, my God, rather than he, and in this matter You helped her so that she might overcome her husband, to whom she was subject as her better, because in this she is also subjected herself to You, especially as You commanded it....

(Augustine is now in Milan.)

VI,1. My hope from my youth (Ps. 71:5), where were You in relation to me, to where had You retreated? For truly, did You not make me and distinguish me from the four-footed beasts and the birds of the air by making me wiser? Yet I walked in darkness and in slippery places, and I sought You outside of myself and did not find God in my heart; I came into the depths of the sea, had no confidence, despaired at finding the truth.

Already my mother had come to me, strong in her piety, following me over land and sea, secure in You against all dangers. For during the hazards at sea she comforted the sailors themselves (to whom inexperienced travellers at sea customarily go for consolation when they become anxious), promising them a safe arrival, because You had promised her this in a vision.

She found me in even more serious danger since I had despaired of tracing out truth. Nonetheless, when I indicated that I was no longer a Manichean, although not yet a

Catholic Christian, she did not leap for joy as if she had heard some unexpected thing. Since now she was assured about that aspect of my misery for which she had lamented me as though I were dead, but were about to be revived. She had carried me in her thoughts as if I were on a bier, in order that You might say to the widow's son, "Young man, I say to you, arise," and he would be resuscitated, begin to talk, and You might hand him over to his mother (Lk. 7:12-15). Thus her heart was by no means stirred up with tumultuous exultation when she heard that already was accomplished in great part that which she daily implored to You might be done, that although I had not yet reached the truth, already I was snatched away from falsehood. Yes, in truth, already she was certain that You who had promised the whole would supply the part that remained. She replied to me very calmly and with a heart full of confidence that she in Christ trusted that before she left this life she would see me a believing Catholic. This much at least she said to me. On You, however, Fountain of mercy, she showered more frequent prayers and tears, that You might hasten Your help and illumine my darkness. She hurried more diligently to church and hung on the words of Ambrose,[45] praying for the fountain of water that flows forth in eternal life. Moreover, she loved that man as if he were an angel of God, because she recognized that it was through him that I had for the moment been led to the present uncertain state of fluctuation through which she most assuredly took for granted that I would pass from sickness to health, in the meanwhile running the more distressing danger through the attack that doctors call the "crisis."

VI,13. There was much activity directed to my getting married. Now I wooed, now it was promised, and my mother gave much attention to the matter. She thought that when I

---

[45]Bishop of Milan, 374-397 A.D.

was indeed married, the health-giving baptism might cleanse me, the baptism for which she daily rejoiced that I was being prepared; she perceived that both her vows and Your promises were being fulfilled in my faith. At the time, to be sure, both by my request and by her desire, we daily begged from You with strong cries of the heart that You would show her through a vision something about my future marriage, but You never would. She saw certain vain and phantastic things, such as a human spirit concerned with inclinations about this matter brings up. She told me about them, not with the confidence she customarily felt when You had shown her something, but rather made little of them. For she said she could tell the difference, although she could not explain it in words, between Your revelation and the dreams of her own mind, I do not know by what sense. Nonetheless, the matter was pursued and a girl was asked for. She lacked about two years of being of marriage-able age, but because she was pleasing, I would wait for her.

> (Augustine, after his conversion experience, abandoned plans for marriage.)

IX,8. "You who make like-minded people to live in one house" (Ps. 67:7 Vg.), brought Evodius, as well, into our company. He was a young man from our city who while serving as agent for Public Affairs was converted to You before I was. He was baptized, and leaving his worldly service, equipped himself for Yours. We were together, and together we were about to dwell in holy teaching. Since we were looking for a place where our services might be more beneficial to You, we were going to return together to Africa. And when we were at Tibertine Ostia, my mother died. Much I omit, because I am in much haste. Accept my confessions and expressions of thanks, my God, for the innumerable things which still rest in silence. But I will not omit anything to which my spirit gives birth concerning Your handmaid, who gave birth to me in the flesh that I might be born in this temporal light, she who gave birth to me in her heart, that I might be born in the light eternal.

I will speak not of her own gifts, but of Yours in her, for she neither made nor educated herself. You created her; neither her father nor her mother knew what sort of person they would produce. The rod of Your Christ taught her in Your fear, the guidance of Your only Son, in the household of a believer who was a good member of Your Church. Yet she did not attribute her training so much to the diligence of her mother as to a certain ancient female servant who had carried her father around when he was an infant, as babies are customarily carried on the backs of quite grown-up girls. By virtue of this relationship and because of her age and excellent character, she was appropriately honored by the masters of that Christian household, whence even the care, of the master's daughters was committed to her, which she diligently carried out. She was vigorous in restraining them with a holy strictness when that was necessary, and in teaching them with a sober prudence.

For aside from those hours in which they were fed most moderately at the parental table, she did not allow them to drink water, even though they were burning with thirst. She thus took advance precaution against a bad habit and added the sensible words, "You drink water only because you don't have it in your power to get wine, but when you get married and are made mistresses of the storerooms and cellars, water will seem contemptible, but the habit of drinking will continue." By this manner of teaching and power of command, she curbed the greediness of their young years and accustomed the very thirst of the girls to a virtuous moderation, so that what was not fitting might already not be found pleasurable.

Nonetheless, there had crept up—as Your maidservant told me, her son—there had crept up upon her a desire to drink wine. For when she as a sober girl was ordered by her parents, as was customary, to fetch the wine from the cask, she would hold the goblet underneath the opening and before she poured the undiluted wine into the flask, would suck a little with the tips of her lips, because she was not able to tolerate more, her sense being unwilling. She did not do this from any desire for intoxication, but from certain over-flowing excesses of her age that boil up in playful move-ments and that are customarily repressed in youthful spirits by adult authority. And to that small amount, daily small amounts were added—since "he who scorns small amounts shall fall gradually" (Eccl. 19:1)—she fell into the habit that she now eagerly drained her little cup of wine, nearly full. Where then was the wise old woman and her stringent prohibition? Can nothing prevail against a hidden desire unless Your medicine, O Lord, watch over us? While fa-ther, mother, and nurses were absent, You were present, You who have created, who call, who even work some good for the health of our souls through those people who are set over us. What did You do then, my God? How did You cure her? Whence did You restore her to health? Did You not bring forth from another woman's soul a harsh and piercing reproach, like a surgeon's knife, from Your hidden supplies, and with one stroke cut out that putrefaction?

For the maid who was accustomed to go to the cask happened to have an argument with her little mistress when they were alone and hurled this vice at her, calling her in a very bitter insult a little drunkard. Struck by this goad, she perceived her foulness, immediately condemned it, and put it aside. Just as friends pervert us by their flattery, so ene-mies often correct us through their charges. Nor do You give back to them what You do through them, but what they themselves intended. For since the maid was angry she wanted to reproach her young mistress, not make her whole. Therefore she uttered the words in private, either because the time and place of the quarrel found them alone, or perhaps lest she herself might also be in trouble for coming forth with the accusation so belatedly. But You, Lord, ruler of heavenly and earthly things, Who turn the deep torrents to Your purpose, Who orders the turbulent flux of the ages, Who even makes whole one soul by the unwholesomeness of the other, lest anyone, when he notices this, should attribute it to his own power if another, whom he wishes to be corrected, is reformed by his word.

IX,9. Having thus been modestly and soberly raised, and more made subject to her parents by You than by her parents to You, when she had sufficient years to be married, she was given to a husband whom she served as a lord. She concerned herself to win him for You, speaking of You through her behavior, by which You made her beautiful, respectfully lovable, and admirable to her husband. Moreover, she thus endured the wrongs to her bed, so that she never had any feuding with her husband on account of this matter. She waited for Your compassion to come upon him, so that believing in You, he might become chaste. Indeed, more than this, just as he was an excellent person when feeling well-disposed, so he was raging when he was angry. She learned not to resist a wrathful husband, not only in deed, but not even by a word. Indeed, when she saw an appropriate moment after he was restrained and quiet, she would explain to him the reason for her behavior, if he had been unadvisedly upset. In short, while many married women with milder husbands nonetheless bore on a dishonored face the traces of beatings, women who would in friendly conversation betray their husbands' lives, she would censure their tongues and, as if she were joking, admonish them in a dignified fashion. She would tell them that from the time they heard read aloud those matrimonial tablets, they should consider them instruments by which they had been made servants; accordingly, remembering the conditions of the marriage contract, they ought not to take the upper hand against their masters. And when these women, knowing what a fierce husband she put up with, marvelled that it had never been heard or made evident by any sign that Patricius had beaten his wife, nor that they had been opposed in domestic strife with each other even for a day, confidentially asked her the reason, she used to teach them her custom, which I related above. The ones who observed it gave thanks when they tried it, but those who did not were vexed in their subjection.

She thus conquered even her mother-in-law, who at first was incited against her by the murmurs of wicked maidservants; she conquered her by submissiveness, persevering in endurance and gentleness. The mother-in-law of her own accord told her son about the meddling tongues of the slaves by which the domestic peace between herself and her daughter-in-law was disturbed, and she wanted the slaves punished. So after that, complying with his mother, caring about the discipline of the household and mindful of its harmony, he corrected with whippings those who were discovered, just as she who discovered them wished. She promised that whoever said something evil to her about her daughter-in-law in order to please her should expect those kinds of rewards. Then no one dared to do so, and they lived together agreeably in remarkable kindness....

At last she won for You even her own husband, now at the end of his earthly life. In him as a believer she did not now bewail that which she endured when he was not yet one of the faithful. She was also the servant of Your servants.[46] Whoever of them knew her, praised, honored, and loved You much in her, because he sensed Your presence in her heart, by the evidence of fruits of holy conversation. For she had been the wife of one man, had given back what we owe in mutual interchange to parents, had managed her house in piety, had testimony to her good deeds (cf. I Tim. 5:4-10).

[46]A phrase used of Church officials.

She raised children, and as many as she gave birth to, that many she perceived straying from You. Lastly, O Lord, because from Your grace You allow Your servants to speak, before she fell asleep in You, to all of us who already were living together as associates and who had received the grace of Your baptism, did she thus manifest care as if she had given birth to all of us and did she thus serve as if she had been brought forth as the child of all of us.

IX,10. Moreover, the day approached on which she was to leave this life, a day You knew, but of which we were ignorant. It happened, arranged by You, as I believe, with Your hidden ways, that she and I stood alone, leaning on a certain window; from it could be viewed the garden of the house we had there in Tibertine Ostia. There, removed from the crowd, we were resting ourselves for the voyage after the difficulty of a long trip. Thus we were talking alone together very sweetly, forgetting past events and stretching out to those ahead of us. We were seeking between us in the presence of truth, which You are, to think how the future eternal life of the saints would be, the life "which eye has not seen nor ear heard, nor had it entered the heart of man" (Is. 64:4; I Cor. 2:9). We opened wide the mouth of our heart to the supernatural streams of Your fountain, the fountain of life, which is with You, so that being sprinkled from it according to our power of comprehension, we might in some way reflect on so great a thing.

And when our discussion arrived at the conclusion that the pleasure of the carnal senses, however great it may be, in however great corporeal light, seemed not comparable to the pleasantness of that life, indeed, not even worth speaking about, we raised ourselves by our more ardent passion toward Him, and we gradually travelled through all corporeal things and Heaven itself, whence sun and moon and stars shine above the earth. We were still ascending by our inner reflection and speech. We admired Your works. We came to our minds and transcended them, that we might reach the region of unfailing fruitfulness, where You feed Israel forever with the food of truth, and where life is Wisdom, through whom all these things were made, both those that were and those yet to be, while Wisdom herself is not made, but is thus as she was and thus she will always be. Rather, indeed to have been and to be in the future is not in her, but only to be, since she is eternal. And while we spoke, we were longing for Wisdom and we touched her moderately with a total beat of the heart; we sighed and left there bound the firstfruits of the Spirit; we returned to the noise of our mouth, where a word both begins and ends. And what is like Your Word, our Lord, who remains in himself without aging and renews all things? (cf. Wisd. 7:27).

Thus we were saying, "If a person's tempests of the flesh were silenced; if the phantoms of the earth, water, and air were silenced; if the poles were silenced; and if the soul herself were silenced within herself and transcended herself by not thinking of herself; if dreams were silenced and imaginary revelations, every tongue and every sign and whatever there is by that passes by—if all these were totally silenced (since if anyone heard, all these things say, "We did not make ourselves, but He made us who remains forever" [Ps. 99:3, 5 Vg.], and if having said this, they now were silent, because they listened in Him who made them)—and He alone speak, not through them but by Himself, that we might hear His word—not by a fleshly tongue, nor by the voice of an angel, nor by the sound of thunder, nor by the riddle of a metaphor—but He Himself, whom we love in these things, that we might hear Him apart from these things, (just as now we both reached out and by quick reflection touched the eternal Wisdom abiding over all)—if we could sustain this, and this one seize us, absorb us, and conceal its beholder in inner joys, so that this life might be eternally of such a kind as it was at this moment of insight for which we sighed, would this not be to 'enter into the joy of your Lord'? (Mt. 25:21). And when is that? 'When we shall all rise up again,' but 'shall we not all be changed?' (cf. I Cor. 15:51)."

Such things I was saying, if not in this way and with these words, You, Lord, know that on that day when we were talking of such things, this world with all its pleasures became worthless to us in the midst of the words. Then my mother said, "My son, as far as it concerns me, I now take pleasure in nothing in this life. What I might still do here and why I might still do here and why I am here, I do not know, for already my hope in this world had been destroyed. There was one thing for the sake of which I was desiring to linger in this life for some time, namely, that I might see you a Catholic Christian before I died. My God has fulfilled this wish for me very abundantly, so that I see you, His servant, even despising earthly happiness. What am I doing here?"

IX,11. What I might have replied to her on these points, I do not well recall. Nevertheless, scarcely five days later, or not much more, she fell into a fever. While she was ill, on a certain day she experienced an eclipse of her spirit and for a little while was drawn away from the things at hand. We rushed to her, but she quickly regained her senses. Looking at me and my brother standing there, she said to us as if she were inquiring, "Where was I?" Then, gazing at us who were stunned with sorrow, she said, "Here you will bury your mother." I was silent, was holding back the tears. My brother, however, said something to the effect that he would have her die in her own country, not a foreign one, because it would be a happier fate. When she heard this, she beat him back with an anxious look in her eyes, thus sensible of such things. She gazed at me and said, "Look at what he said." And soon to both of us she said, "Place this body anywhere; concern over it should not in any way disturb you. I ask from you just this much, that wherever you may be, you remember me at the Lord's altar." And when she had expounded these thoughts in what words she was able, she became silent, being exhausted from her worsening illness. . . .

Even afterwards I heard that already when we were at Ostia, she was conversing with my friends one day when I was away, and with a certain maternal confidence was talking about the despising of this life and the goodness of death. They were amazed by such virtue in a woman—since You had given it to her—and asked her whether she did not fear leaving her body so far from her own city. She replied, "Nothing is far to God, nor should I fear lest at the end of the world He does not know where to raise me up." Thus on the ninth day of her illness, in the fifty-sixth year of her life, and the thirty-third of mine, that religious and virtuous soul was freed from the body.

(Augustine reports that he was dry-eyed at his mother's death, despite his deep grief. Only when he recalled a beautiful hymn of Ambrose, "God, Creator of All," did his grief find outward expression.)

IX,12. . . . Then gradually did I call back my earlier feeling for Your handmaid, her devout conversation with You, her gentleness to and compliancy with us in holiness, of which suddenly I was destitute. It was pleasing to weep in Your sight for her and over her, for myself and over myself. And I released the tears which I had restrained, that they might flow as much as they wished, spreading them under my heart, which rested in them, since Your ears were there, not those of a man, who would interpret my weeping in a haughty spirit. And now, Lord, I will confess to You in writing. Let him read it who will, and let him interpret it as he will, and if he finds a sin in my weeping for my mother for a small part of an hour—a mother who was meanwhile dead to my eyes, who had wept over me for many years that I might live in Your eyes—let him not laugh, but rather, if he is a person of lofty charity, let him weep for my sins against You, the Father of all the brothers of Your Christ.

> (Augustine asks God to forgive any sins his mother may have committed. He ends Book IX as follows:)

IX,13. ...Therefore may she be in peace with her husband, before whom and after whom she married no one, whom she served with patience, bringing fruit to You, that she might also win him for You. And inspire, my Lord, my God, inspire Your servants, my brothers, Your sons, my lords, whom I serve with heart and voice and writings, that however many shall read this may remember at Your altar Monica, Your handmaid, along with Patricius, once her husband, through whose flesh You brought me into this life, in what way I do not know. May they recall with devout affection my parents in this transitory light, my brothers under You, O Father, in our Catholic Mother, and of my fellow citizens of the eternal Jerusalem, for which Your pilgrim people sigh from the time of their departure until their return, so that what she requested of me at her last may be more abundantly executed through my confessions by many prayers, than through my own prayers.

Suggestions for Further Reading

Bailey, Derrick Sherwin. *Sexual Relation in Christian Thought.* New York: Harper & Brothers, 1959.

Campenhausen, Hans von. *The Virgin Birth in the Theology of the Ancient Church.* Studies in Historical Theology 2. Napierville, Ill.: Alec R. Allenson, Inc., 1964.

Clark, Elizabeth A. *Jerome, Chrysostom, and Friends: Essays and Translations.* Studies in Women and Religion 2. New York and Toronto: The Edwin Mellen Press, 1979.

Clark, Elizabeth A. *The Life of Melania the Younger: Translation and Commentary.* Toronto: The Edwin Mellen Press, 1983.

Clark, Elizabeth A. and Hatch, Diane F. *The Golden Bough, The Oaken Cross: The Virgilian Cento of Faltonia Betitia Proba.* Chico, Cal.: Scholars Press, 1981.

Daniélou, Jean. *The Ministry of Women in the Early Church.* Trans. G. Simon. London: Faith Press, 1961.

Davies, Stevan L. *The Revolt of the Widows: The Social World of the Apocryphal Acts.* Carbondale, Ill.: Southern Illinois University Press, 1980.

Pagels, Elaine. *The Gnostic Gospels.* New York: Random House, 1979 (especially chap. 3).

Pomeroy, Sarah B. *Goddesses, Whores, Wives, and Slaves: Women in Classical Antiquity.* New York: Schocken Books, 1975.

Ruether, Rosemary Radford. "Misogynism and Virginal Feminism in the Fathers of the Church," in R. R. Ruether, ed., *Religion and Sexism: Images of Women in the Jewish and Christian Traditions.* New York: Simon and Schuster, 1974.

Ruether, Rosemary Radford. "Mothers of the Church: Ascetic Women in the Late Patristic Age," in R. Ruether and E. McLaughlin, eds., *Women of Spirit: Female Leadership in the Jewish and Christian Traditions.* New York: Simon and Schuster, 1979.

Tavard, George H. *Woman In Christian Tradition.* Notre Dame and London: University of Notre Dame Press, 1973.

Wilkinson, John. *Egeria's Travels.* London: SPCK, 1973.

Yarbrough, Anne. "Christianization in the Fourth Century: The Example of Roman Women." *Church History* 45 (1976), 149-165.